Russian Conservatism

Russian Conservatism

Managing Change under Permanent Revolution

Glenn Diesen

ROWMAN & LITTLEFIELD
Lanham • Boulder • New York • London

Published by Rowman & Littlefield
An imprint of The Rowman & Littlefield Publishing Group, Inc.
4501 Forbes Boulevard, Suite 200, Lanham, Maryland 20706
www.rowman.com

British Library Cataloguing in Publication Data

A catalogue record for this book is available from the British Library

ISBN: HB 978-1-5381-4998-0

Library of Congress Cataloging-in-Publication Data Is Available

Library of Congress Control Number: 2020946879

ISBN 978-1-5381-4998-0 (cloth)
ISBN 978-1-5381-5000-9 (pbk)
ISBN 978-1-5381-4999-7 (electronic)

Contents

Foreword

The topic of Russian conservatism has been the subject of extensive academic research, and the ideology itself has been developing from the times of Kievan Rus until the present day. Many scholars, experts and journalists have sought to analyse the key concepts underpinning the history of Russia's development, its political system and foreign policy. This new book by Professor Glenn Diesen certainly stands out among modern western academic and journalistic publications about Russia.

A feature of Professor Diesen's approach is that his work does not confine itself to existing Western narratives on the development of conservatism in Russia. Such narratives adopt the view that liberal modernisation theory is based on the ideas of universalisation and standardisation of the cultural foundations of public policy. In this context, the predefined list of universal values considered applicable in any society around the world, and national and civilizational differences are perceived as insignificant factors, or as temporary deviations from the "correct" – that is, Western – model of modernisation.

The observation of a broad spectrum of conservative ideologies – from far-right resistance to all socio-economic changes to moderate conservatism as a governing instrument of modernisation (while preserving a nation's precious cultural heritage) – is an extremely important one introduced in this book. It should be emphasised that this differentiation plays an important role in understanding domestic and foreign policy, and in shaping the geopolitical landscape itself.

There is a popular belief that the current contradiction between Russia and the West is a conflict of the postmodern era. It is considered that European countries have already fully rid themselves of the legacy of the Industrial Age and that their societies have outgrown traditional values of the social state, family, mutual assistance, and solidarity, whereas Russia is still struggling in the shadow of modernisation, unwilling to abandon its "backward" traditional values that do not reflect the essence of recent trends of modernisation and the development of socio-economic systems. In this instance, the author's conclusions on the origins and development of the ideology of conservatism in Russia (with his attention to the historical and traditional foundations of Russian statehood) look very reasonable, and are supported with reference to a brilliant constellation of Russian philosophers and thinkers. The author writes that conservatism does not deny the changes necessary for society, but "sets the conditions and limitations" of such changes. In his view, to paraphrase a famous metaphor, "in organic change . . . the future must have a connection with a distinctive past."

An important distinction – and a rare feature among modern western scholars – is that Professor Diesen recognises the historical foundations of Russian conservatism, which crystallised under the extremely difficult conditions across a vast and fragmented territory, amidst constant threats and battles with conquerors, the Tatar-Mongol yoke, revolutions, wars and especially the Second World War in which, according to the latest official figures, Russia lost 26.6 million people. This accumulation of historical, social and even geographical factors leads the author to the conclusion that Russia as a country has civilisational characteristic that cannot be attributed only to Europe or to Asia. Indeed, such a simplified either/or view would be erroneous. Equally erroneous is the widespread view, supported by a number of researchers, that "Russia is not part of Europe". The development of Russia and Europe are deeply interconnected; this can be seen, for example, in the fact that Tsar Nicholas II initiated the international peace conference of 1899 and the creation of the Hague International Court of Justice. It is also worth recalling the creation of the Swiss Confederation, which was ensured by Russia and the diplomacy of Alexander I after the victory over Napoleon and the end of the occupation of Switzerland.

Examining the origins of modern Russian conservatism, the author very clearly focuses on the destructive consequences of the liberal revolution in the USSR in 1991, which later led to the brink of disintegration. The liberal platform for these changes was the concept of "Russia's return to Europe". However, this platform was destroyed by the West itself when Russia was rejected during the formation of a "new Europe" through the expansion of the European Union and NATO to incorporate the countries of Eastern and Southern Europe.

It is worth noting the respectful relationship of the author to his subject of study. He does not try to evaluate Russia and its history through narratives of Western historical and political sciences; rather, he tries to research and define the real differences in the ideologies of the modern West and Russian conservatism. Without creating an opposition, he concludes that there is an objective civilisational difference between the two.

The most important conclusion drawn by the author is that the contradictions between Russia and the West were born not today, nor even in the twentieth century, but formed because of long historical processes. Due to its geographical continuity and interaction with both the West and the East, the Russian Empire was deeply involved in geopolitical challenges and conflicts of interests between the "sea powers" and the forces of the "intermediate region" (Heartland, Halford Mackinder). A large number of different nationalities and ethnic groups lived on the territory of the Russian Empire, and it was natural decision to integrate them with a new transport infrastructure connecting Europe and Asia, outside the dominance of the sea powers. This laid the foundations for further successful development as a state in this territory.

Linking the history of the development of conservatism in Russia with the conservative component of President Putin's modern policy, the author concludes that a comprehensive understanding of contemporary Russia can only be achieved by taking into account the entire history of Russia as an independent civilisation, one that has experienced many tragic and great events, with a history stretching back more than a thousand years.

This book may well become a very significant source for an understanding of Russian conservatism and its impact on the formation of new protocols and instruments of international cooperation. Recognition of a civilizational approach will enable a combination of the positive human potential of civilisational identities, state structures, social and economic features, as well as cultural and historical diversity. The practice of dialogue of civilisations is in fact a way of building the global community driven by values of solidarity, responsibility and a shared commitment to overcoming poverty and inequality. Only by adopting a joined-up approach can we correct and recast the existing global disorder and find a way for greater unity and prosperity for humanity.

Dr Vladimir Yakunin
Chairman of the Supervisory Board,
Dialogue of Civilizations Research Institute
Head of the State Governance Department,
Faculty of Political Sciences, Lomonosov Moscow State University,
Doctor of Political Science

Introduction

Russian history, political system and foreign policy can hardly be understood without appreciating the central role of conservatism. Conservatives aim to navigate society towards a stable middle ground between continuity and change, which neatly summarises the historical challenge for Russia. Pre-communist Russia was primarily devoted to conservatism, and post-communist Russia is now returning to this tradition. Conservatism has a special appeal for Russia as an antidote to its long history of socio-economic disruptions and revolutions. Yet, Russia is commonly studied through the ideological dichotomy of liberalism versus socialism to make sense of the Cold War era.

Conservatism is an ideology about managing change. Conservatism is imperative to ensure that a state does not degrade to a mere geographical description of a patch of land inhabited by people with no special connection. Change and modernisation must build on the culture and traditions that evolved over the centuries to preserve the nation and civilisational distinctiveness. There is a conservative spectrum between resisting change, often termed hard conservatism, and more reform-friendly strand that is commonly referred to as liberal conservatism. The commonality between various strands of conservatism is that the new must build upon the old. The collective must be preserved as human beings instinctively organise in groups.

Conservatism was born out of the Enlightenment and began to take the shape of political ideology following the French Revolution. The endeavour to develop more a rational and modern society creates a counter-reaction as mankind remains influenced by primordial instincts. Conservatism therefore sets conditions and limitations for change. The primary principle for

1

conservatism is the pursuit of *organic change* as the future must have a connection with a distinctive past. Conservatism can be conceptualised as a democracy that includes the votes of previous generations to uphold traditions as a hereditary right. The present generations can reform, modernise and steer society in a new direction, although they do not have the authority to ignore the past.

Human development that breaks with the past causes great social disruptions. Without roots in the past as a source of legitimacy and to define the collective, there is a greater reliance on coercion to establish norms and delineate the acceptable scope for political pluralism. Conservative principles are of greater importance as societies undergo radical changes with fewer ties to the past. Conservatism responds to the emergence of the larger and more complex societies that require a growing bureaucracy, the rule of law, local governance, and to facilitate the cooperation between civil society and the state. Conservative ideas therefore have their roots in the industrial revolution, which restructured work from autonomous work on farms in rural areas towards industry in urban centres. The introduction of capitalism organised the industry into a balance between capital and labour – a relationship managed by the state. These changes have caused social upheavals, ideological rivalries, revolutions and wars across the world.

French nationalism was initially a revolutionary movement that reorganised society by transferring sovereignty from the monarch to the people. Once the transition had been made from monarchies to sovereign nations, conservatism became preoccupied with preserving the nation as the new representative of the collective – a homogenous social group or tribe united by ethnicity, culture, traditions and faith. However, Russia transition to the nation-state was impeded by its geography and history as Slavic lands were divided, and Russia developed as a Eurasian multi-ethnic state following the Mongol invasion.

Russian conservatism became excessively reliant on the autocracy as a representative of the collective and the principal institution to manage change. A strong state became a necessity for conservatives due to the vast geography, low economic connectivity, weak bureaucracy, ambiguity about the nation, and disruptive revolutions. Russian history consistently demonstrated that weakness invites aggression in the form of domestic radicalism and foreign invasions. The Orthodox Church also emerged as a key institution to connect the past with the present.

Russia developed its native conservative concept of "official nationalism" in the 1830s, which focused on unity through the autocracy and orthodoxy, as an alternative to French nationalism. The struggle with defining the nation remains a work in progress to this date as Russia is leaning towards defining itself as a civilisation state with an emphasis on the orthodox faith. The

tensions between tradition and modernity have expressed itself geographically in Russia due to its Eurasian composition. Traditions and spirituality
were linked to an eastern identity where the distinctive was preserved due
to the low economic connectivity and development, while modernity was
represented a Western identity due to the proximity to the industrial societies
in Western Europe.

Russian conservatism has gradually evolved as history reshaped the country. Russian conservatism originated with the cultural ideas of romanticism
in the late eighteenth century that recognised the importance of cultural and
linguistic autonomy required to remain sovereign. By the 1830s and 1840s,
conservatism was spearheaded by the Slavophile movement who lambasted
the Cultural Revolution of Peter the Great for having prevented Russia
from developing its distinctive path to modernity. The balance between
conservatism and liberalism manifested itself in a rivalry with conservative
Slavophiles and Pan-Slavs against liberal Westernisers, while a third ideological path emerged with the socialists in the 1860s. A new strand of conservatism, Eurasianism, emerged in the 1920s in response to the Bolshevik
Revolution. Eurasianism was developed by Russian conservative émigrés
who recognised that Russia had been fundamentally changed imposed by
the communists. The conservative Eurasianists argued that Russia should not
narrow itself to its Slavic origin in Kievan Rus, instead it had to recognise its
Turkic and Ugro-Finnic components. Russia was therefore neither European
not Asian, but it represents a third continent between the Occident and the
Orient. While Bolshevism was conceptualised as Eurasianism by the radical political Left, the conservatives positioned themselves as an alternative
Eurasianism of the political Right.

Striking a balance between change and reproduction of social membership
has profound implications for Russia's identity, geostrategic orientation, and
national cohesion. Russia's uneven and turbulent development has through its
history culminated in two contradictory yet simultaneous imageries – a great
country with excellent literature, potent culture, bold social experiments and
power that casts a shadow across the entire European continent; and concurrently an economically backward and authoritarian state struggling with
literacy and social development that stumbles towards collapse. This contradiction derives from Russia's vast potential that has been unfulfilled due to
the absence of gradual development and modernisation.

REVOLUTIONARY RUSSIA

Revolutionary change is the antithesis to conservatism, as the past is uprooted
to give way to entirely new structures. Revolutionaries believe that the

destruction of the existing state of affairs is a requirement to construct a new and better society. The underpinning logic and justification of revolutionary change suggest breaking with a flawed past is necessary as it corrupts the future. By contrast, conservatism is based on the assumption that a harmonious, stable and modern society must be built on the solid foundation of traditions and continuity.

Yet, radical change creates an impetus for pursuing conservatism. Andrew Sullivan (2007: 9) wrote that "all conservatism begins with loss. . . . If we never knew loss, we would never feel the need to conserve". The intellectual foundations for conservatism are largely based on disruptions to historical continuity. Edmund Burke's (1790), *Reflections on the Revolution in France*, explored the destructiveness of uprooting the entire monarchy and institutions that had organically evolved over the centuries.

Russia's history is one of permanent revolution. Russia has lost much through the centuries, which resulted in a profound appreciation for the importance of conservation. For Russia, conservatism offers salvation to complex geography and troubled history. There is not a single Russia or Russian idea that has persisted through its history. Russia has not grown organically, and the principal constant in Russian history appears to be revolutionary changes. The prolific Russian conservative, Nikolai Berdyaev (1947: 3), recognised that "the development of Russia has been catastrophic" as its history can be segmented into periods with little cohesion or continuity:

> Interruption is a characteristic of Russian history. Contrary to the opinion of the Slavophils the last thing it is, is organic. There have been five periods in Russian history and each provides a different picture. They are: the Russia of Kiev; Russia in the days of the Tartar yoke; the Russia of Moscow; the Russia of Peter the Great; and Soviet Russia. And it is quite possible that there will be yet another new Russia.

Russia's separation from Europe in the thirteenth century was the initial source of its complex history and unique strand of conservatism. The Mongol invasion separated Russia from both Europe and Russia's past by recasting Russia as a Eurasian power with one foot in the west and the other in the east. The event fundamentally changed Russia and the effort to reverse history and set back the clock is in itself a revolutionary act that neglects the principle of organic change. Conservatism is instead directed towards salvaging what it can from a revolutionary past and incorporate it into the national narrative.

The dichotomy of the modern west versus the traditional east resulted in the Enlightenment manifesting itself as a geographical phenomenon in Russia. Peter the Great's modernisation of Russia included a Cultural Revolution to remake Russia as a European nation. The aristocracy rejected traditional Russian values and spirituality of the peasantry as backward and primitive, while European culture was associated with reason and science. The cosmopolitan and Europeanised elite detached itself from the people with its identity based on the traditions of the peasantry. The polarisation into two separate and incompatible cultures and identities also undermined the social contract between the state and society.

While reason and modernisation also countered opposition in Western Europe during the romantic period, it created more antagonism in Russia, China and other states in the east as modernity was conflated with Westernising its culture and repudiating Russia's own past. The conservative Slavophiles recognised that emulating Europe is not possible without sacrificing Russian distinctiveness and social harmony.

The complex relation with Europe has been a defining characteristic of Russian conservatives. While some Russian conservatives seek to detach from Europe to reassert its Russia's cultural distinctiveness, other conservatives argue that Russia is European as Europe is defined by the plurality of nations with different cultures and traditions. Preserving distinctiveness is also a European tradition due to different paths during industrialisation, varying levels of cultural autonomy, and diverse degrees of political freedoms and economic liberalism. Russian conservatism has therefore also been split between a domestic focus that seeks to insulate Russia from the decadence of Europe, and an international conservatism that also aims to save Europe from itself by promoting and infusing the continent with conservatism.

The failure to establish a Russian path to modernity has culminated in a pattern of fierce pendulum swings. Slow socio-economic reforms have through history weakened Russia, which then required rapid development to catch up with the industrialised Western European powers. Russia subsequently was not able to develop gradually based on organic change, and the revolutionary great leaps forward at various periods in its history undermined social stability. Resistance to change and the failure to modernise precipitated Russia's humiliating defeat in the Crimean War in 1856, which incentivised rapid social and economic reforms. The emancipation of the serfs in 1861 shook the entire socio-economic system that could not be managed by a weak bureaucracy and civic institutions. The rapid industrialisation and urbanisation eventually made Russia the fastest-growing state among the great powers. Yet, political and social stability unravelled as radical groups emerged among the socialists, conservatives and liberals.

After the 1905 revolution, Russia implemented democratic reforms and liberalised its political system. Pyotr Stolypin, the Russian prime minister between 1906 and 1911, argued passionately about the great potential of Russian development by continuing reforms under conservative principles. Stolypin famously proclaimed that Russia would be transformed if social and political stability could be maintained: "Give me twenty years of peace, both and home and abroad, and you will not recognise Russia". Stolypin was assassinated by a leftist revolutionary in 1911. Instead of twenty years of peace – Russia was ravaged by the First World War and occupation; which was interrupted by the Bolshevik Revolution in 1917, followed by a destructive Civil War, then a devastating famine and collectivisation, purges and terror by Stalin, until the Second World War that resulted in the loss of approximately twenty-seven million of its citizens. Through the next decades, Russia lived under a revolutionary communist government that sought to create Communist Man liberated from his past by transcending the nation, religion, and the cultural distinctiveness of Russia.

In 1991, Russians abandoned both communism and the Soviet state in a liberal revolution that aimed to establish Russia as a capitalist democracy and a "normal European power". The liberal revolution soon proved disastrous as privatisation became a criminal revolution as a rising oligarchic class began to take control over politics, society began collapsing under alcoholism and other anti-social behaviour, several Russian republics moved towards secession, and the economy collapsed. It appeared that Russians might lose its state for the third time in the twentieth century. Furthermore, the liberal platform had been based on the premise that Russia would "return to Europe", a political platform that collapsed as the West began constructing a new Europe without Russia through NATO and EU expansion.

THE EVOLUTION OF RUSSIAN CONSERVATISM

As Russia itself has changed through history, new conservative strands emerged to adapt to new realities. Nikolai Karamzin was a cultural conservative who emerged in the late eighteenth century during the Romanticist era that opposed the excesses of the Enlightenment. Karamzin was deeply critical of the Cultural Revolution under Peter the Great, aimed to Europeanise Russia, and meant it was neccessary for Russia to return to its roots by reviving the its cultural distinctiveness. Political conservatives emerged in the form of Slavophiles from the 1830s and 1840s. Slavophiles such as Aleksei Khomyakov, Ivan Kireevskii, Konstantin Aksakov and Yuri Samarin considered Russia to be on an artificial European path, and advocated for developing Russia based on its native values and institutions that prevailed before the Petrine reforms. Konstantin Leontiev similarly believed in organic development and romanticised the Byzantine past of Russia, while others drew inspiration for Medival Muscovy. Pan-Slav thinkers like Nikolai Danilevsky advanced a conservative strand that endeavoured to unite Slavs akin to German unification of 1871. Fyodor Dostoyevsky drew from different conservative ideals – he distanced himself from the Slavophiles but was an advocate of pan-Slavism; he looked towards the Byzantine past as a motivation to "retake" Constantinople; he believed that conservatives and the liberal elites should find unity; and he also had some early Eurasianist impulses as the eastern frontier was seen as a remedy to the decadence from living like Europeans. The early twentieth-century Eurasianists such as Nikolai Trubetskoi and Pyotr Savitsky rejected that Russia was defined solely by its Slavic roots as the steppes of Eurasia had altered Russia. The commonality of all conservative epochs has been the central role of the Orthodox Church, which also serves as an instrument to bridge Russian history and different conservative strands.

The conservative turn of Russia from the beginning of the twenty-first century demonstrates both continuity and change. Under the Putin presidency, Russia began seeking refuge and stability under conservative ideas that had been prominent before the Bolshevik Revolution. Conservatives recognise that revolutionary change is destructive, which caused a return to the old question of how conservatives should respond incorporate revolution that has already changed the fundamental character of the state? Conservatism should not be conflated with nostalgia. Grand Duke Nikolai Nikolaevich argued following the loss of Russia to the Bolshevik Revolution: "Nobody should dream that it is possible to turn back the wheel of history. Our task is not to re-create the old order but to build a new Russia" (Robinson 2019: 140).

Conservatives have to salvage what it can from the revolutionary periods of Russian history and incorporate it into the national identity of Russia. The Mongol legacy, the Cultural Revolution by Peter the Great, the Great Reforms of the nineteenth century, the Bolshevik Revolution and other disruptive events are part of Russia's collective consciousness and contributed to what Russia has become today. By expanding and widening the historical memory and traditions, the rifts caused by revolutions become less profound in terms of shaping the identity. In other words, the revolutions of 1917 and 1991 must be incorporated into Russia's identity, although it does not define Russia as the nation was born more than a millennium ago. Contemporary Russian conservatism, therefore, aims to draw a national narrative with historical memory from Prince Vladimir the Great who converted to Christianity in Kievan Rus in the tenth century to the current realities of the Russian Federation.

Finding a Russian path to change and modernisation requires self-awareness and self-esteem, thus rediscovering the traditional in the past is imperative to look confidently into the future. The cultural inheritance is revived, the Orthodox Church is being elevated as a social institution, and nineteenth-century conservatives are commemorated with statues.

Putin rarely cites any socialists or liberals; rather, his speeches frequently include quotes by Nikolai Berdyaev, Ivan Ilyin, Pyotr Stolypin, Aleksandr Solzhenitsyn, Fyodor Dostoevsky, Nikolai Karamzin, and other conservative thinkers.

Unlike the Russian Empire or the Soviet Union, Russia has neither the capacity nor intention to pursue hegemony in Europe or Eurasia. Having made its peace with its existing borders, Russia has positioned itself as a status-quo power seeking to consolidate its existing position. The demographics have changed with a higher percentage of ethnic Russians within its borders, which opens up the question of defining the nation. However, Russian conservatives are more drawn to the identity of a civilisation state as it seized being an ethnic nation-state in the mid-sixteenth century. The tradition of a strong state remains as a source for stability, although as stability boosts the confidence of the Kremlin, there is more ambitious experimentation with gradual democratic reforms.

Russia also aims to resolve the historical challenge of establishing a Russian political economy that pursues organic growth. Infrastructure projects are advanced to tie together the vast territory, with great similarity to the economic policies of Sergei Witte at the end of the nineteenth century. The changing international distribution of power is also influencing Russian conservatism. The rise of Asia, most prominently China, ends 500 years of Western dominance. This has profound implications for Russia as it contributes to resolving the Eurasian schism in its identity and the fixation on Europe and the Western world. The economic rise of Asia ends the dichotomy between a modern European identity and a traditional eastern identity. Eurasian integration by linking with both the east and the west becomes a viable geoeconomic project and a source for bringing harmony to Russian unique identity.

CHAPTER OVERVIEW

This book aims to explain the evolution of Russian conservatism. First, conservatism is theorised to identify the universal assumptions, and why conservative policies evolve in different directions. This approach is important to compare Russian conservative ideas and policies across different periods and even compare Russian conservatism with the Western counterparts.

Without precise theoretical assumptions about conservatism, the analysis of the evolution of Russian conservatism is vulnerable to bias. A key weakness in the literature on Russian conservatism is the tendency in the West to view Russia as the "other" and thus exaggerate the differences and downplay the similarities. Contemporary Western conservatives commonly depict Russian conservatism as a thin veil for self-serving power interests, corruption, imperial ambitions and rationalising anti-Western sentiments. Conservative thinkers in the West often reveal ignorance about Russian history and its conservative traditions to fit within outdated Cold War narratives.

After outlining the analytical framework in the first chapter, the book explores the continuity and change in Russian conservatism. The history of Russian conservatism encompasses central issues in sociology, philosophy, political economy and international relations. While the key principle of connecting the past with the future has remained constant, the Russian past and its future challenges have undergone radical change.

1. Theorising Russian Conservatism

The first chapter outlines the theoretical assumptions of conservatism to explain the distinctiveness of Russian conservatism. Conservatism is an ideology about managing change. While the fundamental assumptions of conservatism are constant across time and space, it culminates in different strands of conservative policies depending on the unique geography and historical development of states. The fundamental assumption is that change towards the rational and the modern must consider the primordial compulsions in mankind that evolved over tens of thousands of years. Conservatism therefore stresses that change must be organic and is averse to revolutionary change, as the new must build on the past. What are these instincts? Human beings are instinctively a social animal, and modernity is primarily limited by the primordial need to maintain the collective and reproduce social membership. The paradox of conservatism is the universal need in human nature for social memberships in distinctive groups, which results in different conservative policies. Parallels are drawn between Western and Russian conservative thinkers and the contradictions they seek to address in human nature and society. However, the West has always been sceptical to the distinctive strand of Russian conservatism – characterised by autocracy, empire, and a safeguarding cultural autonomy from the West.

2. The Eurasian Schism in Russian Conservatism

The second chapter explores the Eurasian schism in Russian conservatism. Russia's origin is commonly traced back to Kievan Rus and the prevalent role of the Orthodox Church. The fragmentation of Kievan Rus and the invasion by the Mongols in the thirteenth century began two and a half centuries of occupation by an Asiatic power. This became the first revolutionary change in Russia, which positioned Russia between Europe and Asia in terms of both national identity and the political economy. Following independence from the

Golden Horde in the late fifteenth century, the Russians had a few decades on independence before conquering the Tatar kingdoms along the Volga. Russia thereby became a multi-ethnic empire that would continue to expand into economically backward regions away from the international trade corridors where traditions and spirituality were preserved. While conservatism entailed seeking refuge in a distinctive eastern identity not corrupted by modern economics, while the need to modernise incentivised a European identity and to reconnect with international maritime corridors.

In the early eighteenth century, Peter the Great interpreted the Enlightenment in terms of geography by transforming Russia into a modern European state. Russian culture and traditions were deemed to be backwards, and Peter the Great sought to turn Russia away from its Muscovite past. The Cultural Revolution deepened the schism in society between Europeanised elites and the peasantry that identified by traditional values. The bourgeois could subsequently not fulfil their social responsibility of producing Russian-language literature as a cultural foundation. Without a distinctive and organic culture that underpinned the morality of Russian society, conservatives cautioned Russia could not remain a sovereign state.

3. The Rise of Conservatism from the Early Nineteenth Century

The romantic era of the late eighteenth century made its way to Russia and laid the early foundation for cultural conservatism. Much like the Enlightenment had been interpreted as the Europeanisation of Russia, romanticism became a movement to reassert Russia's cultural autonomy from Europe. The French Revolution also gave birth to political conservatism to preserve sovereign monarchies. Russian conservatives in the first half of the nineteenth century were largely devoted to managing the liberal political influences from Europe as a result of the French Revolution, and to resolve the problems caused by serfdom. Initially, Alexander I pursued several liberal reforms, and on his behalf, Mikhail Speransky sought to move Russia towards a constitutional monarchy. Albeit, the disruptive changes and the invasion by Napoleon prompted Alexander to halt reforms. The Decembrist Revolt of 1825, an indirect result of the French invasion of 1812, instilled revolutionary myth and spirit in Russia.

Russia launched its nationalist alternative to French nationalism that sought to defend the autocracy. Sergei Uvarov's concept of *Official Nationality* became the foundation for Russia's state conservatism until the Bolshevik Revolution. Building on Russian traditions, the triad of Uvarov's conservatism was "orthodoxy, autocracy, and nationality" to counter the French revolutionary slogans of "liberty, egalitarianism, and fraternity". The political landscape began to fragment between conservative Slavophile and liberal Westernisers.

4. After the Crimean War: The Great Reforms and Revolutions

During the second half of the nineteenth century, conservatism became more preoccupied with managing the Great Reforms. The humiliating defeat in the Crimean War in 1856 made it clear that Russia had to catch up as modernisation was a necessity to survive among the Western European powers. The Great Reforms were enacted. Emancipation of the serfs reorganised the socio-economic foundations of Russian society, although the weak bureaucracy was ill-prepared to manage the drastic changes. Rapid industrialisation and urbanisation similarly disrupted the traditional way of life. With subsequent disorder opened a political vacuum caused by economic inequality and poor conditions for workers was partly filled by the nascent socialists. Much like the conservative Slavophiles, the socialists also claimed to represent the interests of the peasantry. However, unlike the Slavophiles, the socialists desired a revolution to overthrow and destroy the monarchy, the nobility, capitalism, and the Orthodox Church. In 1905, the Tsar accepted deep democratic reforms with the October Manifesto in response to social upheavals. For the socialists, this was merely a practice for the Bolshevik Revolution that would come in 1917.

5. Reforming the Concept of a Conservative Political Economy

The industrial revolution required reforms to the concept of a conservative political economy. Early conservatism was inclined towards resisting change as opposed to managing change. Industrial society was correctly accused of undermining traditional communities and atomising the individual. Much like Thomas Jefferson endeavoured to preserve the morality of agrarian communities, Russian conservatives idealised the spirituality found in traditional communes. Yet, the failure to industrialise creates asymmetrical dependence and core-periphery relationships with Britain, which undermined political and cultural sovereignty. Conservatives subsequently had to develop a conservative approach to industrialisation.

The state requires a central role in a modern conservative political economy. Besides protecting institutions and communities to ensure the reproduction of traditional values and social membership, the state must ensure sovereign control over the economy. Alexander Hamilton, Friedrich List and Sergei Witte all recognised that industrialisation was a central component for nation-building. Managing change required sovereign control over three main pillars of the economy: strategic industries, physical transportations corridors and financial instruments. By the last decade of the nineteenth century, Russia was developing its strategic industries and constructed a pioneering transportation corridor that connected the Eurasian continent as a challenge to the dominance of maritime powers. However, insufficient fiscal sovereignty became a key weakness.

6. Conservatism under Communism and the Advent of Eurasianism

Marxism, as a radical revolutionary movement, sought to liberate Russia from its past to give way to Communist Man. The Bolshevik revolutionaries sought to uproot all institutions that were sacred to the conservatives – the monarchy, the nation, the Orthodox Church, and even the family. Even Russian conservatism diminished from the historical memory in both the Soviet Union and the West due to the binary ideological rivalry of the Cold War of communism versus liberalism/capitalism. Social failures and instability compelled the Soviet Union to revive several conservative ideas by, for example, restoring the status of the family. Similarly, the Orthodox Church and national sentiments proved necessary to mobilise the people. Russian émigré who had left communist Russia continued to preserve and modify conservatism. Eurasianism emerged as a new strand of conservatism in response to the fundamental changes imposed by the Soviet Union. The Eurasianists from the 1920s argued that Russia should not consider the Slavic as the sole component of Russia's ethno-cultural core as Russia had also absorbed Turkic and Ugro-Finnic characteristics as it expanded into the Eurasian steppe.

7. The Liberal Revolution in the 1990s

In 1991, Russia emerged with independence from the Soviet Union. The 1990s was a revolutionary period as Russia gained a new state, ideology, identity, borders and foreign policy. Peter the Great had initiated a cultural revolution to make Russia more European, and Yeltsin similarly initiated a political revolution to model Russia after the political systems of the West to become a member in the family of European nations. The revolutionary changes were informed by liberal ideals, which were implemented in a shock treatment that would not be based on a gradual change or have root in Russian traditions. The liberal revolution caused havoc as privatisation became a criminal revolution with oligarch seizing control over the political system. Alcoholism and anti-social behaviour tore apart society and life expectancy plummeted. Secessionist movements proliferated, and it appeared that Russia would share the fate of the Soviet Union. Furthermore, the West did not share Russia's ambitions about creating a Greater Europe and preserved the zero-sum structures by constructing a new Europe without Russia through NATO and EU expansionism. With the collapse of Yeltsin's liberal platform, there only appeared to be revolutionary political alternatives in the form of a resurgent communist party or the radical nationalists on the right. Yeltsin stepped down early and enabled his Prime Minister Vladimir Putin to chart a new path for Russia.

8. The Return of Russian Conservatism under Putin

Russia's rejection of communism and the liberal revolution of the 1990s created a demand for rejuvenating conservatism as a third alternative. The conservative commitment to organic growth presents a challenge in terms of preserving the legacy of a proceeding revolutionary state that sought to eliminate Russia's distinctiveness. What should conservatives salvage from the Soviet history that eviscerated much of what was sacred for conservatives? Both the Soviet era and the liberal revolution of the 1990s have to be incorporated into the national narrative as it laid the foundation for contemporary Russia. Furthermore, conservatism as an ideology had to be rediscovered at a moment when liberal reforms were needed and globalisation could not be ignored. Rather than resisting change or embracing revolutionary change by denouncing its past, Putin became increasingly conservative to manage change. The troubled and revolutionary history of Russia can be woven into a unifying and coherent identity if it is placed within the context of Russia's more than 1,000 years as a civilisation. Contemporary conservatives seek to address the Soviet legacy in a balanced manner, rehabilitate tsarist history, restore the role of the Orthodox Church in society, embrace traditional family values and restore the historical memory of Russia.

9. The End of the Occidental Era and the Birth of Greater Eurasia

Three centuries of Russia mirroring itself in the West has come to an end. Since the reforms of Peter the Great in the early eighteenth century, Russia has largely defined itself by its relationship with the West. The liberal international order propagated by the West after the Cold War caused a mutual rejection and ended the occidental era for Russia. First, the liberal international order left no legitimate space for Russia in Europe. Second, the excesses of the liberal international order convinced Russia that there was nothing left to learn from the West. Concurrently, the rise of China and the wider East has ended 500 years of Western dominance. The geographical manifestation of a modern West versus an economically backward east has been rendered obsolete, and Eurasianism is reconceptualised as a geoeconomic concept. Greater Europe has been abandoned and replaced by

Greater Eurasia. The endeavour to find a distinctive Russian path to modernisation appears to be within grasp, a centuries-long struggle of Russian conservatives. A Eurasianist political economy is established as a multipolar ideology. In cooperation with China and other powers in the East, Russia is seeking to develop Eurasian strategic industries, transportation corridors and financial instruments that rescinds US geoeconomic dominance of Eurasia from the Rimland. The relationship with Europe is also transformed as geoeconomic revisions convert Europe into the western peninsula of Greater Eurasia.

10. Russia as an International Conservative Power

From the fall of Constantinople, the French Revolution, to the Napoleonic Wars – Russia's efforts to immunise itself from the turbulence outside its borders shifted quickly to a universal mission to "save Europe" from itself. As the West undergoes a crisis in liberalism, Russia is yet again taking on a wider role as an international conservative power. Russia's efforts to reject universalism and restore its Eurasian distinctiveness is paradoxically creating a common cause with classical conservative movements around the world and thus fuelling Russian soft power. The liberal international order has largely been an international revolutionary movement aiming to reorganise the world around liberal ideals, which had both domestic and international repercussions. The neoliberal consensus prevented the political Left from re-distributing wealth and obstructed the political Right from preserving the community and traditional values. Russia and classical conservatives in both the West and the East are redefining the dividing lines in the world as being national-patriotism versus cosmopolitan-globalism.

Chapter 1

Theorising Russian Conservatism

INTRODUCTION

Conservatism postulates that society must develop organically from the roots of its particular culture, history and traditions. The most important task for conservatives is therefore to manage gradual and organic change and oppose disruptive change that disconnects the present from the past. By contrast, revolutionary change implies liberation from one's past as tradition can be heavy luggage that slows down progress. Conservatism is commonly confused with nostalgia that resists change. Conservatism acknowledges that the failure to renew and change causes stagnation, decay and eventual collapse. Conservatism, therefore, aims to manage change by recognising limitations set by human nature.

The core principle of conservatism is that human behaviour is informed by both reason and primordial instincts, which sets conditions and limitations for societal change. This duality within mankind is the principal source of internal contradiction that conservatives set out to manage. Mankind is far from being a completely rational creature as ancient instincts that evolved over countless of millennia has a profound influence on behaviour. As society undergoes change and modernisation, stability depends on harmonising the rational and modern with the instinctive and traditional. The concept of organic change is therefore the most important consideration for conservatives as the new must build on and renew the past.

The most dominant instinct in mankind is the need for social memberships in a group. Human beings are a social animal, and the collective is necessary for meaning and security. Herein is another contradiction for managing change: conservatives must embrace the liberty and autonomy of the individual to modernise society, while concurrently preserve the

15

authority of the collective such as the family, church, community, culture, nation, and other institutions that socialise and restricts the autonomy of the individual.

Social groups must preserve their cultural distinctiveness by adhering to inside versus outside dynamics, which is why conservatism is averse to universalism. Culture represents the achievements of the collective that offers a bridge between the past and the present. Culture must be reproduced as it provides nourishment for the collective consciousness by providing a deeper meaning and purpose for society. Culture lays the foundation for morality, as the standards, principles and rules of conduct for a social group, which are encoded in the particular history and traditions of a shared religion or culture. Conservatism does not oppose the liberty advanced by liberal ideology; rather, it aims to preserve the collective as the necessary foundation for individual liberties.

The concept of *organic change* explains why conservatism is based on fundamental assumptions about human nature and society that transcends time and space, although these universal assumptions do not translate into consistent and uniform policies. While human nature is static, the state as a political entity evolves in terms of what modernity entails and what to preserve. A universal trait in human nature is to organise in distinctive social groups, which paradoxically limits the ideals of universalism. Different conservative policies therefore emerge as nations or other social groups have all been shaped by distinctive geography and historical complexity.

Russian conservatism has been influenced greatly by autocracy, empire and efforts to disassociate Russia from the West. These conservative policies derived from the unique geography and history that caused ambiguity about the nation and fuelled economic inefficiency. Russian conservatism has been greatly shaped by the failure to pursue gradual modernisation, which has culminated in stagnation or disruptive great leaps forward. Russia's history of revolutionary change creates an attraction of conservatism, as the impulse to preserve emerges when something sacred or instinctive is lost. Yet, these are not inherent features of Russia or its unique strand of conservatism as change appears to be the only constant.

The purpose of this chapter is to outline the theoretical assumptions behind the concept of conservatism. The theoretical assumptions charted here informs the analysis of Russian conservatism. Conservatism is based on some common fundamental assumptions irrespective of the distinctiveness of societies and various stages of development. Nonetheless, a variety of conservative strands emerge depending on what is aimed to be preserved and the development that threatens its reproduction. Russian conservatism differs from its Western equivalents, although the fundamentals remain similar.

REASON VERSUS INSTINCT

Conservatism as an ideology was born out of the Enlightenment when societies began to be organised according to rationality rather than superstition. The sovereignty of reason and science as evidence were the foundation for advancing sublime ideals such as liberty, tolerance, justice, constitutional government and the separation of church and state. Structuring society along the rational was revolutionary in every sense of the word as the organisation of humanity had evolved from instincts that developed over many millennia as a means of survival, which was then codified into religious doctrines.

Both liberalism and conservatism are children of the Enlightenment, although with one basic discrepancy. The liberal idea posits that mankind advances by continuing to embrace the rational and shed the irrational. By contrast, conservatism cautions against exaggerating the rational capacity as human beings still act upon ancient instincts that have developed over tens of thousands of years to survive (Huntington 1957; Herder 1966). Completely overcoming ancient instincts such as reliance on social groups such as the family and the community requires thousands of years of evolution, not a few centuries (Luttwak 1995: 80).

The Enlightenment did not enable humanity to transition from the instinctive to the rational – rather it left mankind with one foot in reason, the modern and calculative; and the other foot in the innate, traditional and spiritual. The so-called duality of mankind has caused a schism between nature and civilisation, the soul and intellect, spirituality and reason. Blaise Pascal, the seventeenth-century philosopher, famously advised in Pensées against: "Two extremes: to exclude reason, to admit reason only". Mankind therefore moves between the material world and emotional consciousness (Voegelin 1974).

Conservatism is therefore critical of liberal advancements to the extent it entails liberating the individual from communitarian influences that provides purpose and unity. Neglecting the instinctive is not an alternative as it merely manifests itself in new forms. The excesses of the Enlightenment subsequently produced the Counter-Enlightenment movement and Romanticism that revived admiration for medievalism, nature and the past.

Conservative ideology has its support psychology, the study of the mind, which affirms that the instinctive has a powerful influence over behaviour what is inaccurately believed to be rational choices. Sigmund Freud (1963: 119) succinctly argued that "the primitive mind is, in the fullest sense of the word, imperishable". Carl Jung (1973: 227) similarly recognised that the collective consciousness is influenced by archetypes, imagery that has been inherited by early ancestors and evolved throughout evolution: "Free will only exists within the limits of consciousness. Beyond those limits there is mere compulsion". These ideas from psychology have evidence in the natural sciences as brain scans reveal that people reach conclusion based on instincts, and then use reason to justify the predetermined inference (Haidt 2012). Neglecting instincts that evolved for self-preservation, such as reproducing culture, community or the family, is punished with psychological anxiety and other mental health issues that culminate in a variety of destructive and anti-social behaviour.

While conservative ideology emerged out of the Enlightenment, the duality of mankind has been coded into ancient religions and mythology. In Greek mythology, Zeus had two sons: Apollo was the God of rational thinking, logic and order, while Dionysus was the God of the irrational, instincts and chaos. The mythology of ancient Mesopotamia tells a similar story about two original Gods: Abzu, the father, representing order, and Tiamat, the mother, embodying primordial chaos. Correspondingly, the Egyptian God of Osiris embodied a paternal spirit by ruling with wisdom and virtue, and his wife, Isis, was the Goddess of Darkness and Chaos. The commonality with these ancient stories was the recognition that the rational and instinctive were mutually contradictory and mutually dependent, and the effort to advance one at the expense of the other caused disaster. Aleksei Khomyakov, a leading nineteenth-century Russian conservative, argued that every state or society

is made up of two elements: the living historical element, which embodies all the society's vitality, and the rational or speculative element, which can achieve nothing by itself, but gradually imparts order to the fundamental or living element, sometimes pushing it aside and sometimes developing it. (quoted in Saunders 2014: 1)

In the progressive ideologies of liberalism and socialism, there is an intrinsic and misguided belief that mankind will become happier and more evolved by advancing reason and shedding the instinctive and spiritual. Fyodor Dostoyevsky (2017: 255) opined that the development of humanity and society can not only be based on reason:

Reason has never had the power to define good and evil, or even to distinguish between good and evil, even approximately; on the contrary, it has always mixed them up in a disgraceful and pitiful way; science has even given the solution by the fist. This is particularly characteristic of the half-truths of science, the most terrible scourge of humanity, unknown till this century, and worse than plague, famine, or war.

Furthermore, the struggle towards utopia is commonly depicted as the absence of hardship, even though human beings find meaning in adversity and struggle (Frankl 1985). Dostoyevsky thus argued that the path towards utopia based solely on reason will lead to nihilism and destruction:

> Reason is an excellent thing, there's no disputing that, but reason is nothing but reason and satisfies only the rational side of man's nature. . . . Even if man really were nothing but a piano key, even if this were proved to him by natural science and mathematics, even then he would not become reasonable, but would purposely do something perverse out of simple ingratitude, simply to win his point . . . then, after all, perhaps only by his curse will he attain his object, that is, really convince himself that he is a man and not a piano key! If you say that all this, too, can be calculated and tabulated . . . then man would purposely go mad in order to be rid of reason and win his point. (Dostoyevsky 2009a: 21, 23)

Conservative theory suggests that the principal challenge for Russia to manage change derives from the inability to harmonise the instinctive and the rational. The traditional and modern has been polarised by history. Russia was largely severed from Europe, the Nordic Rus, and Byzantine heritage when it was conquered by the Mongols in the early thirteenth century. The duality of mankind manifested itself geographically in the schism that had taken root in Russia's identity between the east and the west. Russia's eastern identity represented the traditional and spiritual, while its western identity represented modernity.

The Enlightenment was expressed in a cultural revolution in the early eighteenth century as Peter the Great sought to replace Russia's culture based on religion and tradition with a European substitute that represented the rational. The Romanticism and Counter-Enlightenment movement that reacted to the excesses of the Enlightenment shared many similarities with its European counterparts, although it entails scaling back Russia's Europeanness and instead reasserting its distinctive cultural roots.

ORGANIC CHANGE VERSUS REVOLUTIONARY CHANGE

The progressive ideologies of liberalism and socialism tend to be agnostic about traditions and history as the experiences of the past may no longer be relevant and could even corrupt the present. By contrast, conservative ideology has a profound reverence for the institutions and orthodoxies of the past as it is the foundation for a stable and viable present and future.

Conservatism is commonly misunderstood as resisting change as opposed to managing change. The central theme in conservatism is the belief in *organic change* due to the need for harmonising the instinctive and the rational. Organic change implies that the new must build on and renew the old, which requires society to guard against alien corruption of the system. The best-known pre-revolutionary philosopher in contemporary Russia is Nikolai Berdyaev (1923: 100), who argued: "The conservative principle is not by itself opposed to development, it merely demands that development be organic, that the future does not destroy the past but continue to develop it". Conservatism "unites the future with the past" and this link must not be severed (Berdyaev 1923: 90).

Huntington (1957: 461) calls conservatism a *positional ideology* as it responds to attack against important institutions that represent the collective. Conservatism functions as a balance and corrective mechanism to the excesses of progressive ideologies such as liberalism and socialism that embark on the misguided mission to transcend the instinctive reliance on social groups, faith and tradition. An early Bolshevik cautioned that conservative impulses restrain and reverse revolutionary change: "History is full of examples of the transformation of parties of revolution into parties of order. Sometimes the only mementos of a revolutionary party are the watchwords which it has inscribed on public buildings" (Cohen 1980: 186).

The positional nature of conservatism that adapts to social situations produces different strands of conservatism, depending on the institutions and traditions that are threatened. Hence, conservatism does not adhere to a uniform tradition, and the policies cannot always be comfortably positioned on a left-right political scale.

Edmund Burke's famous maxim, "we must reform to conserve", suggests that the old must perpetually be reformed to avoid decadence and revolution. The old stagnates and dies, which suggests that change and renewal is the sole alternative. Resisting societal change will result in the inevitable collapse of the old, although without the new to replace it. Failing to manage change will therefore produce *revolutionary change* as the new makes a break with the past. Destroying the societal structures without replacing it with institutions that build on the past leads to nihilism, anarchy and collapse (Nietzsche 1968: 64).

The origin of European conservatism is commonly recognised to have been a reaction to the excesses of the French Revolution. Conservatism is thus often reactionary or counter-revolutionary. Carl Schmitt (1986: 62) argued that "history is the conservative God who restores what the other has revolutionised". Huntington (1957: 470) similarly argued that

> Men are driven to conservatism by the shock of events, by the terrible feeling that a society of institutions which they have approved or taken for granted and with which they have been intimately connected may suddenly cease to exist.

Democracy can only sustain itself when limited by conservative principles. The consensus of society that defines interests, values and the acceptable scope of political pluralism is based on a collective consciousness inherited from past experiences. Organic and gradual changes enable the new to have a solid root in the legitimacy of the past. By contrast, fundamental breaks with the past will be fiercely resisted as an attack on the sacred, and national cohesion will then need to be imposed by authoritarian and coercive means.

Edmund Burke's ideas of conservatism derived from the contrast between the destructiveness unleashed by the French Revolution and the benign results of the American Revolution. In France, the former regime and its structures had to be eliminated in order not to corrupt the new order. The terror that followed the French Revolution demonstrated for many the contradiction of achieving freedoms through revolutionary change. In the early nineteenth century, Nikolai Karamzin (2005: 135) believed that the French terror had "cured Europe of the dreams of civil freedom and equality". By comparison, the American Revolution stands out as a unique case as it resulted in a very liberal constitution. Unlike other revolutions, the American Revolution was to some extent a secession as the American colonies sought to liberate themselves from the rule of a monarch on the other side of the Atlantic. The core liberal ideals and identity of the British were not uprooted to give way to something new; rather, these ideals were advanced further by rejecting taxation without representation.

The Bolshevik Revolution shared the destructiveness of the French Revolution by attempting to create Communist Man, untainted by his past, by purging all capitalist and religious institutions that organised society. Without building a future based on the legitimacy of the traditions and culture of the past, revolutionary leaders became reliant on brutal means to impose a new system. Disconnecting with the past results in revolutionaries often eating their own with accusations of not being pious enough, and the most extreme and brutal revolutionaries tend to float to the top. By relying on brutal means to form a new centre, the revolutionaries eventually destroy the intended ends of advancing human freedoms.

Change can be accommodated and ideas can be imported, although they need to adapt to the distinctiveness of one's own culture. Oswald Spengler (1991) famously argued that civilisations falter when they outgrow the culture they emerged from and depended upon for nourishment. Charles Lindbergh used a similar analogy for organic growth: "We root into the primitive as a tree roots into the earth. If we cut off the roots, we lose the sap without which we can't progress or even survive" (Whitman 1969). Konstantin Pobedonostsev likewise compared the cultural development of society to the biology of a flower:

A flower develops from a bud, and the makeup of the bud fully defines its development. If we want to give the latter a different character, which contradicts the constitution of the bud – then we will achieve nothing but death. (Gusev 2001: 55)

Gradual development is similarly undermined by periodical great leaps forward. Boris Chicherin, a nineteenth-century Russian liberal-conservative, recognised: "There are those who demand sudden changes and do not admit the gradualness of historical evolution. . . . History, like nature, does not make leaps" (Hamburg 1992: 169). Herein lies the principal source of disruption that has defined Russian history. Due to its complex geography and history, Russia has not excelled in managing change by pursuing gradual development and modernisation. Instead, Russia has through its history pursued periods of rapid and disorderly modernisation that amounts to revolutions. The schism between Europe and Asia during the "Mongol Yoke", Peter the Great's cultural revolution to Europeanise Russia, the emancipation of the serfs, rapid industrialisation and urbanisation, the Bolshevik Revolution and the destructive liberal revolution of the 1990s represented revolutionary changes that failed to build on the past.

Russia's geographical make-up makes it predisposed to revolutionary change by making great leaps rather than gradual and organic development akin to its European counterparts. Leon Trotsky explained Russia's *unbalanced development* and reliance on great leaps as the result of its contradictions:

A population of 150 million, 4.4 million square kilometers of land in Europe, 17.5 million in Asia. Within this vast space every epoch of human culture is to be found: from the primeval barbarism of the northern forests, where people eat raw fish and worship blocks of wood, to the modern social relations of the capitalist city, where socialist workers consciously recognize themselves as participants in world politics and keep a watchful eye on events in the Balkans and on debates in the German Reichstag. The most concentrated industry in Europe based on the most backward agriculture in Europe. The most colossal state apparatus in the world making use of every achievement of modern technological progress in order to retard the historical progress of its own country. (in Neumann 2016: 76)

Nikolai Berdyaev (1947: 1) similarly attributed the vast geography of Russia for its unique identity, mentality, and propensity towards extremes:

In the Russian soul there is a sort of immensity, a vagueness, a predilection for the infinite, such as is suggested by the great plain of Russia. For this reason the Russian people have found difficulty in achieving mastery over these vast expanses and in reducing them to orderly shape. There has been a vast elemental strength in the Russian people combined with a comparatively weak sense of form. The Russians have not been in any special sense a people of culture, as the peoples of Western Europe have been, they have rather been a people of revelation and inspiration. The Russians have not been given to moderation and they have readily gone to extremes.

THE INDIVIDUAL VERSUS THE GROUP

Conservatism has a communitarian foundation as the collective must restrain individualism (Huntington 1957: 456). The quintessence of the communitarian idea is that the community can be a conveyer of freedoms and rights, which may require that the community is prioritised above individual rights and interests. Freedom demands that citizens embrace virtue and responsibility towards the community. Thus, freedom must not be confused with radical individualism that entails throwing away responsibilities.

The principal instinct of mankind is to seek refuge in social groups, which limits rationality and individualism. Human beings are a social animal that must reproduce social membership to ensure organic change. The group offers security, belonging and even a sense of immortality by reproducing the group. Social groups offer safety and order from chaos. The most important group is the family, which is why its preservation as an institution and traditional family values are always a key priority for conservatism. Beyond the family, the individual requires the local community and to strive towards larger units. The largest tribe that defines a distinct group is a civilisation (Huntington 1996).

The need for some extent of social exclusion in conservatism clashes with liberal ideals of inclusion and fairness. Tribalism is deeply entrenched in human nature after organising according to kinship and united by common faith through the millennia. Tribalism is commonly associated with negative connotations, for good reasons, as the loyalty towards the group members is at the expense of non-members of the group. A social group by definition is exclusive as it also identified by what it is not. A group such as a family, tribe, nation or civilisation has external walls that uphold order for those on the inside to protect from the chaos on the outside. Groups that completely isolate themselves from the external stagnate and decay as engagement with the external is a condition to renew and update the internal.

Liberals such as Thomas Paine denounced the idea that traditions and the past should influence the present as undemocratic, and John Stuart Mill (2001: 65) even referred to the "the despotism of custom" as a "hindrance to human advancement". By contrast, conservative intellectuals such as Gilbert Keith Chesterton ([1912] 2002: 58) argued that democracy does not oppose tradition as "tradition is only democracy extended over time". Tradition is "the democracy of the dead. Tradition refuses to submit to the small and arrogant oligarchy of those who merely happen to be walking about" (Chesterton 2002: 58). Edmund Burke similarly rejected the liberal concept of a social contract as an agreement among the living. Burke argued that society is an association between the dead, the living and the unborn. Burke, therefore, defended the virtues of tradition and continuity as a counterweight to destructive revolutionary movements that would destroy the moral underpinnings of society and association with the dead and the unborn. Nikolai Berdyaev outlined the Russian conservative position on incorporating the past:

> The nation speak([s] not only the living, but also the dead, the great past and the enigmatic future. In a nation enter not only human generations, but also the stones of churches, palaces, and estates, gravestones, old manuscripts, and books. In order to catch the will of the people one has to listen to these stones, read the rotting pages. But with your revolutionary-democratic noise you want to drown the voices of the dead, of past generations, you want to kill the feeling of the past. (Robinson 2019: 131)

The communitarianism of conservatives that builds on a shared past should not be conflated with Marxist communitarianism as a revolutionary ideology. Much like his liberal counterparts, Karl Marx (1912) expressed hostility to the concept of democracy for the dead: "The tradition of all dead generations weighs like an alp on the brains of the living."

The nation-state made Western societies remarkably capable of managing the schism between liberal individualism and conservative communitarianism. Nationalism established a larger social group based on ethno-cultural kinship. Johann Gottfried Herder's concept of nationalism in the eighteenth century celebrated the nation as an organic structure that transcends all other features on social differentiation. Preserving the nation was imperative, although for Herder, the nation should not be conflated with the state and the military. For Herder, the state was merely a means to an end – the nation (Schmidt 1956). George Kennan (1993: 76–77) recognised that nationalism is "the greatest emotional-political force of the age". The nation establishes clear and natural inside-outside dynamics and represents the "essence of our being which defines us against the background of the world" (Lippman 2008: 66–67). The European nation-state became the most successful institution in history to manage change as it formed a strong ethno-cultural core as the foundation of the community, which was used to elevate individual rights and human freedoms.

Nationalism was initially a revolutionary liberal cause by transferring sovereignty from the monarchy to the people, and early conservatives sought to preserve the order and institutions of kingdoms and duchies. Once the nation-state became the main institution that represented the collective, conservatives altered their position to become ardent defenders of the nation-state. By contrast, liberals challenge the arbitrary authority of ethnicity, religion and culture as the representation of the collective in the nation-state, which is deemed to be an infringement on the autonomy of the individual.

The contemporary decoupling of liberalism from the nation-state in the West is deeply problematic because the nation-state is not replaced with a clearly defined collective with roots in the traditions of a specific group. Rather than evolving into a global village without civilisational dividing lines, society fragments into sub-identities as evident by identity politics. The rational drift towards individualism is destructive as mankind instinctively responds by seeking out old communities or construct new ones if the old have seized to exist. Berdyaev even portrayed his prison sentence favourably as an escape from individualism: "I never experienced so fully such a feeling of oneness with the *communauté*, I was in a less individualistic mood than ever" (Rancour-Laferriere 1995: 227).

CONSERVATISM AND LIBERTY

Conservatism is not an ideology that seeks to restrict liberty; rather, it maintains that liberty can only be built on a foundation that adheres to the collective and traditions of the past. Conservatism strives to maintain the collective as the foundation of a cohesive social group, with the unifying and common rules outlined in a shared morality. Passing on the lessons of the past generation to the new is imperative to ensure cultural continuity as a precondition to advance a complex society and liberties. Sowell (2002: 162) argues that "each new generation born is in effect an invasion of civilisation by little barbarians, who must be civilised before it is too late".

Altruism is self-interest in disguise as the social group represents an extension of the self (Harman 2010). The willingness of human beings, much like animals, to assist each other depends on kinship and in-group loyalty as self-preservation is advanced by defending the group is required to sustain protection and even achieving immortality by reproducing the distinctive group. An early theorist on civil society from the mid-eighteenth century, Adam Ferguson (1767), argued that civil society depends on in-group loyalty as the source of morality, benevolence, trust and mutual obligation.

A united and cohesive social group lays the foundation for individual rights. In the struggle towards establishing a cohesive collective, the scope for individual liberties have been marginal as the alternative to autocracy has not been democracy, but anarchy. Russian conservatism has therefore relied heavily on autocracy as the principal source of power to maintain stability.

In the absence of the distinctive social group and morality as the foundation of conservatism, liberty diminishes. The organisation of society shifts from restraints based on a benign internal compulsion to the heavy hand of external compulsion. The challenge for states with autocratic traditions is not merely to relinquish power along with liberal dogmas; rather, it also requires the establishment of alternative sources of the collective as a source of legitimacy for the existence of the state as a political unit. Autocracy can be a necessary form of government when the alternative is anarchy due to the lack of socio-economic, normative and political connectivity of society. However, with the central government taking responsibility for organising all aspects of society, other institutions will be deprived of the oxygen required to develop.

Much like its European counterparts, Russia relied on strong rulers during the troubled sixteenth and early seventeenth century. However, Russia took a much longer time to transfer sovereignty to the people due to its vast and scattered geography with a multi-ethnic population. Catherine the Great was a strong proponent of the Enlightenment and was enthused about the writings of Voltaire. However, following the French Revolution erupted; Catherine recognised that Russia did not have the political foundations for such liberal reforms as the collective was held together by a strong leader. Liberty was rooted internally, and strong faith was deemed required as an internal compulsion to organise morality.

Russia's historical difficulty in managing the relationship between the collective and the individual is rooted in the difficulty of defining the collective. The ethno-cultural nation-state failed to establish itself due to the Mongol yoke for roughly 250 years, which was followed by an independent Russian state becoming a multi-ethnic empire by conquering and absorbing Tatar kingdoms. Nationalist movements like Slavophilism or Pan-Slavism always threatened to invoke nationalist sentiments among the ethnic minorities within Russia. Subsequently, the community was organised with the state at the centre rather than the nation, which culminated in loyalties towards the monarch, bureaucracy or orthodoxy as opposed to the nation-state. Efforts to reduce the reliance on the state resulted in Russian conservatism becoming split politically into two branches – the "state-protective conservatism" and the cultural "Orthodox-Russian conservatism" (Gusev 2001: 40, 70). The Russian Empire and the Soviet Union had a weak ethno-cultural core as the Russians did not form a strong majority, although the post-Soviet Russian Federation has more in common with the European nation-state.

Russian conservatism has through history developed excessive reliance on the state. In an autocratic state, the revolutionary changes usually come from the top. Russian conservatives have therefore historically been placed in the awkward position of supporting the state but opposing its revolutionary policies. This has been a profound challenge as top-down reforms tend to be countered by a conservative backlash. The need to support organic change has entailed conservative support for local governance to incentivise bottom-up modernisation. Albeit, the decentralisation of power has also given oxygen to revolutionary movements and conservatives have therefore also supported the central government to impose direct control over regions and clamp down on the education system.

The weakness of the Russian state has paradoxically also been a source of tyranny, which has been countered with a strong central government. In the past, the underdeveloped bureaucracy of the Russian state made it impossible to govern its vast and growing territory. Moscow resolved this problem by outsourcing governance to noble landowners, although there was no social contract between landowners and peasants in the Russian feudal system to protect the peasants. Thus, a strong central government meant less reliance on the nobility and thus improved conditions for the peasantry. Similarly, the societal reforms in the late 1980s were pushed by Moscow, and several Soviet republics subsequently relapsed after the Soviet Union broke up. After the oligarchs asserted their control over Russia in the 1990s, the regions became especially susceptible to oligarchic rule and lawlessness. Putin's policy of centralising power was therefore instrumental to scale back the arbitrary rule of the oligarchs (Sakwa 2008: 891).

THE UNIVERSAL AND THE DISTINCTIVE

Conservatism presents a paradox as the organisation of humanity in distinctive and exclusive groups is a universal trait in human nature. While the fundamental assumptions of conservatism are constant, the policies will vary over time and space. A contradiction seemingly appears in conservative thought as it opposes moral relativism, although arguing against universalism. Conservatism changes in terms of what to preserve.

Russian conservatism has similarly positioned itself between the distinctive and universal. While Russian conservatives have sought to shield Russia from the decadence of universal ideals, it has also paradoxically taken upon itself messianic missions to save Europe and the world. Russian was distinctive from Europe due to the east-west schism of the Russian character. Russians absorbed Asiatic peoples into its ethno-cultural core, yet the ability to accommodate distinctiveness also gave Russia a universal character. The foundation of Russia's state conservatism was outlined by Sergei Uvarov was "orthodoxy, autocracy and nationality", which entailed both distinctiveness and universalism. In 1869, Danilevsky (2013: 76) wrote that history did not follow a single path towards modernity: "The principles of civilisation for one cultural-historical type are not transferable to the peoples of another type". Yet, among some conservatives, such as the Pan-Slavs, Russia had a mission to liberate the Slavs of the world and unite under a Pan-Slavic Empire.

Orthodoxy signifies Russia's unique link to original Christianity, which represents divine and universal truths. When Moscow became the "Third Holy Rome" after the fall of Constantinople, Russia began to embrace a mission to recapture Constantinople on behalf of the Christian world. Autocracy in Russia has been central for conservatives as it was a necessity to rule over a vast multi-ethnic empire. Last, "nationality" for Uvarov was conceptualised as loyalty to the monarchy (Zevelev 2009). Dostoyevsky wrote in 1880: "For what else is the strength of the Russian national spirit than the aspiration, in its ultimate goal, for universality and all-embracing humanitarianism?" (Rancour-Laferriere 1995: 239).

The alleged "anti-Western" bent of Russian conservatism should be understood in terms of repelling the threat to Russia's cultural autonomy. While leading Russian conservatives expressed profound admiration for the West, they nonetheless cautioned against Russia's fixation on the West and emulation. The objective was to establish an organic path to modernise that is sustainable by incorporating the particularities of Russian culture and history (Ilyin 1956). Similarly, Herder's concept of German nationalism did not disparage other nations or claim cultural superiority; rather, he recognised that a nation must assert its culture to remain a sovereign and united people. Conservative ideas suggest that by abandoning organic growth and instead of emulating the West, Russia would merely become subservient. By contrast, by upholding its historical and cultural distinctiveness, it contributes to the diversity and greatness of Europe.

Russia's splintered origin and difficulty in terms of defining itself based on the distinctive have also resulted in its identity shaped by civic ideals with universalism. Russian history demonstrates a schism between defending the distinctive by severing itself from Europe, and taking on universal missions by claiming to be the "real Europe" and saving the continent from itself. Following the fall of Constantinople in the fifteenth century, Russia took on the self-declared role as the "Third Holy Rome" to safeguard Christianity on behalf of the entire continent. Following the French Revolution, Russia declared its intention to preserve the French ideals that the revolutionaries were seeking to eliminate. Even when Napoleon's invasion had been pushed back, Russian conservatives were divided in terms of whether to remain within Russian borders to prevent its soldiers from being exposed to the influence of liberal decadence in Western Europe, or continue to Paris to liberate Europe Napoleon's tyranny (Robinson 2019: 30). After the defeat of Napoleon, some Russian conservatives aspired to unite all strands of Christianity (Grisbrooke 1967: 210).

The universalist impulses within Russia were also found among the socialists, as the Soviet Union declared the universal mission of liberating the workers of the world from the capitalist elites. By defeating Hitler, Russia yet again saved Europe from one of its own monsters. In more recent times, a similar dilemma can be posed in terms of whether Russia should pursue its particular path or provide support for conservative populists in the West that contest the excesses of liberalism.

COMPLEX SOCIETY: THE INDUSTRIAL REVOLUTION AND CAPITALISM

The industrial revolution and the subsequent introduction of capitalism represent a significant revolutionary moment in human history that continues to challenge the cohesion of social groups. Polanyi (1944) argued in *The Great Transformation* that the Industrial Revolution and market economy caused major disruptions to society as the new economic activity was "disembedded" from the institutions of society. Carl Jung (2014) cautioned that technology would estrange Man from his consciousness, usefulness and instincts. Societal change must develop based on profound familiarity with the past, as modernisation often displays "ineradicable aversion to traditional opinions and inherited truths" (Jung 2014). Industrial market society fuelled two contradictory movements: a rational movement towards the self-regulating market that would maximise individualism and economic efficiency, and a counter-movement resisting market forces disruptive to society (Polanyi 1944: 136).

Ferdinand Tönnies (1957) similarly posited that industrial society has caused a schism within mankind, which is pulled towards two opposite directions – smaller communities (gemeinschaft) and complex society (gesellschaft). Human beings are conditioned by evolutionary biology to gravitate towards smaller, tribal communities based on kinship. Concurrently, human beings strive towards larger and more complex societies defined by technological innovations, rational and calculative behaviour. Russian intelligentsia in the 1840s similarly worked along the *gemeinschaft-gesellshaft* or *obshchina-obshestvo* dichotomy. Max Weber (1924: 413–414) cautioned that the rational calculations that define the organisation of industrialised society dispossess people of their humanity as it "reduces every worker to a cog in this [bureaucratic] machine", which eventually "drives us to despair".

Russian conservatives shared the ideas and concerns of their American contemporary, Thomas Jefferson, who advocated in favour of developing the United States as an agrarian democracy. The common argument was that gemeinschaft was the source of virtue and agrarian communities were subsequently more qualified to preserve Christian values and morality. The Slavophiles termed the concept *sobornost* to encapsulate the spiritual harmony within communities that prioritised cooperation over individualism. The same dilemma and challenge that had faced Jefferson also became evident in Russia, which had to modernise society and preserve sobornost (Khomyakov 1895; Lossky 1952). Russia can be considered a natural gemeinschaft-based civilisation as its Eurasian geography and societal structures contributed to delaying the introduction of property rights, industrialisation and capitalism. The need to rapidly modernise to catch-up with the West over various periods further diminished Russia's ability to balance traditional community and complex society.

Disruptive and destructive pendulum swings between preserving the traditional or modernising were exacerbated as the modern manifested itself in a European identity and the traditional as distinctive Russian identity. Russian conservatism also carries with it a tradition of anti-capitalist sentiments and the tradition of government-led top-down growth that funnelled money and power to affluent industrialists, financiers and oligarchs. Russian conservatism efforts to use redistribution of wealth to support traditional social institutions and family values differ from contemporary Western conservatives, who are often more concerned that a strong state displacing the family as an institution.

CULTURE, RELIGION AND MORALITY

Culture represents a renunciation of pure individualism as it entails socialisation by a community and values formed in the past. The renewal of culture is the process of indoctrinating the individual into a collective community. Culture also enables societies to manage contradictions such as the tension between reason and religion (Bloom 2008: 197). Culture becomes even more important as humanity has migrated into cosmopolitan cities, coexisting with millions of people with diverse backgrounds. The purpose of culture is to maintain a connection with the past, and culture itself can degrade into a commodity that instead celebrates egotism and hedonism (Burckhardt 2010). Conservatism subsequently refutes universalism due to its encroachment on the distinctiveness of culture and the need for organic change (Mannheim 1936: 116; Strauss 1953: 13).

Religion is a central feature of culture to conservatives as it is passed down from generation to generation without corrupting the eternal and divine truth. Faith does not become an irrelevant historical artefact belonging to a bygone era; rather, it must remain intact and unadulterated for a civilisation to renew itself and survive. The divine and transcendent therefore inevitably make up the centre any organic culture. The shared and perpetual truth of religion lays the foundation for the collective consciousness, which becomes the principal source of authority and social membership of the community.

Christianity also represents a branch of power that can balance the unrivalled power of the state. Tyrants have therefore throughout history sought to limit the role of the church in society as a constraint on absolute loyalty and as a source of resistance. Edmund Burke (1792: 353) argued:

> Despots govern by terror. They know, that he who fears God fears nothing else; and therefore they eradicate from the mind, through their Voltaire, their Helvetius, and the rest of that infamous gang, that only fort of fear which generates true courage

Morality is a set of values and standards that are based on the instinctive and a particular religion or culture. The internal cohesion and endurance of societal groups are therefore dependent on upholding and reproducing morality as it sets the basic framework for conduct and behaviour. For Otto Von Bismarck in the nineteenth century, Christianity was instrumental to develop unifying values and morality to unify German states (Kissinger 1968: 898). Religion is also an important component to elevate social capital and cohesiveness in society. Research confirms that the religious are more trusting, generous and happy, and engage more in charity, neighbourhood organisation and civic society (Putnam and Campbell 2010).

In modern and complex societies, moral and religious guidelines are encoded into law to advance liberty and just society. A well-functioning rule of law can make a society complacent concerning upholding morality, and decay commences when the legal system outgrows its moral and religious foundation. Conservatism therefore focuses intensely on maintaining faith and morality. Law rests on the foundation of morality, which is profoundly different from the expectation that the rule of law can replace the role of morality or Christianity. Both morality and the rule of law define what is right and wrong, although they should not be conflated. Morality refers to an internal compulsion to resist certain behaviour, while the rule of law relies on external compulsion. In other words, morality is what you would not do when nobody is looking, while the rule of law is what you do when you think somebody is looking.

The difference between internal and external compulsion is imperative is susceptible to radical and disruptive change. Solzhenitsyn (1986) cautioned that replacing morality with the law would set the West on the path to totalitarianism, as the reliance on external compulsions for restraints make the people agreeable to whatever is legislated. Conrad (1996) similarly portrayed the moral hollowing of European society as a pernicious development as the fear of being reprimanded in public replaced the ability to exercise internal control over dark impulses. Once the authority of the state and the law rescind or be under the control of tyrants, Europeans would be predisposed to commit horrific acts (Conrad 1996). Societies without common and strong moral codes that are enforced by convention will rely more on courts and prisons.

Manners are a reflection of morals, and have the highest importance in society: "Manners are of more importance than laws. Manners are what vex or soothe, corrupt or purify, exalt or debase, barbarize or refine us, by a constant, steady, uniform, insensible operation, like that of the air we breathe in" (Burke 1796). Ivan Ilyin, one of the Russian conservatives quoted most by president Putin, aimed to develop the rule of law based on morality. The rule of law, Ilyin argued, had to derive from a legal consciousness rooted in natural law. The alternative would be laws that merely reflect an external compulsion by threatening punishment.

The decline of Christianity is a challenge for conservatism as it is the foundation for the common rules and collective consciousness that uphold any social group ranging from a family to a civilisation. Change and modernity require consciousness about the old values and laws that are destroyed to make space to what can replace it (Nietzsche 1968: 64). What replaces the old? Reluctance to let go of the past causes stagnation and decay, although destroying the past without a replacing it with a viable alternative creates nihilism and anarchy. Nietzsche cautioned that the Enlightenment would gradually increasingly cause the "death of God" as the source of meaning and morality. The loss of a divinely ordained moral order represented a revolutionary disruption if it is replaced with something entirely new. According to Mikhail Katkov, a nineteenth-century Russian conservative, the failure to renew the sources of morality will unleash nihilism and then eventually a revolution (Katz 2017: 154).

Is there a replacement for religion to ensure morality and unity? Without a viable replacement, the decline of Christianity causes moral fragmentation and corrupted concept of tolerance. Conservatives tend to be deeply sceptical about the feasibility of the effort in the West to replace Christianity with human rights. Scruton (2015) cautioned that "Europe is rapidly jettisoning its Christian heritage and has found nothing to put in the place of it save the religion of 'human rights'". The concept of human rights derived from the unique characteristics of Christianity. However, replacing Christianity with human rights does not offer a collective consciousness and morality. Human rights, standing on its own, become a very subjective concept. For example, whether it should be accepted to marry a partner of the same sex, take on more than one spouse, or marry a sibling will all depend on subjective narratives of who is discriminated against (Scruton 2015). The focus on non-discrimination as a human right is no longer balanced by the conservative moral principle of preserving the inside-outside dynamics and in-group loyalty. Human rights without its Christian roots construct a path towards moral relativism, which undermines the pursuit of unifying truths as the source of collective consciousness.

Tolerance in Christianity is expressed in the concept of "brotherly love", which suggests that the sin should be hated, yet the sinner should be loved. Moral relativism is rejected by clearly delineating between moral behaviour and sins, while the idea of equality of the unequal is repudiated. Plato (2008: 94) warned that the egalitarianism within democracy had a destructive component by "distributing equality to equals and unequals alike", while Aristotle referred to "tolerance is the last virtue of a dying society". Chesterton similarly argued that "tolerance is the virtue of a man without convictions" (Carson 2012: 124). Konstantin Leontyev (1885), a Russian conservative, similarly advocated in favour of healthy inequality and bourgeois culture to shame deviance from moral values rooted in the Orthodox Church.

There is an inherent contradiction in morality that reflects the schism in human nature between individualism and communitarianism. Five key moral instincts can be identified that are embedded in human nature and are displayed through time and space: fairness, reciprocity, authority/respect, in-group loyalty and sanctity/purity (Haidt 2012). The contradiction emerges as advancing individualism and inclusivity demands fairness and reciprocity, while preserving the collective requires some degree of respect/authority and exclusivity to maintain in-group loyalty. Research demonstrates that liberals do not recognise authority/respect and in-group loyalty as moral virtues, which implies they are less capable of preserving the collective (Haidt 2012).

The Orthodox Church had a central position in Kievan Rus as the origin of Russian civilisation, and was a key cultural feature that preserved Russian distinctiveness throughout two and a half centuries of the "Mongol yoke". For a country living that has spent much of its history under occupation, with authoritarian traditions, or under Stalin's purges – Christianity becomes a source of inner freedom that the state, nobility or other external sources cannot suppress. Khomyakov (1895) posits that the West lacks the community strength that Russia gains from the Orthodox Church: "Rome kept unity at the expense of freedom. Protestants had freedom but lost unity".

For Russian conservatives, the Orthodox Church must have a central role in society to represent the shared community and the rules that govern it. The Orthodox Church provides continuity in Russia history and collective consciousness. The Orthodox Church represents distinctiveness from the West stretching back to the Roman Empire that was consumed by barbarism, while the eastern part of the Roman Empire broke away and formed the Byzantine

Empire for the next thousand years. The Orthodox Church is also tied to Russia's narrative of being the real European, the Third Holy Rome" that kept Christianity in its original form and has not been tainted and corrupted by the changes in the Catholics and the Protestants (Evdokimov 2011).

The Orthodox Church represents a paradox as a central authority over the collective. The Orthodox Church has been used by all Russian leaders to mobilise the masses, even leaders with open hostility towards the clergy – such as Peter the Great. Even Stalin during the Second World War was able to tap into the cult of martyrdom in support of Holy Russia during the Second World War as the Orthodox Church was a stronger source of community than communist ideology. Reasonable arguments can be made that the power elites have corrupted the church throughout the years. However, the Orthodox Church has through history also demonstrated its capacity to resist the pressures of the state and organise a collective consciousness independent of the state.

CONCLUSION

Conservatism aims to pursue gradual and organic growth that builds on distinctive traditions. The advancement of rational and calculative society must account for the instinctive impulses in human nature. The main primordial instinct in mankind is the organisation in social groups, which lays the foundation for liberty, advancement, morality and law. Political and economic liberalism advances individualism, which must be balanced by the need to reproduce social membership in the collective.

Contemporary conservatism is largely devoted to preserving the nation-state as a representative of the collective, which has become a sturdy vessel for liberal rights. European conservatives initially opposed nationalism as the transfer of sovereignty from the monarchy to the people, although in modern time, the conservatives embrace the nation-state as the principal entity that represents a distinctive political entity. Russia's geography and demographics are not consistent with the concept of a nation-state, and Russian conservatism has relied on varies degrees of autocracy to manage an empire or in more modern time – a civilisation state.

Since the early nineteenth century, Russian conservatism has emerged to develop an organic path to change by decoupling modernisation from westernisation of Russian culture. The development of national identity with a unifying historical memory leans strongly on orthodoxy and cultural distinctiveness. Conservatives seek gradual economic development rather than great leaps forward. While conservatism has changed as Russia evolved, the theoretical assumptions that underpin conservatism remain constant.

Chapter 2

The Eurasian Schism in Russian Conservatism

INTRODUCTION

Geography and history inform the aptitude of a state to manage change. Russia's origin and complex history create ambiguity about what Russia is and what should be preserved. The Eurasian geography created a schism in Russia's identity that greatly influenced its unique strand of conservatism. Russia's eastern territories have been defined by a unique identity and strong communities based on tradition and spirituality, largely due to economic backwardness, poor physical connectivity and engagement with different peoples along the expanding Eurasian frontier. The western territories tend to incentivise a return to various European identities and economic development models, although the European identity is also commonly associated with moral decadence and a hostile environment with powerful European adversaries. Russia's ability to manage change by harmonising the modern and traditional translated into balancing its western and eastern identity.

This chapter first explores the revolutionary origin of Russia from Kievan Rus to the Mongol yoke. Russia had already begun shifting from trade to agriculture under Kievan Rus and its fragmentation, although this trend was strengthened under the rule of the Golden Horde. While the socio-economic and political traditions of Kievan Rus suffered under the Mongols, the Christian Orthodox Church became immensely powerful in terms of political, economic and cultural power, and laid the foundation for a future Russian state.

Second, the emergence of a Russian Eurasian Empire is discussed. The need for security created an imperial impulse that defined Russian conservatism. After conquering Kazan in 1552, Russia became a multi-ethnic empire that rapidly expanded towards the south and the east. Serfdom and autocracy became important institutions to adapt to the challenges of a rapidly growing territory. After falling under and liberating itself from the European yoke at the beginning of the sixteenth century, also known as the Times of Trouble, Russia also expanded control over its western periphery as a defensive strategy.

Last, Peter the Great launched deep and rapid reforms to modernise Russia in the early eighteenth century. While modernisation and establishing Russia as a European maritime power was supported by most conservatives, the neglect and derision of Russian culture and faith broke with all the principles of conservatism. Peter conflated the Enlightenment and modernisation with European culture, and subsequently launched a Cultural Revolution to remake Russia as a European state.

It is concluded that the Eurasian geography and topography of Russia created a schism in which modernisation is conflated with the Europeanisation of Russian culture. The failure to establish a Russian path to modernity has subsequently become the key task for Russian conservatives.

THEORISING THE IMPORTANCE OF
GEOGRAPHY AND TOPOGRAPHY

The geography of a nation represents the soil from where its unique culture emerges and the propensity towards modernisation. The ability to manage change cannot be understood without exploring historical development, which grows from distinctive geography. George Kennan commonly referred to the German concept of "Realien" to elucidate why geography and topography shaped the character of Russia (Engerman 2009: 247).

Geography and topography define Russia as a large land-power without sufficient access to maritime corridors. The lack of reliable, efficient and secure transportation corridors limits the ability to develop a competitive economy. These limitations are exacerbated by the vast and cold territory with poor physical connectivity between population centres. Russia's geography evolved largely from security considerations as opposed to acting according to economic incentives. The topography is characterised by the lack of natural boundaries, such as seas, deserts or mountain ranges for protection. The open topography made Russia vulnerable to invasions and obscured the borders between distinctive peoples and culture. Subsequently, Russia had strong incentives to expand its borders as a defensive strategy and merge with other peoples in a melting pot. Defending the lengthy borders with the establishment of strategically scattered population centres, with great distances between, resulting in weak infrastructure within Russia and the need to redistribute wealth to economically isolated regions. Furthermore, the outsourcing of governance to the nobility to manage the large territory had to be balanced with a centralised state. Hence, the lack of a competitive economy undermines the ability to manage change, which placed Russia in a pattern of stagnation and disruptive efforts to rapidly catch up.

By comparison, the geography and topography of Britain as an island state on the periphery of Europe has been conducive to manage change. The relatively small territory with a coastline has demarcated the borders of a distinctive nation. Without any land-borders with other European states, more resources were devoted to augments its maritime power that created a competitive advantage for trade and conquests. Britain was also more disposed towards liberal reforms due to the lack of extensive land-powers. Without the need for a large standing army during peacetime, which could also be turned against its own population, the monarchy had a greater need to compromise with the population and parliament (Quigley 1961). A government seeking to preserve stability was thus balanced by a population seeking change. The leverage of parliament vis-à-vis the monarch resulted in land rights and enclosures that fuelled modernisation of the agriculture industry and labour for industrialisation. The United States, as the successor of Britain, shares its characteristics as a maritime power. Protected by two great seas, the United States became a virtual island much like Britain. There was traditionally little need for a large and powerful federal government in the United States that could trample on individual liberties due to the absence of great powers in the Americas.

Germany's geography as a European land-power has more resemblance to Russia. Before unification in 1871, German territories were largely disconnected and power decentralised. German territories were largely self-contained, and education was highly regarded as a competitive advantage in a fragmented region surrounded by European giants. As a unified state, Germany became a natural cosmopolitan trading state endowed with navigable waterways and arable land in the heart of Europe. However, Germany's position within Europe has been vulnerable due to rivals – the French in the West, the Russians in the East, and the British controlling the maritime corridors in the north. This makes it imperative for an industrialised Germany to integrate Europe through either diplomacy or war.

The geography of Russia reveals the foundations of conservative policies defined by autocracy, great leaps forward, an ambiguous and complex concept of nationalism, and the enduring role of the Orthodox Church that should incentivise resistance towards radical secularism. Russia's origin was revolutionary – it began as a European trading state that transitioned to a Eurasian empire severed from the arteries of international trade. Russian conservatism has many challenges and internal contradictions that can be traced back to the complex history of its origin. Conservative ideologies would only be formed by the late eighteenth century and early nineteenth century, although the geographical schism emerged in the thirteenth century as Russia disappeared from the European political map for centuries. Subsequently, the dualism of mankind between the rational and instinctive manifested itself a modern European identity versus a traditional and spiritual Eurasian identity.

FROM KIEVAN RUS TO THE MONGOL YOKE

The origin and civilisational roots of Russia demonstrate a complexity that continues to influence its identity. Russian civilisation was born from the Slavs' interactions with the Vikings in the north and the Byzantine Empire in the south, before being invaded by the Mongols in the east (Quigley 1961: 81). Borders have remained elusive, and identities have been fragmented.

Early Eastern Slavic states had grown organically and not been constructed through external force. These Eastern Slavic tribes had *knyaz*, consisting of nobles who submitted to the rule of princes to establish a united, peaceful and harmonious community. Some tribes eventually formed a common capital in Novgorod in the ninth century. The Norman theory, a leading yet contested historical narrative, suggests that the divided Eastern Slavic tribes invited Rurik, a Viking prince, to unify and lead the Eastern Slavs (Riasanovsky 1947). The subsequent Rurik dynasty ruled Russia until the end of the sixteenth century. The purported role of the Scandinavian Vikings in establishing the land of Rus reflected the Vikings prominent position across Europe and beyond due to their maritime capabilities, which translated into commercial and military power. For historians such as Mikhail Pogodin, the Norman theory revealed roots of a unique Russian civilisation. Russia had been formed by invitation and harmonisation of interests as opposed to the other European states that were shaped by conquest and subjugation. The Viking raids to the West, towards Britain and Western Europe, were more brutal and offered lessons about pillaging and colonisation. The Viking expeditions to the East were more benign and cooperative, which therefore created a different legacy. The unique character of the Russians was therefore the aptitude of accommodating and absorbing conquered peoples without establishing dividing lines between the natives and the newcomers.

Rurik's successor, Prince Oleg, captured Kiev in 882 and made it the capital of a new state, Kievan Rus. Russian conservatives tend to identify Kievan Rus as its civilisational birthplace, which was largely a typical European power. Kievan Rus formed strong ties with the Byzantine Empire in the south, which became the domineering influence on both the culture and religion of the Russians. Kievan Rus adopted Christianity in 988 with the baptism of Prince Vladimir the Great. A few years later, in the Great

Schism of 1054, Christianity split into the Christianity of the East (Orthodox Church) and the West (Roman Catholic Church), and the Catholic Church was yet again divided as a result of the reformation in the early sixteenth century. Narochnitskaya (2003) argues, the rupture in Christianity occurred earlier, in 800 when the spiritual and political was merged as Charlemagne was crowned emperor by the pope. Subsequently, Kievan Rus linked its cultural heritage to the realm of the Byzantine Empire. The distribution of power in Kievan Rus was divided between the prince and the head of the church to ensure a harmonious relationship between the earthly world and the heavenly world, which was based on Byzantine political traditions (Daniel 2006: 12). The power-sharing between the monarch and the Orthodox Church became a defining feature of Russian conservatism for the centuries that followed, which reflected the dualism in mankind.

The cultural link to the Byzantine Empire, as the successor of the Roman Empire, represented a schism in Russia's relationship with Europe. Russia shares the civilisational roots with Western Europe due to the common Roman legacy, although the Byzantine Empire would last for another thousand years after the collapse of the Western Roman Empire.

Yaroslav the Wise conquered new lands and codified laws in the eleventh century, making Kievan Rus a powerful European state. However, after the death of Yaroslav, the autocracy weakened as his sons fought among themselves, and Kievan Rus fragmented into a patchwork of princedoms. The break-up of Kievan Rus was a critical moment as "Slavdom ceased to exist as a single whole, while still preserving a mutual comprehensibility of the [Slavic] languages or linguistic closeness as a reminiscence of the former unity" (Gumilev 1989: 31). The closeness of fragmented Slavdom became a double-edged sword as indistinct cultural, ethnic and linguistic borders can be interpreted as eternal brotherly bonds and an invitation to invade. While the English and Germans (and later the Americans) have throughout history sought to deepen the divide between the Slavs, Russia as the power centre has traditionally downplayed differences to create a gravitational pull.

The lesson from the fragmentation of Kievan Rus was that the weakness of the autocracy would precede internal fragmentation, which would create opportunities for hostile foreign powers. The fragmentation of Kievan Rus occurred at the worst possible time as the Mongols invaded from the East in the early thirteenth century. The Rus princes became mere vassals of the Golden Horde. Russian historians disagree on the extent of the cultural and political influence of the Mongols, although for approximately 250 years Russia disappeared largely from the European political map and was relegated as tributaries of an Asian power (Hosking 2001).

Kievan Rus had been prosperous with Kiev located on the Dnieper River, while the Russian cities in inhospitable forests in the north-east were not connected to major maritime corridors for trade. The Mongol yoke also detached the Russians culturally from the Byzantine Empire. However, the cultural differentiation between Kievan Rus and Muscovite Rus should not be exaggerated, and Russia still considers itself as the principal successor of Kievan Rus. The history and legacy of Kievan Rus were central in Russia's struggle towards independence in the fourteenth and fifteenth century (Likhachev 1963).

The Mongol invasion destroyed many of the political institutions of Kievan Rus, although religious freedoms were upheld. Subsequently, the cultural legacy of the past was preserved in the Orthodox Church as the foundation of Russia's historical memory and national consciousness. In the absence of independent political structures, the national unity through shared cultural heritage became all the more important as a conservative impulse. The Mongols also endowed the Orthodox Church with substantial tax benefits, which strengthened its economic prowess in society (Halperin 1987: 113). The Orthodox Church became the centre of culture, politics and economics – thus becoming the unifying force of a collective Rus before the nation or state emerged. The Orthodox Church was, however, not corrupted by the support of the Mongols. On the contrary, the Orthodox Church became a powerful supporter of Russian princes seeking to expel the Mongols from Russian lands.

While the Mongols supported the Orthodox Church, they treated conquered peoples as inferior, compelled to obey their authority and pay tribute. The autocratic political structures and lack of a social contract between the ruler and its subjects were accentuated under the rule of the Golden Horde. The split from developments in Europe insulated Russia from exposure to the emerging commercial culture and the binding loyalty between the lords and vassals (Pipes 2005: 181).

The principality of Moscow was formed in the late thirteenth century and grew rapidly in power. Moscow's emergence as the power centre of Russia was largely a result of politics rather than economics. Moscow, a settler colony in the cold forests in the north-east, was largely disconnected from major trade corridors. However, the Golden Horde delegated an administrative role to Moscow, and was tasked to with collecting tribute from Rus principalities. The administrative role of Moscow fuelled its rise as an unexpected leader in Rus principalities in the early fourteenth century. This administrative role would continue even after the rule of the Mongols ended.

In the second half of the fourteenth century, Moscow consolidated its rule over Rostov, Suzdal, Nizhny Novgorod and new territories in the north-east (Hosking 2001: 78). The year 1380 became a turning point in the Mongol domination of Russia, as various Russian principalities under the leadership of Moscow defeated the Mongols in the historical battle of Kulikovo.

The Mongols supremacy continued, although Moscow had placed itself at the centre of a future Russian state. Moscow also became the spiritual centre of the Russians as devout Orthodox Christians. After the fall of Constantinople in 1453, Moscow claimed the role of the spiritual centre of the Christian world by becoming the "Third Holy Rome" (Neumann 2016: 7).

Moscow began expanding rapidly to the north from the mid-fifteenth century in the search for new lands. Avoiding the Mongols in the east and the south, and Poland-Lithuania in the West, only the north offered room for expansion without triggering a hostile response from foreign powers. These forest regions were, however, weak in terms of economic potential. Territorial expansion into economically backward regions shifted the economy from trade to agriculture. The growing territory was therefore largely defined by illiteracy, economic backwardness and a lack of modernisation.

When the Mongols were invading in 1480 to regain their former control over the Russians, they were defeated at the Ugra River. The battle ended the Mongol/Tatar yoke. However, the Russian culture and political system had changed as it inherited a centralised and autocratic system from the Mongols. The patrimonial system continued after the Mongols left, and Russia had not embraced the key foundation of the West such as private property rights, Roman law, feudalism, Catholic theology and commercial culture.

A schism revealed itself in Russia's identity and its relationship with Europe as it represented the real Europe, and concurrently a distinctive civilisation. During diplomatic contacts with the Europeans in the years following the Mongol yoke, Russia insisted on its European character and rejected the need to external recognition as the Tsar claimed status equal to the Holy Roman Emperors (Neumann and Pouliot 2011: 135). Russia deemed itself the true centre of Christianity, and as the successor of the Byzantine Empire. For Russian westernisers, the Mongol occupation had severed Russia from its native European home and its future path depended on returning to Europe. By contrast, for some Russian conservatives, the Mongols had defended the Orthodox Church and Russian culture from the decadence of the Roman-Germanic world (Mirsky 1927).

The complex historical make-up of Russia created several dilemmas in terms of defining its heritage and successor status. The Russians had a close affinity to the Byzantine Empire, although they were hesitant to claim the transfer of imperial authority from Constantinople as it might obligate them to reconquer Constantinople. It was also problematic to claim the successor role and heritage of the Golden Horde as it would relegate Russia to the status of an Asiatic power (Hosking 2001). Even claims of heritage to Kievan Rus could cause a clash with Lithuania.

Due to the lack of consensus about a clearly articulated successor role – legitimacy became more dependent on tradition, imperial authority and the orthodox faith. The church became central in Muscovite Russia, which further strengthened the autocracy as the monarch enjoyed a divine mandate from heaven. For sixteenth-century Russian writer, Peresvetov, the fall of Constantinople to the Ottomans was caused by the disloyalty of the aristocrats and disorganisation of the ruler. Peresvetov pleaded with the Russian Tsar to strengthen the autocracy to ensure that Moscow would not share the fate of Constantinople (Cherniavsky 1968: 204).

TOWARDS A EURASIAN EMPIRE

After two and a half-century of Mongol rule, Russian security and independence were not safeguarded. The Grand Principality of Moscow had no natural geographical frontiers and defensive lines in terms of mountains, deserts or significant rivers. Peter Hitchens (2014), a British classical conservative, points to the geography of Russia as the source of its historical security concerns:

> The country has no natural defensible borders. . . . From every direction, the heart of Russia lies open to invaders. Moscow has been invaded or occupied by Swedes, Poles, Lithuanians, The Golden (or Great) Horde, Crimean Tatars, and Napoleon. No wonder the Russian word for "security" (*byezopasnost*) is a negative construction ("byez" means "without"; "opasnost" means "danger"). The natural state of things is danger.

In the West was the threat of Lithuania-Poland, Sweden and other European powers that would later invade. In the south and east the Tatars, the successors of the Golden Horde, presented a lingering threat. Muscovy expanded into regions away from the corridors of international trade to avoid provoking a reaction from rival powers. Vasili III began expanding Moscow's influence to the east in the early sixteenth century. His successor, Ivan the Terrible, was coronated as the first Tsar of Russia conquered large swathes of Tatar lands to the east.

The victory and conquest of Kazan in 1552 enabled Russia to secure its periphery and escape isolation. Kazan is on the Volga River and by annexing the city, the Russians had access to a maritime corridor it could use as a supply route. One after the other, the Tatar kingdoms along the Volga River that had previously been the rulers of the Russians became vassals of the Tsar. Russia continued downwards the Volga River until reaching the Caspian Sea and thus establishing a valuable trade route to the Middle East. To the east of the Volga River, the vast open Eurasian space laid open for Russian colonisers. Not all of Russia's expansion was driven deliberately by the state, as hunting became a key impulse to colonise new lands in the east (Etkind 2011: 79). The Eurasian landmass and Russia subsequently changed ever since, as the Russians began to assert dominance over an immense territory held previously only by three great nomadic powers: the Scythians, Huns and Mongols.

The lesson learned from conquering the Tatars was that offence is the best defence. From Ivan the Terrible, Peter the Great and Catherine the Great, the common knowledge was that large buffer zones were required for security. Attacks and expansion became a defensive strategy. Newly acquired territories were consolidated by expanding further. Catherine the Great is attributed with the statement that the best way to defend Russian borders is to continue expanding them. With the open plains, Russian security depended on using its vast territory to absorb invading forces through attrition and cutting off their supply lines. This strategy passed the test of time as the large territory was capable of absorbing the invading forces of both Napoleon and Hitler, which were swallowed up by the vastness of Russia as reliable supply lines could not be sustained. The huge territory also defended Russia from a US nuclear first-strike by reducing the feasibility of a successful surprise attack and interception of Russia's retaliatory capabilities (Diesen and Keane 2018).

Over the three centuries of the Romanov dynasty, from 1613 to 1917, Russia expanded on average with approximately 140 square kilometres per day (Heller 2015). Russia became an empire and, in the absence of a topography suitable for defence, developed a large protective chain of cities stretching towards the East. While the vast and growing territory was a strategy for security, it also became a source of insecurity as the extended borders were porous and vulnerable – which thus led to expansion often as an accidental policy. Kotkin (2016) described Russian expansionism as a defensive impulse:

> Whatever the original causes behind early Russian expansionism – much of which was unplanned – many in the country's political class came to believe over time that only further expansion could secure the earlier acquisitions. Russian security has thus traditionally been partly predicated on moving outward, in the name of pre-empting external attack.

In the Long Telegram of February 1916, George Kennan argued that Soviet communism had inherited the historical insecurities of Russia:

> At the bottom of Kremlin's neurotic view of world affairs is a traditional and instinctive Russian sense of insecurity. Originally, this was the insecurity of peaceful agricultural people trying to live on vast exposed plain in neighbourhoods of fierce nomadic peoples. To this was added, as Russia came into contact with the economically advanced West, fear of more competent, more powerful,

more highly organized societies in that area. But this latter type of insecurity was one which afflicted rather Russian rulers than Russian people; for Russian rulers have invariably sensed that their rule was relatively archaic in form, fragile and artificial in its psychological foundation, unable to stand comparison or contact with political systems of Western countries. For this reason, they have always feared foreign penetration, feared direct contact between the Western world and their own, feared what would happen if Russians learned the truth about the world around them or if foreigners learned the truth about the world within. And they have learned to seek security only in the patient but deadly struggle for total destruction of rival power, never in compacts and compromises with it.

Nikolai Berdyaev argued that empire is at the heart of Russian identity, and the act of expanding borders thus became a conservative policy. Russia rapidly acquired an immense amount of territory, although much of the expansion was into regions that were not economically competitive. Russia's rivers would freeze at winter, and its regions subsequently moved towards inefficient economic autonomy. Retreating into economically backward regions, away from the arteries of international trade, also assisted to conserve traditional values and spirituality.

AUTOCRACY AND EMPIRE

Russia's expansive geography translated into a conservative inclination that relied on autocracy. The large territory with weak infrastructure and unforgiving climate created weak economic connectivity between its regions populated by a multi-ethnic population. Russia's vast regions with poor physical connectivity between them increased the reliance on an autocratic ruler (Starr 1972: 47).

The consolidation of power in Muscovy required co-opting privately owned estates by conditioning their privileged socio-economic position on loyalty and service to the monarch. The societal role of peasants began to change from the 1540s as they migrated away from the Moscow region to develop new lands. The landowning nobility began losing the labour they relied upon, which then threatened their position as the intermediary between the state and the people. Subsequently, the peasants began to be tied closer to the land as a step towards serfdom (Pipes 2005: 19). These developments intensified as Russia expanded beyond the Volga. After conquering the Tatars, Russian colonisers could expand outside the Russian forests and found new rich soil along the steppes with more rewarding harvests. The peasants did not have any rights to own property or land, although in an open system they would have been able to get better conditions for working on the land of other landowners. The landlords of the forest regions had the value of their estates falling, which could become worthless as the labourers required to work the land left for better regions. The peasants were therefore legally bound to the land.

The paradox for the Russian peasant was that they did not prosper when the rich fertile region finally became available; instead they drifted towards serfdom (Robinson 1967: 15). The expansion and consolidation of Russian lands by Moscow required the Tsar to further strengthen control over the landowners, which was compensated by strengthening the landowners control over the peasants. The demand for military power increased as Russia conquered its adversaries at the periphery and had to manage its empire. Payments for military service had previously been a problem, although the access to new territories acquired after 1552 provided the state with a solution. Military service was paid with land rights and peasants tied to the land. Serfdom thus became the price for empire. The poor condition of the peasantry greatly influenced the ability of Russia to manage change. The communes became the foundation for tradition and spirituality, albeit they also became a source of economic backwardness, stagnation and revolutions (Bartlett 1990).

By absorbing the Tatar kingdoms, Russia transitioned into a multi-ethnic Eurasian empire, which became even more diverse as the expansion continued towards the Pacific Ocean. The multi-ethnic empire with possible nationalist and secessionist sentiments demanded centralisation of power in authoritarian structures. Logistic problems across the large territory made it difficult to prosper economically, as the economic centre in European Russia had to subsidise the eastern regions. Last, the insecurity from expansive border required a large standing army during peacetime, which gave the state more power vis-à-vis the people.

European empires, much like the Russian Empire, relied on centralised control and coercion to manage its territories. At its heyday, Russian territory included Poland, Finland, Central Asia and Alaska. A land-based empire made Russia less capable to trade as compared with the European maritime empires. However, being connected by land made the empire convertible into a civilisational-state rather than breaking into a multitude of smaller political entities. Russia did not develop as a traditional Westphalian state and focused instead its energy towards consolidating control over a civilisation state without any natural borders.

TOWARDS THE EUROPEAN YOKE

Ivan the Terrible had been successful in defeating Tatar kingdoms along the Volga and reached the Caspian Sea, however, he faced defeat against the

Europeans in the Livonian War. Since the early sixteenth century, Western Europe began to grow rapidly in strength. Western European maritime powers established economic prowess with vast sea-based trade-post empires, which laid the foundation for 500 years of global dominance. By contrast, Russia developed as land-power as it had been pre-occupied with casting off the Tatar yoke.

Ivan the Terrible began pushing into the Baltics in the mid-sixteenth century to improve maritime connectivity for trade with the English, its only trading partner. Ivan also sought to establish fortifications along the coast as a natural defensive line against hostile powers. Albeit, Ivan was not able to establish a permanent presence as Russia's incursion was repelled by other European powers (Hosking 2001: 120). Russia's expansion to the north and foundation of a port in Arkhangelsk finally endowed the Russians with a seaport for trade. However, positioned on the shore of the White Sea, Arkhangelsk was an Arctic transportation corridor that made it difficult to navigate, especially during winter.

In final years of the sixteenth century, the childless son of Ivan the Terrible died, and the Rurik dynasty ended. The succession crisis weakened the autocracy, which brought about the Time of Troubles. A Russia weakened by internal divisions emboldened the invasion by Poland in 1605, which resulted in the occupation of Moscow by 1611. The Time of Troubles (*Smutnoe vremya*) also enabled Sweden to seize Novgorod and expand its influence over the Russians. With widespread famine, plague and terror that killed approximately a third of the entire Russian population, the Russian state lurched towards collapse and the Russian people possibly towards extinction.

Russian militias eventually ended the Polish occupation of Moscow. Recognising the need for unity of Russians, The Zemsky Sobor, consisting of the nobility, Orthodox clergy and commoners, elected a new Tsar in 1613 – Mikhail Romanov. The Romanovs would rule Russia for more than three centuries until the revolution of 1917. Mikhail Romanov exchanged territories in return for peace to give Russia some breathing space to recover. The Treaty of Stolbovo in 1617 with Sweden deprived Russia of direct and independent access to the Baltic Sea. Sweden, acting according to modern geoeconomic logic, sought to ensure that all Russian trade had to transit through Swedish waterways. However, Russia was able to maintain control over its port in Arkhangelsk to maintain some trade with England.

The Time of Troubles deepened the schism or divide between modernity and tradition within Russian society. On the one hand, the Swedish control over Russian trade and Polish invasion and occupation resembled a European version of the Mongol Yoke, as a spiritually inferior people dominated the Orthodox capital and spiritual centre of the world. One the other hand, Russia defeat had been caused by backwardness and lessons could be drawn from the modernity in the West (Neumann 2016: 10). Sweden failed to take control over the Russian White Sea region, and the Arctic route became the last direct maritime corridor for trade with Europe. The ability of Russia to grow its economy and gradually modernise was thus undermined by foreign powers.

Having shaken off the European yoke, Russia sought to cement its security by controlling its Western periphery. The Cossack rebellion against the Poland-Lithuania in 1654 changed the power balance in Eastern Europe. In the Cossack-Russian Treaty of Pereyaslav in 1654, Russia provided military support in what became the Thirteen Years War (1654–1667) between Russia and Poland-Lithuania. In victory, Russia acquired Smolensk and the eastern half of what is today Ukraine. Three centuries later, on the reunion in 1954, Khrushchev commemorated the Treaty of Pereyaslav by altering the administrative borders of the Soviet Union by positioning Crimea within Ukraine. In 1686, the Treaty of Eternal Peace was signed with Poland-Lithuania. Having pacified the threat from the west, Russia instead pushed south against the Ottoman Empire and east across the Eurasian steppe.

PETER THE GREAT'S CULTURAL REVOLUTION

The lack of modernisation and maritime power made Russia increasingly vulnerable to the Europeans, and survival required Russia to modernise rapidly. Peter the Great had travelled enthusiastically across Europe to seek fellow European allies against the Ottoman Empire. Peter was inspired by Western European innovations and learned everything he could about shipbuilding science, and culture. A treaty was eventually reached with the Ottomans in 1700, which bequeathed Russia the territorial possession of Azov, a strategic corridor where the Don River enters the Black Sea.

In the early eighteenth century, Peter the Great endeavoured to make Russia more European and modern by turning his back on the Muscovite past and instead look towards Europe. The reforms were aimed at not only solely developing Russia as a European naval power and build its industry but also developing a new national culture. The radical Petrine reforms changed the duty of the autocracy – from maintaining the status-quo to delivering change and progress (Whittaker 1992). The military reforms under Peter the Great laid the foundations for the power of Imperial Russia.

The rule of Peter the Great represented the beginning of three centuries-long occidental era as Russia would see the West as both a model and a competitor. Modernising the Russian economy and developing required establishing a maritime trade corridor by re-establishing a presence on the Baltic Sea, which Russia had lost in 1617. Peter the Great achieved this momentous task in the Great Northern War (1700–1721) against Sweden. Russia subsequently replaced Sweden as the dominant naval power in the Baltic Sea, which also positioned Russia as a European great power. Furthermore, the victory in the Great Northern War officially resulted in empire, as Russian Tsardom was officially replaced by the Russian Empire in 1721.

Even critics of Peter the Great, such as Nikolai Karamzin (2005: 120–121), recognised his achievements in terms of modernising Russia:

> He reorganised and increased the army, he achieved a brilliant victory over a skilful and courageous enemy, he conquered Livonia, he founded the fleet, built ports, promulgated many wise laws, improved commerce and mining, established factories, schools, the academy, and, finally, he won for Russia a position of eminence in the political system of Europe.

For eighteenth-century conservatives, such as Ivan Pososhkov, Peter the Great was celebrated for political reforms of modernisation with education and commerce, and the development of maritime power (Hamburg 2016). Pososhkov's (1987) *Book of Poverty and Wealth* is commonly referred to as the Russian Adam Smith. Pososhkov recognised that European modernisation coincided with the construction of the European nation-state. Pososhkov celebrated modernisation, although he was appalled by the failure of shoring up the traditional and spiritual. Pososhkov scorned the Cultural Revolution was as Russia abandoned its Church Slavic traditions. Pososhkov also cautioned against the failure of converting Russian subjects to Orthodox Christianity, similar to the process of religious homogenisation taking place in Europe:

> These people have been the subjects of the Russian Empire for two hundred years, but they did not become Christians, and their souls perish because of our negligence. The Catholics are sending their missionaries to China, India, and America. [Despite] the fact that our faith is a right one – and what could be easier than converting the Mordvas, the Cheremis, and the Chuvash? – yet we cannot do this. And our pagans [inovertsy] are like children, without a written language, without a law, and they do not live far away, but within the Russian Empire, along the Volga and the Kama rivers. (in Khodarkovsky 1997: 19)

For conservative thinkers, the socio-economic disruptions from such rapid and extensive changes must be mitigated by rejuvenating cultural traditions, as a growing nation requires deeper roots. Peter the Great did the exact opposite. Emboldened by his successes, such as the victory over Sweden, Peter the Great used his legitimacy to transform Russia culturally into a European power. Simply put, Peter the Great conflated the Enlightenment and modernisation with the Europeanisation of Russia through a Cultural Revolution.

Peter the Great demonstrated a simplistic view of modernity that was merely contrasted with the primitive and backwards. By imitating a foreign culture with alien traditions instead of building on domestic and organic institutions, the modern is built on a superficial foundation without the ability to express intellectual or cultural depth:

> The Western culture of Russia in the eighteenth century was a superficial aristocratic borrowing and imitation. Independent thought had not yet awakened. At first it was French influences which prevailed among us and a superficial philosophy of enlightenment was assimilated. The Russian aristocrats of the eighteenth century absorbed Western culture in the form of a miserable rehash of Voltaire. (Berdyaev 1947: 17)

In his effort to make Russia more European, he founded the coastal city of St. Petersburg in 1703 as the "window to Europe" and passed reforms to reorganise society. In 1712, St. Petersburg became the new capital of Russia. Even the name *St. Petersburg* was intended to sound Germanic as opposed to Russian. As a coastal city connected to the arteries of international trade, St. Petersburg soon began developing as a cosmopolitan society where foreign merchants entered and various European cultures mixed. It also gave Russia a port on the Baltic Sea and thus joined the family of European maritime powers.

The Europeanisation of Russia was not an organic development based on an evolving morality focusing on the individual. Instead, the great leap forward to Europe was reliant on external compulsions by an autocratic leader. The construction of a new European capital on the swamps became an artificial construct with the tremendous human costs as it was anything but an organic development. Russian writer, Boris Mozhaev, questioned the foundation of St. Petersburg:

> How many people died in the swamps when they built the new capital? Millions! And what for? The artificiality of that capital could still be felt even two hundred years later. You can't bend history to suit your wishes, as if you were bending a stick over your knee. (in Gillespie 1989: 205)

The Cultural Revolution was based on the premise that Europe to represent progress, which contrasted with Russia as ignorant, backwards and barbaric (Zhivov 2009: 49). Peter was hostile to the clergy and ended the independence of the Orthodox Church as an impediment to reforms and obstruction to the Europeanisation of Russia. In 1721, Peter ended the patriarchate and subordinated the church under state control. Peter made himself the head of the church to manipulate the core of civic virtues. The Petrine reforms of the Orthodox Church represented a perverted interpretation of secularism, as the state subordinated the church rather than dividing the state and the church.

However, the Orthodox Church nonetheless was to some extent capable of upholding its historical role as an independent branch of power. By resisting to submit to the authority of the state, Russia maintained a separation between the nation/faith and the autocratic state. The nobility was encouraged and supported by Peter the Great to travel to Western Europe to learn and bring these new ideas back to Russia to modernise and maintain political control (Chamberlain 2020: 2).

Petrine reforms included oddly specific policies such as the change in clothing and the requirement to shave away beards. A certain paradox became evident in the obsession with Europe and tearing up Russian traditions under the banner of the Enlightenment, as cultural changes had little to do with the scientific principles: "The Russian dress, food, and beards did not interfere with the founding of schools. Two states may stand on the same level of civil enlightenment although their customs differ" (Karamzin 2005: 122).

The Petrine language reform was a significant alteration of Russia. Inspired by his time spent in the Netherlands, Peter the Great assigned workers in Amsterdam to alter the Russian alphabet to make it more similar to the Latin alphabet. Problems did not only derive from the loss of knowledge and traditions passed down through the written word, but the language was also attributed to the old culture. The new alphabet and the subsequent alterations in the language broke with the organic linguistic development and it was imposed from the top down. Even after the alteration of the language, the Russian elites would commonly speak French as the language of culture and high-society, while Russian was deemed to be the language of the peasantry.

While Peter the Great authored important reforms, he also created deeper economic and social divisions in society. Peter imposed class divisions and endowed landowners with new rights, including tying the serfs to the land. Under the reign of Peter, serfdom subsequently began resembling slavery and "the gravity of the economic situation that followed the reign of Peter the Great was compounded by the legacy of serfdom" (Gerschenkron 1962: 135).

DUAL IDENTITY

Peter the Great's radical modernisation and Cultural Revolution sowed a deep disconnect between the people and the elite. The cosmopolitan and Europeanised elites sought modernity, while the peasantry embraced an identity closely linked to the land, distinctive Russian culture and traditions (Lieven 1998: 258). The Russian commune was one of the few institutions that survived the Petrine revolution and thus became a pivotal conservative anchor to the past.

The growing the schism of culture within Russian society would unavoidably tear away at the legitimacy of the elites. The gulf between the elites and the peasantry would only continue to deepen. Karamzin lambasted the revolutionary changes: "Having transformed the fatherland with his mighty arm, Peter the Great made us similar to other Europeans. Complaints are useless. The link between the minds of the ancient and of the modern Russians was cut forever" (in Riasanovsky 1992: 73). Karamzin (1959: 124) hinted towards wider ramifications from the policies of Peter the Great by transitioning Russia from distinctiveness to universalism:

> It must be admitted that what we gained in social virtues we lost in civic virtues. Does the name of a Russian carry for us today the same inscrutable force which it has in the past? No wonder. In the reigns of Michael and his son, our ancestors, while assimilating many advantages of which were to be found in foreign customs, never lost the conviction that an Orthodox Russian was the most perfect citizen and *Holy Rus'* the foremost state in the world. Let this be called a delusion. Yet how much it did to strengthen patriotism and the moral fibre of the country! Would we have today the audacity, after having spent over a century in the school of foreigners, to boast of our civic pride? Once upon a time we used to call all other Europeans *infidels*; now we call them brothers. For whom was it easier to conquer Russia – for *infidels* or for brothers? . . . We became citizens of the world but ceased in certain respects to be citizens of Russia. The fault is Peter's. (Karamzin 2005: 123–124)

Culture reflects a set of moral principles that guide the behaviour of people. Karamzin (2005: 121) argued:

> Peter was unable to realize that the national spirit constitutes the moral strength of states, which is indispensable to their stability as physical might. . . . By uprooting ancient customs, by exposing them to ridicule, by causing them to appear stupid, by praising and introducing foreign elements, the sovereign of the Russians humbled Russian hearts. Does humiliation predispose a man and a citizen to great deeds?

Karamzin (2005: 121) recognised that modernisation and greatness must be built on a conservative foundation:

> But shall we Russians, keeping in mind our history, agree with ignorant foreigners who claim that Peter was the founder of our political greatness? . . . Shall we forget the princes of Moscow, Ivan I, Ivan III, who may be said to have built a powerful state out of nothing, and – what is of equal importance – to have

established in it firm monarchical authority? Peter found the means to achieve greatness – the foundation for it had been laid by the Moscow princes.

By becoming more European, Russians also abandoned the virtues of their Asiatic character: "Russian women ceased to blush at the indiscreet glances of men, and European freedom supplanted Asiatic constraints. . . . As we progressed in the acquisition of social virtues and graces, our families moved into the background" (Karamzin 2005: 123).

Russia would in the future switch between two capitals, St. Petersburg and Moscow, which represented competing visions. For the liberal Westernisers, St. Petersburg represented Russia's path to becoming Europeans, while the Slavophile conservatives saw St. Petersburg as a symbol and embodiment of the corruption of Russian civilisation.

The rest of the eighteenth century became a continuity of Peter the Great's European era. The new geography pulled Russia into the great power politics of Europe. By the Seven Years War (1756–1763) Russia had another profound impact on Europe by occupying both East Prussia and Berlin. Under Catherine the Great, who ruled Russia from 1762 to 1796, Russia's territorial expansion to the West would further embroil Russia in the great power rivalries of the Western Europeans. Russia conquered much of Poland in the west, and in the south finally seized Crimea in 1783. As Russia's land-based empire expanded, the centre had to subsidise the continued expansion of the periphery.

CONCLUSION

Russia's geography, topography and history have set the foundations for a unique strand of conservatism. The principal challenge in Russian conservatism has continuously been to pursue organic change – a Russian path to modernisation. This objective has been complicated by a revolutionary origin. The Mongol invasion imposed a geographical schism as Russia was drawn between the modernity and reason of the West, which contrasted with the traditions, spirituality and distinctiveness of the East. Autocracy became a necessity following the Mongol legacy and the establishment of Russia as a Eurasian empire with a vast and poorly connected geographical expanse. The Orthodox Church became a powerful institution that defines the collective and granted legitimacy to the autocracy, harnessed significant economic power and laid the foundation for Russia's cultural distinctiveness. The land-based empire capable of absorbing foreign peoples into the native population created apprehensions towards the concept of ethno-nationalism. These peculiarities made Russia ill-prepared for the French Revolution that would follow at the end of the eighteenth century. French nationalism that entailed the transfer of sovereignty from the monarchy to the people/nation became a problematic concept for a state that relied heavily on the autocracy and was not a traditional Westphalian nation-state.

Chapter 3

The Rise of Conservatism from the Early Nineteenth Century

INTRODUCTION

At the beginning of the nineteenth century, both cultural and political conservative movements emerged in Russia. The cultural conservatives responded to the Europeanisation of Russia throughout the eighteenth century from Peter the Great to Catherine the Great. The political conservatives reacted to the French Revolution, which threatened to unravel Russia's most important political institution – the autocracy.

As Russia developed and became increasingly complex, a social contract was required between the state and society expressed in a constitution and the rule of law. The historical peculiarities of Russia had created a powerful nobility as an intermediary between the Tsar and the people, which had become an impediment to reform. A paradox is evident as the concentration of power in the Tsar could improve the liberties of people by weakening the heavy hand of the nobility.

Emancipation of the serfs was the main focus in the first half of the nineteenth century. Serfdom had contributed significantly to the foundation of societal culture and the agricultural economy. However, serfdom was abhorrent to the concept of justice and it stifled modernisation. Stability relied on the Tsar managing relations with the nobility. Several assassination attempts and palace coups had made it evident that any meaningful reforms required the engagement with and support of the nobility. Any effort to sideline or take away the privilege of the land-owning nobility could be extremely disruptive. How could Russia alter one of the fundamental structures of its society, without sparking social upheaval and revolution? On the other hand, if Russia did not adjust to the tides of time, the prospect of revolution would also visit Russia.

This chapter will first explore the adverse impact of the French Revolution on Russia's path to gradual development. The liberal reforms of Alexander I had to be scaled back due to the revolutionary forces from France that manifested themselves in domestic movements. Second, the conservatism of Nicholas I is assessed. The cultural conservatives that appeared towards the end of the eighteenth century, especially Nikolai Karamzin, wielded a great influence on the Tsar. Furthermore, the political conservatism of Nicholas was articulated and formalised primarily by his minister, Sergei Uvarov. Russia launched its Official Nationality consisting of "Orthodoxy, autocracy and nationalism" as a conservative alternative to the revolutionary creed of liberal French nationalism. Last, the rise of conservative Slavophiles laid the intellectual foundation for Russian conservative thought, which offered a counterbalance against the westernisers. Russia's capacity to immunise itself from the revolutions that swept across Europe in 1848 also obstructed Russia from modernising its economy and technology. It is therefore concluded that the conservatism of Nicholas I leaned excessively towards preventing change as opposed to managing change.

THE FRENCH REVOLUTION OF 1789

The French Revolution became the greatest shock to the status quo in Russia since the Cultural Revolution by Peter the Great. Before the French Revolution, Russia had experienced a golden period of development under the rule of Catherine the Great who ruled from 1762 to 1796. Catherine's objective was to complete the transformation of Russia initiated by Peter the Great by elevating Russia's status as a modern European power (Dixon 2015: 6). The stability achieved under Catherine provided her with room for manoeuvre in the pursuit of liberal reforms. Catherine was a student of the French Enlightenment and admired liberal French thinkers, and she even corresponded with Voltaire. Russia thrived as the monarch embraced reason, education, culture and art. Europeans were invited, especially Germans, to settle in Russia and bring with them their ideas and innovations.

However, the French Revolution shook the entire European order and threatened Russia's state structures. Catherine the Great was alarmed by the radicalism and violence of the French Revolution as a contradiction to the liberal principles under which it was launched. While the revolution brought havoc in France, Catherine believed that Russia would be destroyed by a similar revolution due to the unpreparedness for nationalism. The nationalism of the French Revolution was a liberal and democratic idea as the sovereign mandate transitioned from the monarchy to the people. The French Declaration of

Rights proclaimed: "Each people is independent and sovereign, whatever the number of individuals who compose it and the extent of the territory it occupies". Russia did not have any natural tradition of liberal political ideas, and a revolution would likely unravel the entire foundation of the Russian state as it relied heavily on the autocracy as an institution. Unlike in France, the collapse of the Russian state would likely disintegrate the vast territory.

Russia became more apprehensive as the French Revolution continued its descent into barbarity. The Jacobin movement advocating radical measures and the Reign of Terror to purge the old order had a profound impact on Russian conservatives as a caution against revolutionary movements. When Louis XVI was guillotined in 1793, Russia's opposition to the French Revolution intensified. Catherine severed diplomatic relations with revolutionary France and declared Russia as a counter-revolutionary power that would uphold, conserve and continue the old French order. Catherine declared: "We are raising the hope of France, and it is these young people who will restore the monarchy" (Chamberlain 2020: 8). The announcement was reminiscent of another international conservative duty – when Russia took on the responsibility to preserve Christianity by taking over the Orthodox Church following the fall of Constantinople in 1453. Catherine subsequently embraced a conservative role for Russia and the conservative renewal in Europe. The conservatives supported the state, the Orthodox Church and a distinctive cultural identity against European cosmopolitanism and the influence of revolutionary France (Hamburg 2015).

After the death of Catherine the Great, Tsar Paul I came to power in 1796 and responded to the liberal influences of the French Revolution with fierce suppression. The brutality and rule by fear made Paul I a truly unpopular leader and damaged the legitimacy and moral standing of the autocracy. The golden years under Catherine the Great had established clear expectations of the monarch in terms of the ability to deliver positive change, and the failure to continue along this trajectory empowered revolutionary forces.

Paul also became deeply unpopular among the military and the nobility as he reversed a central tenet of Russia's foreign policy, which was to fight the French in cooperation with the other European monarchies. While Paul I was opposed to the French Revolution, he established an agreement with the French against the British for geostrategic reasons. Rather than confronting France in Europe and working towards taking back Constantinople on behalf of the Orthodox Christian world, Paul took the advice of Napoleon and sent a Cossack army to march through Central Asia to take British India (Schimmelpennick van der Oye 2015). Britain was the domineering maritime power and a leading geostrategic threat to Russia. However, Paul I was eventually killed in a palace coup in 1801 and replaced by his son, Alexander I, who immediately called on the return of the Cossacks.[1] The European continent was yet again envisioned as Russia's main geopolitical chessboard, although Russia would later that century return to the unique Eurasian vector of Russian foreign policy.

THE LIBERALISM OF ALEXANDER I (1801–1825)

Alexander I returned Russia to a liberal path. Following the tradition of Peter the Great and Catherine the Great, liberal reforms were pursued in the education system to prepare the population for a more complex and advanced society. More universities were built, and liberal education reforms were passed. Much like Peter the Great and Catherine the Great, Alexander I also recognised the centrality of the autocracy. The concept of an enlightened autocracy was preferred as the empire may otherwise collapse. The reforms to modernise Russia were eventually disrupted by Napoleon's invasion in 1812.

Mikhail Speransky, known as the godfather of Russian liberalism, became the chief minister of Alexander I between 1807 and 1812. Speransky did not aim to dismantle the autocracy; rather, the objective was to moderate the autocracy by transitioning Russia towards a constitutional monarchy (Zyrianov 1997). Speransky even met Napoleon at the Congress of Erfurt in 1808. By 1809, Speransky attempted to introduce the rule of law, representative government and a State Duma to limit the power of the autocracy. While Speransky's policies were liberal, he was nonetheless cautious not to equate the autocracy with oppression. Speransky recognised that a strong state was necessary for stability, prosperity and security. Speransky's plan entailed providing voting rights for all land-owning citizens of Russia. A major achievement was the establishment of the State Council in 1810, which would mediate between the autocrat and the Duma (Raeff 2012: 115). The State Council provided a legal foundation that Speransky aspired to use for decentralising power in Russia (Von Mohrenschildt 1981: 15). The additional reforms of Speransky did not come to fruition.

Speransky's efforts to reorganise the Orthodox Church became a step too far, and it created enemies among the conservatives. Furthermore, the liberal reforms were causing disgruntlement from the nobility that Alexander I had to appease as a war with France appeared on the horizon. The reforms of Alexander I were therefore interrupted by the pending war and Speransky was the personification of these reforms. In March 1812, a few months before Napoleon invaded Russia, Speransky was exiled to Nizhny-Novgorod. Alexander I acknowledged that Speransky had been "sacrificed to public opinion" (Zyrianov 1997: 109).

VICTORY OVER NAPOLEON AND
THE DECEMBRIST REVOLT

The French-led Continental System was imposed on Europe to undermine British maritime power. However, the Continental System was not sustainable for Russia as the blockade with Britain deprived Russia of essential trade that could not be replaced due to insufficient land corridors with European continental powers (Broers et al. 2012). Following Russia's withdrawal from the Continental System, Napoleon invaded Russia in 1812.

Russia's victory over the invading forces of Napoleon initially appeared to bequeath greatness to Russia. The war against Napoleon became Russia's first "great patriotic war", which implanted a strong national sentiment based on heroism and victory. Much like Peter the Great had established Russia as a European power by defeating Sweden in the Great Northern War, the victory over Napoleon cemented Russia's role as a European great power. Furthermore, the spoils of war enabled Russia to finally reunite with the historical and European land of Kievan Rus and bring the Belarusian and Ukrainian peoples back into the Russian Empire.

Russia's victory also reasserted political conservatism in both Russia and Europe. The Concert of Europe was established at the Congress of Vienna in 1815 and was the principal European institution for a century until 1914. The Concert of Europe was intended to curtail the liberal and revolutionary impulses of the French Revolution. The export of the liberal revolution was obstructed, and a European security system based on conservatism and the balance of power was established.

With the external French revolutionaries defeated, Alexander I revived the controlled liberal reforms that had previously been advocated by Speransky. In 1815, following the Congress of Vienna, Alexander I approved a constitutional charter to the Grand Duchy of Warsaw (Poland). In 1818, Alexander I instructed the development of a Russian constitution. Elements from Speransky's former plan and ideas were also incorporated. The concept of separation of power reappeared throughout the charter (Vernadsky 1947: 60). By 1820, the "Constitutional Charter of the Russian Empire" was completed. According to the plan, Russia would develop a federal structure that endowed each region with a political representative body.

However, the charter was never signed by Alexander I. The nobility resisted further liberal reforms. The killing of Alexander's father, Paul I, was a reminder about the cost of pushing the nobility too far (Zakharova and Owen 2005: 34). The failure to sign the charter fuelled resentment within Russia as a constitutional charter had been granted to defeated Poland but not the Russian people. Orlov, an army officer and favourite of the Tsar, argued: "Many hoped that, having granted Poland a constitution, the emperor would

in turn not forget Russia" (O'Meara 2019: 156). The subsequent disenchant-
ment of Orlov and several other officers motivated a revolt against the autocracy after the death of Alexander I.

The victory over France had several hidden costs. The threat from the
Europeans increased as Russia's position on the continent paradoxically
declined by defeating France. The seemingly never-ending conflict between
Britain and France for dominance had finally come to an end, and Britain
enjoyed superiority. This paved the way for British-French cooperation
throughout the nineteenth century that would not bode well for Russia.

While Napoleon had been defeated on the battlefield, the liberal influences had permeated across the main capitals of Europe. Russia's victorious
army had also been "infected" by liberal ideal during the march across the
European continent and entering Paris in 1814. Furthermore, Russian cultural power had demonstrated its weakness as the Russian elites themselves
seemed at times more French than Russian. Well-educated Russian officers
returned to Russia and desired fundamental change to the authoritarian political structures of Russia.

The war augmented existing pressure to end serfdom, which was already
opposed both many conservatives and liberals due to the injustice and socio-
economic impediment for development. The large military draft in Russia,
required to defeat Napoleon, revealed that military service was incompatible
with serfdom. The military draft was primarily from the peasantry, and the
serfs were liberated from the land once they entered military service. Military
services lasted for twenty-five years and neither the communities nor families
of the recruits expected to ever see them again. The former serfs could also be
promoted into higher military ranks and achieve a status that had previously
been impossible. The incompatibility between serfdom and military service
was evident as no landowner would want to have former military men work
for them (Lieven 2009). Military service had exposed the men to the wider
world and become more aware of the injustices of serfdom. With military
training and the ability to rally up discontent in the communes, the former
serfs were dangerous to the landowners (Lieven 2009). Before Napoleon's
invasion, one of the most senior advisors of Alexander cautioned against
preparing for war by establishing a militia: "At present in Russia the weakening of ties of subordination to the landowners is more dangerous than foreign
invasions" (Lieven 2009).

When Alexander I died in December 1825, the line of succession was
not followed. Alexander I's younger brother, Konstantin, had renounced his
claim to the throne. Instead, Nicholas I became the Tsar – who would rule
Russia from 1825 to 1855. The confusion about succession during inter-
regnum was seized upon by disgruntled Russian army officers and approximately 3,000 soldiers, who attempted to take advantage of the opportunity to

end the autocracy. Some of the military officers leading the rebellion were members of the secret organisation – Northern Society, which advocated liberal reforms such as abolishing serfdom, advancing the rule of law, and electing the legal assembly (Trigos 2009).

The Decembrist Revolt was easily defeated; however, the myths of the rebellion became a powerful force as it demonstrated the influence of European ideas and the consequences of failing to reform. The Northern Society's Decembrist Revolt developed competing myths about its significance (Trigos 2009). Supporters of the Decembrist Revolt glorified the event to inspire future rebellions of different strands against the state. Nicholas used the rebellion as a case for strengthening the autocracy and elevating conservatism as Nicholas considered the Decembrist Movement to be the result of Western liberalism (Wortman 1994: 265).

The Decembrists did not have a clear platform for what would follow the autocracy. The possible alternatives included a centralised Rechsstaat based on law, a centralised Jacobin republic or a constitutional monarchy. By the 1830s, Russia's culture, political identity and place in history were in a limbo between the liberal West and the conservative East. Intellectuals identifying as Westernisers sought liberal socio-economic development that would emulate the European experience. Organic development was largely rejected as Russia's distinctiveness was associated with backwardness, which was exactly what they sought to overcome. By the 1840s, the influence of the Decembrist Revolt had manifested itself as a revolutionary wing among the Westernisers. Nicholas I was determined to resist the radicals by leading Russia along a conservative path.

THE CONSERVATISM OF NICHOLAS I

Nicholas I sought to counter the liberal creed of the French Revolution with conservative values consistent with Russia's distinctiveness. Nicholas was convinced that the French Revolution, much like the fall of Constantinople, had been caused by the weakness and indulgence of the monarch. The challenge for Nicholas was to defeat revolutionaries, while concurrently delivering the required socio-economic reforms to prevent stagnation that gave fuel to the revolutionary forces.

Reforms were required for Russia to survive in Europe, although the conservatives were adamant that traditional life and faith had to be preserved for stability. In 1826, Nicholas began to root out revolutionaries and potential traitors. Russian conservatism as a state ideology was yet again strengthened following the suppression of the Polish Rebellion in 1830–1831 against the Russian monarch, also known as the November uprising. Nicholas revoked the autonomy of Poland and subsequently its new constitution to enforce the internal cohesion of the Russian Empire.

Nicholas recognised that serfdom was problematic and efforts were made to improve the life of peasants, although emancipation was considered too disruptive as the stability of the state had the highest priority. Nicholas sought to respond to the challenge of the growing might of rapidly industrialising Western powers – a problem that would only become more unmanageable. Serfdom was at the centre of focus as Russia's entire socio-economic order rested on this antiquated institution. Reforming serfdom was obstructed by the inadequate bureaucracy in the provinces of Russia, which would be a fundamental requirement to manage socio-economic disruptions. Furthermore, emancipating the serfs without granting them land would cause exploitation and poverty, although seizing territory from the land-owning nobility could similarly unleash destructive forces (Christoff 2019).

Cultural conservative movements that emerged in the early nineteenth century had to a great extent been neglected by Alexander I, although they would shape the policies of Nicholas (Pipes 1959). Much like the Enlightenment manifested itself in Peter the Great's Cultural Revolution to remake Russia as a European state, the counter-Enlightenment or romanticism that followed was similarly motivated by the goal of rediscovering Russia's distinctive culture.

Paradoxically, the romanticist ideas of reviving traditional culture and spirituality were borrowed primarily from German philosophers from the 1770s such as Johann Gottfried Herder and Johann Georg Hamann. The focus on the particularities of German culture had been imperative to resist French cultural universalism and unite Germany. Herder was averse to the cosmopolitan influence the Enlightenment had on Germany, especially in the cultural sphere of language. In the *Treatise on the Origin of Language*, Herder (1772) argued that language laid the foundation for culture and *the nation as* "a poet is the creator of the nation around him". A particular and unique culture that unites people was recognised as a condition for stability and to preserve the autonomy of the nation.

At the turn of the nineteenth century, romanticism and cultural conservatism made its way to Russia. For the Russians, it was in response to Peter the Great's Cultural Revolution that had rejected Russian culture and language. Cultural conservatives such as Aleksandr Shishkov, Fedor Rostopchin and Sergei Glinka critiqued and sought to roll back the Petrine policies of Peter the Great (Martin 1998; Hamburg 2015: 118). They defined Russia politically as a European power, although Russia had to assert its cultural identity to remain a distinctive nation.

The romanticist author, Vladimir Odoyevsky, became an inspiration and a forerunner to the conservative Slavophiles. Odoyevksy's influential novels such as *The City without a Name* and *Russian Nights* offer a profound critique of the economic rationality of the British political economy that absorbed individual life. Spirituality, philosophy, art and time itself was commodified, and life itself was reorganised to enhance economic efficiency. Odoyevsky suggested that in the rapid advance towards industrial society, the British had left something important and immeasurable behind. Economic and political freedoms were deemed to eviscerate the internal freedom of mankind. As the nation is an organic entity, Odoyevsky also feared that Russia's efforts to emulate the West prevented Russia from developing along an organic path and thus have something of value to contribute to the family of European nations.

An important defence of Russian culture took place in the language sphere by pushing back use the French language. Shishkov published an essay in 1803, *Discourse in Ancient and Modern Style of the Russian Language*, which was largely inspired by Herder. Shishkov Rostopchin and Glinka all denounced the contempt by the nobility for the Russian language and culture. The obsession with French culture and language was seen as a revolutionary act by severing ties with previous generations and the Russian people. Language is not merely a way of communicating but a source of identity. The bourgeois tendency to favour the French language prevented Russian cultural enrichment as an underpinning of the survival of the nation. Instead of enriching Russian litera-ture and language, the cosmopolitan elites were plunging their native country "deeper and deeper into ignorance" (Shishkov 1824: 10–11). Furthermore, the Russian language was also a transmitter of culture and spirituality.

Nikolai Karamzin, the state historian of Alexander I, stressed the centrality of the autocracy for Russian statehood. Russian history provided empirical evidence that when the state had been weak and divided, it descended into anarchy and became preyed upon by hostile foreign powers. By contrast, dur-ing periods of strong centralised power, the Russian state and its people had prospered (Karamzin 2005).

The autocracy would restrain the descent towards hedonism internally, and defend against aggressors externally. Under the revolutionary forces of the French Revolution, Karamzin argued that Russia and Europeans had to defend the traditional forms of government. The destructiveness of the French Revolution had a Hobbesian lesson for Karamzin as the threat to order, justice and security came primarily from too little government – not too much government. The limitations on autocracy were set by the Orthodox Church, customs and the central role of the nobility.

SERGEI UVAROV AND OFFICIAL NATIONALITY

Cultural conservatism made its imprint on politics as Nicholas I appointed Count Sergei Uvarov in 1832 to reform the education system, and then became the minister for national enlightenment. In 1833, Uvarov established

"Official Nationality" that would remain Russia's guiding conservative ideology until the Bolshevik Revolution. Thus, Uvarov is commonly referred to as the godfather of Russian political conservatism (Chamberlain 2020).

Official Nationality represented a drastic shift as Russia had been averse to nationalist ideas as a monarchy ruling over a multi-ethnic empire. Yet, the nationalist sentiments proliferating across Europe and Russia could not be ignored. Instead of resisting nationalism, Russia sought to shape the concept of nationalism to fit its distinctiveness. French nationalism of transferring sovereignty from the monarch to the people was not feasible for Russia. Uvarov's Official Nationality consisted of the Holy Trinity of: "Orthodoxy, autocracy, and nationality" as a repudiation of the anti-monarch nationalism of the French Revolution under the slogan "Liberty, Equality and Fraternity" (Riasanovsky 1959: 74). The ideology of Official Nationality linked national identity and faith to the Tsar, which subsequently endowed the autocracy with what can be characterised as soft power. A strong ideology that strengthened the loyalty of the people directly to the Tsar would improve governance, and also make the Tsar less reliant on the nobility that was often a thorn in the side of both the monarch and the people.

Russia's official conservative ideology aimed to establish a solid foundation to make Russia resilient and capable of managing change in a rapidly changing world. The tripartite focus on orthodoxy, autocracy and nationality also encapsulated the distinctiveness of Russia and thus its unique strand of conservatism. As a multi-ethnic empire without any natural borders, Russia could not emulate the homogenous European nation-state. First, the strong and unique spiritual roots of Russia before the Petrine reforms was deeply embedded in the national history, and thus a source of legitimacy for the devout. Second, Russian history had demonstrated the important role of the autocracy and Uvarov argued it was "a necessary factor in the survival of the Empire in its present form" (Miller 2008: 142). The national memory and heritage were recognised to be harmonious with the central role of the Orthodox Church and the autocracy. Uvarov's triad was envisioned as three branches of power that would define a common purpose to ensure Russia remained united and resilient.

Uvarov's conservatism was motivated by resistance to revolutionary change and an unwavering belief in Russian national traditions and culture as the foundation for organic growth. The nationalism that Uvarov developed was aimed to immunise Russians from the seductiveness of foreign ideologies that would divide Russia. The new political conservatism eased the tensions between the national prestige of modernisation and maintaining domestic order (Chamberlain 2020). Uvarov is described as a Burkian conservative who shaped modern Russian conservatism with all its unique characteristics (Chamberlain 2020: 3). The "sustaining principles" of Uvarov were to manage Russia's path to modernisation or "conservative renovation" while maintaining both social and political stability (Whittaker 1984: 4).

UVAROV AND CIVILISATION

Uvarov subscribed to the theory of civilisations undergoing cyclical development from infancy, youth, maturity, decay and death. The cyclical thesis suggests that culture is the spiritual scaffolding that enables civilisations to grow. Culture provides a refuge for connectivity to the primordial and instinctive that provides humanity with meaning and cohesion. When civilisations eventually outgrow their own culture, they decay and eventually die.

Many Western philosophers have shared this influential thesis about the cyclical development of civilisations. In the early eighteenth century, Giambattista Vico (2002), argued that the advancement of reason eventually eschews the culture and spirituality, and thus descends into barbarism. Brooks Adams (1897), Oswald Spengler (1922), Arnold Toynbee (1946), Carroll Quigley (1961) and other leading scholars on the rise and fall civilisations have similarly contributed to this cyclical thesis. Others, such as Pitirim Sorokin (1941), were more optimistic in terms of the ability to recover culture and spirituality that has been lost to excessive reason, individualism and materialism.

Uvarov posited that the dawn of Christianity represented a unique event in world history as it laid the foundation for the moral equality of mankind and thus basic rights. The concept of human rights developed from Christianity and presented a conservative path towards emancipation. Europe had entered the civilisational stage of youth during the emergence of powerful kings and its emancipated people and had since begun its decay (Whittaker 1978: 161). Uvarov's concept of enlightened constitutional monarchies was also prevalent in Europe as an alternative to disruptive revolutionary change. Many Western contemporaries shared the scepticism of the ability of democracies to preserve the traditional, spiritual and collective creed required for a society to maintain its internal cohesion.

Uvarov's concept of a constitutional monarchy was similar to what had been presented by Speransky, which represented the height of civilisation that should be implemented in Russia. The powerful monarch would be constrained, although strong enough to protect against domestic upheavals and foreign aggressors. A constitutional monarchy was intended to facilitate gradual and organic growth by positioning Russia between the despotism and democracy as two decadent forms of government. Preserving the monarchy was consistent with Russia's autocratic traditions and geographical challenges. Gradual development would be embraced by "the spirit of a strong, humane, enlightened autocracy" (Uvarov 1818: 52). Emancipation of the serfs was desirable, although Uvarov considered that Russia was not yet ready for it. Serfdom as an institution underpinned the socio-economic structures and the relationship between the Tsar and the land-owning nobility.

Uvarov considered Russia to be a European state and he was a great admirer of European civilisation. However, in the tradition of Herder, Uvarov recognised that Russia should not attempt to emulate Europe as it would be a revolutionary act breaking with the distinctiveness of Russian culture. Furthermore, Russia was a young member of the European family and should not be in a rush to mature. Delivering a speech in 1835, Uvarov argued that Russia had to adjust and prepare itself rather than spearhead the new changes taking place in Europe:

> We, that is the people of the nineteenth century, are in a difficult position: we are living amidst political storms and political unrest. Nations are changing their way of life; they are experiencing rebirth, are in ferment, and advancing. . . . But Russia is young and virgin, and she should not taste, at least for the time being, these bitter troubles. We must extend her youth and educate her in the meantime. That is my political approach. (Nikitenko 1975: 62)

UVAROV AND EDUCATION

The liberal reforms of Peter the Great, Catherine the Great and Alexander I focused heavily on the education system to modernise Russia. Nicholas I similarly sought to advance conservatism through the education system. The universities had become a source for revolutionary ideas and movements, which had to be moderated by advancing unifying ideals of the collective. Uvarov had an excellent record of implementing extensive reforms to elevate the quality of the Russian university system.

Uvarov's aimed to ensure that these advancements were rooted in Russian distinctiveness to ensure organic growth. As Education Minister, Uvarov recognised the importance of education as the foundation for development and a central function of the state. Education became the natural space for conservatism as a patrimonial government could guide the nation towards modernity while also rejuvenating the national identity based on the past. Uvarov's viewed governance to be similar to raising children since the state had to socialise the public to influence public opinion. Much like the parent, the state would use its unrivalled authority to develop and emancipate its citizens, while concurrently using autocratic control to suppress destructive behaviour. Russia's prominent universities would also be instrumental to Russify its Polish and Baltic provinces with a common culture.

The national memory advocated by Uvarov entailed the study of Greek civilisation as the common cradle of all European civilisations and the history of Russia as a unique branch. Positioning the national history in the context of Europe was intended to avoid the destructive polarisation of either attempting to emulate Europe or severing itself from Europe. Some Eurasian inclinations also became evident as oriental studies were deemed to be important. Russia was to be positioned between European civilisation and Asian wisdom as a source of strength rather than neglecting either its European or Asian components (Whittaker 1978: 173).

As the roots of a shared national identity were cultivated and dug deeper into the shared consciousness, Uvarov grew more confident in the ability of Russia to manage change. As democratic theory suggests, political pluralism can only exist within "accepted boundaries" and "cleavage must be tempered by consensus" (Diamond 1990: 49). Without social unity and a clearly defined scope for political pluralism, "the pressures towards moderate middle-of-the-road attitudes are absent" (Lijphart 1969: 208–209). In 1847, Uvarov argued that Russian universities had developed a consensus concerning the scope of political pluralism that remained committed to the autocracy. Uvarov, therefore, favoured to further liberalise the universities and accept academic freedoms akin to the German education system (Whittaker 1978: 173).

RISE OF THE CONSERVATIVE SLAVOPHILES

Slavophilism was an intellectual framework for Russian conservatism. The Slavophiles have been described as nationalists and "the intellectual disciples of to the Johann Gottfried Herder and Friedrich von Schelling" (Szvák 2011: 308). Slavophiles emerged in the 1830s, and by the 1840s, they had become a powerful movement of conservative intellectuals. The early Slavophiles were Aleksei Khomyakov, Ivan Kireevsky, Yuri Samarin and Konstantin Aksakov. The Slavophiles repudiated both the Cultural Revolution by Peter the Great and the French Revolution as a foreign corruption of Russia's cultural and political sovereignty. Konstantin Aksakov posited that the former harmonious relationship between the monarch and the people had been interrupted by the policies of Peter the Great (Riasanovsky 1956: 79).

Pyotr Chaadayev, a Westerniser, framed the debate between Slavophiles and Westernisers with his eight "Philosophical Letters" between 1826 and 1832. In a rejection of Slavophilism and an indictment of Russian culture, Chaadayev posits that Christianity is the vessel of universal historical development and Russia's separatism from the Western Church had been the

source of its backwardness. Russia's Byzantine history and Orthodox faith
had decoupled Russia from universalism and prevented meaningful development. Chadaaev (1965: 117) opined:

> We have given nothing to the world, we have taught nothing to the world; we
> have not added a single idea to the mass of human ideas; we have contributed
> nothing to the progress of the human spirit. And we have disfigured everything
> we have touched of that progress.

While the predecessors of the Slavophiles were preoccupied with constitutional reforms under the rule of Alexander I, the Slavophiles were more
preoccupied with societal and cultural change. The Slavophiles considered
custom and culture to be a central component of nationalism, which informs
politics (Rabow-Edling 2012: 119). The Slavophiles were concerned that the
Russian elites and intellectuals did not appreciate the importance of custom
in state affairs. The deep identity gulf between the Europeanised elites and
the Russian people fuelled distrust to the legislators. Kireevsky therefore
considered customary laws to be preferable as it is not constructed by distant
and detached elites. Khomyakov similarly argued:

> Law and custom rule the social life of the peoples. Law, written and armed with
> compulsion, brings the differing private wills into a conditional unity. Custom,
> unwritten and unarmed, is the expression of the most basic unity of society. . . .
> The broader the sphere of custom, the stronger and healthier the society and the
> richer and more original the development of its jurisprudence. (Riasanovsky
> 1995: 96)

Slavophiles embraced romanticism and nationalism. The objective was
to cultivate solidarity through a collective identity based on the Orthodox
Church, the traditional communities of the peasantry, the monarchy and the
cultural uniqueness of Russia (Lieven 1998: 258). The Orthodox Church
was upheld as a key institution for organic unity. Unlike Western branches
of Christianity, Orthodoxy had maintained its links to the past. By contrast,
the reformed Protestants was criticised as they had obtained more freedom at
the cost of unity (Khomyakov 1895). Internal freedom through the Orthodox
faith was imperative as an internal compulsion that did not compel excesses
by the state.

The peasantry was revered as it had preserved the traditions, spirituality
and soul of Russia. Khomyakov (1895) argued that agrarian communities
were better Christians, had higher moral standing and were more unified. The
peasantry was deemed to have preserved the primordial embedded in Russian
culture and *sobornost*, which denotes the spiritual unity found in religious

communities (Khomyakov 1895). The virtue of rural regions is central in the political economy of conservatism as the absence of economic development and connectivity preserved tradition. Khomyakov believed that the excesses of the Enlightenment, introduced into Catholicism and Protestantism, resulted in its religious social structures losing the true sense of community (Ware 2011). Ivan Kireevsky (1911: 226) similarly argued:

> Rome preferred abstract syllogism to sacred tradition, which is the deposition of the common mind of the whole Christian world, and in which that world coheres as a living, indissoluble unity. This elevation of syllogism over tradition was in fact the sole basis for the rise of a separate and independent Rome. . . . Rome left the Church because of a desire to introduce new dogmas into the faith, dogmas unknown to sacred tradition, which were by nature the accidental products of Western logic.

Serfdom was a contentious topic among the Slavophiles. Serfdom made the majority of the population static and almost impermeable to change. While the traditional was maintained, the ability to modernise was limited. Some Slavophiles believed that serfdom had to be maintained to preserve sobornost, while others viewed the injustice as unacceptable. Conservative Slavophiles such as Samarin and Khomyakov argued that to preserve the social order after emancipation, the peasants should be awarded land collectively to protect traditional communes from disruption (Christoff 2019). From the 1840s, the dichotomy of gemeinschaft/obshchina versus gesellshaft/obshestvo was radicalised by serfdom.

Maintaining serfdom stifled modernisation, although conservatives were concerned that there was an absence of other societal institutions to represent the community if serfdom was abolished. As Nietzsche had cautioned, creative destruction within culture and society can unravel the sources of morality and values. If the creators of new values and moral codes do not emerge (Übermensch), then society descends into nihilism and anarchy.

In the absence of a substitute for the communes of the serfs, Karamzin and Samarin argued in favour of preserving serfdom. The aversion to liberty for peasants was rooted in the belief that they did not have the required moral foundation and freedom would be squandered on "drinking and villainy – what a gold mine for taverns and corrupt police officials, but what a blow to morals and to the security of the state!" (Karamzin 2005: 165–166). Serfdom was the epitome of the state's paternal role that would be to provide the peasantry with stability and purpose, while emancipation would stabilise both the peasants and the state. The prioritisation of ensuring stability reflected the fragile condition of such a large country not connected strongly with either infrastructure or institutions to uphold the socio-economic and political:

The primary obligation of the monarch is to safeguard the internal and external unity of the state; benefitting estates and individuals comes second. Alexander wishes to improve the lot of the peasants by granting them freedom; but what if this freedom should harm the state? And will the peasants be happier, freed from their masters' authority, but handed over to their own vices, to tax farmers, and to unscrupulous judges? (Karamzin 2005: 166)

Karamzin did not rule out the future emancipation of the serfs but suggesting this had to be a gradual process. Rights would have to be accompanied by new responsibilities, and it was feared the serfs would lose their communities, become buried in debts and engage in disorderly behaviour to the extent in undermined the stability of the state: "Freedom demands preparation through moral improvement – and who would call our system of wine-farming and the dreadful prevalence of drunkness a sound preparation for freedom?" (Karamzin 2005: 166). By contrast, conservatives such as Glinka made arguments in favour of abolishing serfdom to prevent the moral corruption of Russia. Count Arakcheev believed in gradual emancipation by allowing serfs to buy their freedom.

The monarchy was respected as the main authority that had throughout Russian history been the bedrock for order and stability. Samarin blamed the outsourcing of governance to the gentry as the source of tensions, since they were positioned in-between the Tsar and the people (Christoff 2019). Ivan Aksakov aspired for Slavophile ideas to bridge the spiritual gap between the gentry and the people, which would strengthen the connectivity between the monarch and the people (Lukashevich 1965).

The Slavophiles relationship with the West was complex and often confused as "anti-Western". Leading Slavophiles such as Kireevsky and Khomyakov expressed profound admiration for the West and built on romanticist and conservative ideas from their European counterparts. However, they maintained that Russia had to preserve its distinctiveness. By imitating Europe, Russia would become an imposter and could not stand tall and proud among its fellow Europeans. The paradox was that imitation had been used to catch up with the West, which had become a source of falling behind as cultural decline would inhibit the mobilisation of the Russian people and the collective consciousness to achieve greatness. Furthermore, the Slavophiles frequently pointed out that the West was heading down a wrong path, and the criticism of the West was also intended to assist the Western Europeans to preserve their traditional culture. The Russian identity was not in direct opposition to the West; it merely recognised that the fixation on the achievements of the West undermined the development and advancement of Russian culture. Admiration of the West thus prevented Russia from defining itself (Rabow-Edling 2012: 98).

THE LEGACY OF THE SLAVOPHILES

The Slavophiles did not conform fully with conservative principles by treating the Cultural Revolution as an aberration that could be overturned and thus return to the romanticised pre-Petrine Russia. The effort to reverse more than a century of Russian history and development becomes a revolutionary act. True conservatism is not nostalgic and recognises that organic growth must encompass recent history. Even the Cultural Revolution must thus be recognised as having influenced Russia and will continue to shape future development.

The next generation of conservatives, such as Apollon Grigoryev and Fyodor Dostoyevsky, challenged this aspect of Slavophiles by including the different and often contradictory features of Russian history into a consistent narrative. The crux of their argument was that Russia was an amalgam of its pre- and post-Petrine history. This conservative approach to dealing with Russia's revolutionary history was also intended to build a bridge that was growing between the Europeanised elites and the peasantry (Dowler 1982).

Nikolai Berdyaev, who became a leading conservative thinker of the twentieth century, criticised his Slavophile predecessors for being too divisive. The Slavophile tended to view the Westernisers as almost treasonous due to their aspirations for Russia. Berdyaev (1947: 56) argued that while the ideas of the Westernisers were misguided, "the Westernizers were just as much Russians as the Slavophils; they loved Russia and were passionately desirous of its highest good". The unique East-West geography of Russia was a curse when either side sought full victory over the other, and Russian civilisation triumphed when the instinctive and traditional East was balanced with the rational and modern West:

> The inconsistency and complexity of the Russian soul may be due to the fact that in Russia two streams of world history – East and West – jostle and influence one another. The Russian people is not purely European and it is not purely Asiatic. Russia is a complete section of the world – a colossal East West. It unites two worlds, and within the Russian soul two principles are always engaged in strife – the Eastern and the Western. (Berdyaev 1947: 1)

Nikolai Gogol (2009), a fellow conservative, had similarly intervened in the 1840s to alleviate the polarisation between the westernisers and Slavophiles, as they were both deemed to be one-sided and thus undermined what Russia needed the most – unity. Conservatism suggests that human beings are trapped between instincts and reason by embodying both Apollo and Dionysus; thus mankind prospers when positioned between nature and civilisation to accommodate both chaos and order. In *Dead Souls*, Gogol suggested that both a dull home life and perpetual wandering fuels spiritual decadence. Order is a necessity, yet engaging in chaos is necessary for renewal.

Nikolai Gogol opined that wisdom and meaning derived from struggle and suffering. The strength of Russia had evolved over the centuries of fighting against the Tatars, Mongols, Turks and other peoples in the East. The open steppes had elevated a warrior morality among the Russians that strengthened the cultural core. Furthermore, incorporating Cossacks and other people into the Russian Empire had infused Russians with new energy. Gogol believed that capitalism and engagement with Europe had drained the energy from Russia and corrupted its development. Gogol desired to change Russia through a spiritual renewal based in orthodoxy. In his 1835 novel, *Taras Bulba*, Gogol depicted Russia's energy as deriving from the chaos and wildness inherited from the Cossacks and the East. Gogol believed that the wildness of the East was inaccurately depicted as negative since it was contrasted order. However, order, meaning and cultural strength derive from engaging with chaos. Russia's energy and culture derived from its ability to position itself between order and chaos. Gogol, therefore, cautioned against attempting to fit Russia within the format of the European nation, which had already reached old age and decadence. With Russia still in its youth, Gogol argued: "We are still molten metal, not moulded into our national form" (Singleton 1997: 44).

PAN-SLAVISM

Pan-Slavism originated from the unresolved issue of nationality. Pan-Slavism emerged as a wider concept than Slavophilism as it strived towards uniting all Slavs. The rise of German nationalism in the first decades of the nineteenth century as a driving force for unifying Germany had a great influence on the emergence of Pan-Slavism. The success in unifying Germany inspired the unification of Slavic lands. While Slavophilism was a strand of conservatism, Pan-Slavism was to some extent a revolutionary child of the French Revolution. The ambition of uniting all Slavs had gained some momentum during the romantic era, although it was the revolutionary spirit of France in the late eighteenth century that envisioned a Slavic nationality.

Russia became the natural centre for pan-Slavs as Russia was the only truly independent Slavic state as other Slavic peoples were ruled by non-Slavic empires. While Russian Pan-Slavism was often seen as an extension of Russian nationalism, the first Slav Congress meeting in Prague in 1848 rejected Russian expansionism.

Danilevsky (2013), a leading Pan-Slav, argued that the Slavs had to be liberated from the rule of the Turks and the Austrians, or remain divided vassals with marginal significance. The Pan-Slavic mission would unavoidably cause conflict with Europe, although when the unified Slavs had recaptured Constantinople they would make an important and valuable part of Europe:

> Russia, being foreign to the European world by virtue of its inner workings, and furthermore, being too strong and powerful to take its place as just one of many members in the European family – as just one of many great states – Russia cannot take a place in history worthy of itself and of Slavdom unless it becomes the head of a unique, independent political system of countries and unless it serves as a balance to Europe in all its community and wholeness. (Danilevsky 2013: 402)

The Russian monarchy had previously been sceptical and even resistant to the revolutionary idea of liberating all Slavs from neighbouring states and absorb them into a greater Slavic empire. Both Alexander I and Nicholas I had been opposed to the Pan-Slavist nationalist movement as defining the empire by ethnicity unravel the multi-ethnic empire and stroke conflicts with neighbouring states.

CONSERVATIVE INTERVENTION DURING THE REVOLUTIONS OF 1848

Russia had proved itself to be remarkably immune to revolutions, unlike its European counterparts. Russia circumvented the revolutionaries of the 1820s and the 1830s, and even the revolutions of 1848 that shook the European continent. Industrialisation, urbanisation and agriculture were rapidly changing society, and the old forms of governance were becoming outdated. Liberal movements advocated for both political liberalism and economic liberalism.

In February 1848, King Louis-Philippe vacated the throne in France, and the revolutionaries proclaimed the birth of the Second Republic. In 1848, revolutions also broke out in the Austrian Empire, Denmark, Italian states, German states and Poland. The foundation of the entire European order was suddenly put in question and monarchies appeared to move towards extinction as the revolutionary movement quickly spread. The revolution also fuelled unification movements of both German and Italian lands.

Fearing that the revolutionary tide would reach Russia, Nicholas I intervened on the continent as a conservative internationalist. Russia sent 300,000 troops to assist against the Hungarian revolution in the Austrian Empire, which earned Nicholas I the nickname *Gendarme of Europe*. Before 1848, Russia had begun to question the autocracy-serfdom model as the source of socio-economic stability. However, Russia became more defensive in response to the revolutionary movements. Reforms were scaled back, and the Russian autocracy spoke more cautiously about abolishing serfdom. By contrast, the 1848 revolutions had ended the last remnants of serfdom in eastern Europe, and Russia was left as the last European state with serfs.

The revolutions across Europe in 1848 had largely been liberal. However, another strand of revolutionaries also emerged in 1848, which advocated for a communist revolution. In 1848, Karl Marx and Friedrich Engels published *The Communist Manifesto*. Capitalism was deemed to be an exploitative and transitional system as wealth in a liberal economic system gradually transfers wealth and power from labour to capital. A class struggle was expected to grow and eventually unleash a revolution, in which the proletariat would seize the means of production.

The Slavophiles viewed the revolutions with great concern and argued that the state had the responsibility to restore order (Hughes 2000: 169). With the collapse of the revolutions, Russia emerged again in a dominant position as the defender the old order (Riasanovsky 1993: 334). However, the strengthened position of Nicholas I would not last long as the authoritarian means created a backlash.

CONCLUSION

During the first half of the nineteenth century, conservatism emerged as a state ideology. The French Revolution disrupted Russia's path towards gradual and organic development, which undermined the ability to balance continuity and change. The spectre of a liberal revolutionary approach to development incentivised Russia to counter it with state conservatism that subsequently halted Speransky's liberal reforms.

Uvarov's Official Nationalism presented an official conservative position that recognised the different path Russia had to follow in its modernisation. Yet, the split between Slavophiles and Westernisers demonstrated that a social consensus had not been established in terms of whether development entailed establishing an organic path or pursuing a universal/Western path to modernisation.

The defeat of Napoleon became to some extent a pyrrhic victory for Russia. By following the French back to Paris, the Russian military was exposed to liberal ideas and developments that eventually fuelled the Decembrist Revolt. The reluctance to embrace reforms due to the fear of revolution had caused stagnation and thus elevated the risk of revolution. Furthermore, the total defeat of France disrupted the balance of power, which strengthened Britain as a maritime power and even brought about a British-French partnership. Russia had marched from victory to victory for the past 150 years since Peter the Great, which came to an end by the 1850s.

NOTE

1. It is widely believed that the British were involved in the assassination.

Chapter 4

After the Crimean War

The Great Reforms and Revolutions

INTRODUCTION

The humiliating defeat in the Crimean War (1853–1856) challenged the conservative ethos established by Nicholas I and Sergei Uvarov. Economic and technological backwardness had deprived Russia of the necessary tools to fight a war. Falling far behind the Europeans threatened the legitimacy of key Russian institutions, including the autocracy.

The Great Reforms were designed to make a great leap forward to survive in the European neighbourhood. The 1860s subsequently became the second Russian Enlightenment. Not since Peter the Great had so many reforms been pushed forward so swiftly. The abolishment of serfdom, extensive judicial reforms, decentralisation of power, educational reforms and industrialisation were some of the top-down reforms imposed on Russia's underdeveloped bureaucracy and an ill-prepared society. Limitations on further development included a lack of tradition with individualism, entrepreneurship and the market. The modernisation policies initiated by the government compelled conservatives to shift focus from gradual change to rooting revolutionary changes in something that resembled the collective and other conservative values. Industrialisation required a format for a conservative political economy that linked a catch-up strategy to the state and the nation.

Much like the first Enlightenment caused the counter-Enlightenment and romanticism as a reaction, so did the Second Russian Enlightenment cause reactions to the excesses of materialism and individualism. The extensive and disruptive reforms following the Crimean War eventually destabilised society beyond control. The Great Reforms created economic disparity and failure of institutions and provoked foreign adversaries. The failure to manage change, as evident by delayed reforms followed by a great leap forward, eventually brought down the Russian state in the Bolshevik Revolution.

This chapter first explores the consequences of Russia's defeat in the Crimean War as it delegitimised Russian conservatism, its European identity, great power status, and the entire political system. Second, the subsequent Great Reforms are assessed, and the deep divisions they created, as conservatives had to address the rise of socialists, nihilists, radical liberals and even divisions within conservatism. Rapid industrialisation and urbanisation added further strain. Conservatism underwent reform as there was a growing need to develop a centrist liberal-conservative position to bridge the widening gap with the westernisers, and thus prevent the country from unravelling. Third, the development of transportation corridors enabled Russia to expand towards the southern and eastern coastlines of the Eurasian continent, which placed Russia in direct conflict with maritime powers. The defeat to Japan in 1905 replicated some of the failures in Crimea and sparked the revolution of 1905. The drastic changes to Russian institutions were imposed as a result of domestic instability and did not have roots in Russian history or traditions. The Democratic Revolution of 1905 was subsequently followed by the Bolshevik Revolution of 1917.

It is concluded that the Great Reforms set Russia on the path to becoming an immensely powerful state. However, key conservative principles were neglected. The socio-economic disruptions fuelled political radicalism domestically, and the connectivity with major international trade corridors caused a balancing by imperial maritime powers.

DEFEAT IN THE CRIMEAN WAR

The Crimean War revealed the dualism of Russia as an immensely powerful state, yet with profound weaknesses due to backward institutions, economy and technology. Britain had already by the late 1820s become apprehensive about Russian expansionism towards the maritime borders of the Eurasian continent, as Russia annexed Ottoman and Persian territory. The Russian victory in the Russo-Persian war of 1826–1828 displaced British influence in the region. The Persians became alarmed by the feebleness of British support and began instead looking towards Russia as the regional power. A future Russo-Persian conquest of British India thus became a possible prospect. The shadow of the Paul I ambition to conquer British India at the turn of the nineteenth century still hung over the British Empire. By the 1850s, Britain and France were intent to cooperate to obstruct Russia's southern expansion and possible conquest of Constantinople, which would make Russia a leading maritime power on the Mediterranean.

Subsequently, in 1853, Britain and France allied themselves with the Ottoman Empire in a war against Russia. The Crimean War was one of the first conflicts to use the modern technologies of the industrial revolution, such as steamships, gunboats, ironclad warships, railways and telegraphs. Furthermore, the development of sanitary hospitals was imperative since the vast majority of fatalities were caused by disease. The war displayed the might born out of Britain's industrial revolution in terms of technology, economic strength and entrepreneurship, which could be documented with the invention of photography.

Conversely, Russia's technological and economic backwardness was on display for the entire world. Russia had made efforts to industrialise, although it had not kept up with the pace of the Europeans. Russia's expansion to the coastal regions of Eurasia required a strengthening of infrastructure for defence. In the early nineteenth century, Russia could defeat the French invading by land as the massive territory enabled victory by attrition as supply lines were cut. By contrast, the Crimean War was fought from the sea, which enabled Britain to use its strengths as a maritime power. Russia's vast geographical expanse, detached from key transportation corridors, exacerbated the problems of its underdeveloped technology and infrastructure. Britain and France laid siege on the ports of St. Petersburg and Crimea to cut off Russia from waterways, which devastated Russian mobility as it had only completed its first railway in 1851 that connected Moscow with St. Petersburg. The absence of railways to Crimea and the overall underdeveloped transportation infrastructure was instrumental to Russia's defeat. Russia had an excellent river system, although the rivers would freeze for several months every year. Britain and France could transport supplies faster by the maritime corridor from Gibraltar to Crimea than Russia could bring supplies from Moscow.

Sustaining a prolonged modern war required modern infrastructure for logistical support. Furthermore, an industrialised economy was required as the commercial sector could then be converted to an autonomous supplier for Russia's war efforts during conflicts. During the Crimean War, Russia did not have a supply of commercial vessels that could aid the navy, modern technologies and supplies were scarce, and armaments had to be imported.

Russia could also not mobilise a large army without emancipating the serfs. Serfs achieved the standing of soldier citizens by serving in the armed forces, and they were not returned to serfdom after completing the military service. Even the effort to establish a militia created widespread confusion. While participating in a militia did not award emancipation, entire villages left for military service with the expectation of obtaining freedom (Saunders 2014: 213).

In 1856, Russia conceded defeat in the Crimean War. The devastating loss revealed that autocratic rule was not keeping the country strong and secure, which undermined the entire foundation of Russia's political system. Only eight years after the 1848 revolutions against European royals, the legitimacy of the Russian monarchy was also at stake. The loss of legitimacy subsequently fuelled both internal and external challenges.

Russia's claim to being a European great power was based largely on its large military power, which endowed Russia with a seat at the European table. Russia's future inclusion in the European system was in question and all the advancements that had followed Peter the Great's victory in the Great Northern War. Russia's status as a European great power following the victory over Napoleon had been shattered.

The Treaty of Paris stipulated demeaning terms of surrender, which included scaling back Russian maritime power by disallowing it from stationing its navy in the Black Sea. The treaty became a reminder of the Treaty of Stolbovo in 1617 with Sweden, which had cut Russia of from direct maritime access on the Baltic Sea. Without reliable access to maritime corridors, Russian power on the continent would fade. European diplomats had spoken openly about the intention of pushing Russia back into Asia and excluding it from European affairs (Kipp and Lincoln 1979: 4).

Russia's civilisational belonging in Europe had also been shaken. Russia was alarmed that the Europeans had sided with the Islamic Ottoman Empire, which had three centuries earlier conquered Constantinople. Russia's ambition to retake Constantinople would have cemented Russia civilisational roots to the Byzantine Empire and Europe. Russia also had seen itself as having a wider mandate by retaking Constantinople on behalf of the Christian world. Nikolai Danilevsky (2013) later argued that the Europeans reacted fiercely in 1853 as they deemed Russia to be inherently different and not part of the European family. The rebuke from Europe did not make Russia retreat into Asia, and make peace with its gemeinschaft-based civilisation. Instead, modernisation became all the more necessary. The Russian economy had been devastated, and the survival of the state depended on catching up with industrialisation and restructuring society (Blackwell 2015: 184).

THE GREAT REFORMS

In 1855, the year before Russia's defeat in Crimea, Nicholas I had died. His son, the more reform-friendly Alexander II, would rule Russia from 1855 to 1881. Alexander II was a conservative like his father. However, Nicholas I had allegedly expressed deep regrets on his deathbed that he was leaving the empire in such a bad state. Alexander was warned that the failure to embrace reforms had led to stagnation, decay and eventually defeat (Eklof et al. 1994).

The war exposed problems that had been festering for years, such as the antiquated institution of serfdom, economic backwardness, the lack of industrial development, and poor infrastructure. The Russian state no longer had the luxury of embracing conservative principles as it required rapid and pragmatic reforms to catch up and survive. The expectation that modernisation would be accompanied by gravitating towards Europe stoked increased expectations among Westernisers and resistance among the Slavophiles. The series of reforms would be referred to as the Great Reforms.

The Great Reforms were intended to restructure almost every aspect of Russian society, and the social reforms became nothing short of revolutionary. The spectacular reforms of the 1860s, the revolutionary movements of the 1870s, and the rapid industrialisation of the 1880s and 1890s caused immense challenges to the political structures of Russia (Berdyaev 1992).

In March 1856, the same month as signing the Treaty of Paris that ended the war, Alexander II informed the nobility about his intention to emancipate the serfs. In 1961, Alexander II finally passed the decree that abolished serfdom. The reforms also included reforming local governance, the judiciary, education, the military, the financial system, scaling back on censorship and other key spheres of society. Alexander II even gave exiled Decembrists amnesty and allowed their return in 1856. The amnesty for political prisoners also included a pardon for Fyodor Dostoyevsky in 1857.

EMANCIPATION OF THE SERFS

Emancipation was intended to intensify economic and social development. The issue of justice was also prevalent as abolishing serfdom ended more than two centuries of virtual enslavement. Societal structures were shaken, traditional life was reorganised, and new political movements subsequently emerged. The emancipation of the serfs was referred to by the Russian leadership as nothing short of a revolution, with the French Revolution as the only comparison in terms of scale (Rogger 1966: 197).

Even those who argued in favour of emancipation had to agree that the revolutionary change of civil liberties created chaos. The shock from the radical restructuring of society could not be adequately absorbed by remaining social structures, the justice system and government institutions. The abolition of serfdom altered the economic foundations of the power structures and the social structures, which implied that radical political changes were also on the horizon. Russian conservatives began to resemble their European counterparts as they focused less on static preservation, and instead consider pragmatic solutions as the foundations of the existing order had already unravelled (Pipes 1971: 123). Conservatives shifted their focus to managing change by ensuring the new would have some attachment to the old.

Emancipation caused profound problems among the peasantry. The breakup of traditional communities had social repercussions. Chicherin had recognised that emancipating the serfs without land would lead to rebellion (Hamburg 1998). The peasantry had to be given their own land otherwise they would become impoverished and thus also rebellious. The traditional communes could thereby be preserved to ensure social stability and security for the peasantry.

Conservatives argued that Russia would not be capable of managing the tensions from the subsequent deep class divisions. The alternative to serfdom therefore had to be a landowning peasantry that would be elevated to the middle class. Mikhail Katkov, a prominent nineteenth-century Russian conservative with a close relationship with Alexander II, cautioned: "If we abolish the commune, Russia won't last twenty-four hours. The peasant commune is the only conservative element that we have" (Khristoforov 2002: 312).

Several Russian aristocrats desired to reorganise the peasantry according to the British model, which entailed abolishing the commune based on the private property and free-market capitalism. The British experience of legislating land ownership and enclosures to break up its communes had sparked the agricultural revolution (Quigley 1961). The conservative argument against dismantling the communes could also be based on the British experience. The breakup of the communes in England resulted in profound exploitation the state outsourced governance of Game Laws to the aristocracy, who could then force the common people into the labour market (Perelman 2012: 55). A strong British state had been required to mitigate social disruption by ensuring society was not completely subjugated to market forces. The English peasantry was able to withstand the "grave damage the calamity of the enclosures" because the strong state had been able to "slow down the process of economic improvement until it became socially bearable" (Polanyi 1944: 38).

In Russia, the state was not as strong, and the vast geographical expanse further exacerbated the problem. Abandoning the communes was feared to create intolerable social disruption as the peasantry would be ravaged by unfettered market forces and the heavy hand of the aristocracy.

LOCAL GOVERNANCE, JUDICIAL
REFORMS AND EDUCATION

Zemstvo was established in 1864 to develop local governance. Assemblies and boards were elected within districts and provinces, which included the participation of peasant communes, landowners and towns. Zemstvo never developed what can be defined as self-government, and the tensions arose due to unfamiliarity with these institutions. Without tradition as a source of legitimacy and unity, deep divisions exposed themselves. The autocracy reluctantly lost some control over governance, and revolutionaries believed the extent of reforms were insufficient, and they were passed too slow. The state feared the rise of revolutionary movements that could grow within local government. This fear appeared to be validated after the assassination attempt on the Tsar in 1866, which resulted in the central government scaling back on local government and civil society (Starr 1972: 347).

The judicial reforms of 1864 created a radical shift in Russian legal culture as it embraced an independent, modern, liberal and westernised legal system. By 1870, the city authorities were organised according to non-estate principles. While changes were required to the old system, there was a backlash from conservative writers such as Dostoyevsky – who argued in favour of alternatives. Dostoyevsky and other conservatives initially offered praise of the reforms, although the criticism then arose as the laws had outgrown their moral foundations much like a civilisation outgrows its culture. Dostoyevsky believed that by westernising its legal system – the laws would no longer reflect Russia's distinct morality as a force for internal compulsion, and instead introduce foreign and alien laws by corrupt immoral courts and lawyers as an external compulsion. Consistent with other conservatives, Dostoyevsky had therefore been a proponent of customary law.

Much like in the past, the efforts to restructure Russia's political culture demanded reforms in the university system. Education advances scientific discoveries and prepares the population for a changing economy, albeit it also established class differences and distinctive sub-cultures. Underpinning the education debate was the conservative question about the need to exclude, even if it created class differences. Kostomarov desired open-university systems according to the French model where lectures were open to the general public. This was intended to prevent the emergence of a student caste ranking itself above general society. By contrast, the liberal-conservative Chicherin argued that exclusiveness is required as universities should not become public spheres of entertainment as it would diminish both the scientific quality and the student culture. Chicherin posited that universities were instrumental to foster a civic culture that supported the ideals of scientific research, hard work and civility (Kassow 1994: 250–251).

THE RISE OF RADICAL MOVEMENTS

By the 1860s, deep divisions in Russia had become evident as the country adjusted to vastly new realities. In addition to revolutionary reforms, the Polish Rebellion of 1863–1864 contributed to more extreme positions. Nihilists, socialists and the Narodniki movement presented new challenges to conservatives, while even the conservatives were growing more divided.

The revolutionary changes of the 1860s had given birth to the "nihilist". The abolishment of serfdom opened the doors to question all institutions of society. Nihilism embraces the logic of liberalism to its fullest extent by challenging the influence of all institutions that impose collective identities and norms on the individual, such as the state, church, ethics, manners and even the family. Yet, these institutions also instil the individual with responsibilities, meaning and purpose. Conservatism subsequently became increasingly focused on countering the growth of nihilism (Pipes 1971: 124). Katkov referred to nihilism as a "social disease" that eventually produces revolution (Katz 2017: 154).

Similar conclusions about nihilists have been reached by conservatives in the West. Nihilism becomes unavoidable when individuals are liberated from all authority and institutions that represent the collective, as they are then only defined by themselves (Deneen 2018). Heidegger (1953) posited that failing to reproduce the traditional would fuel nihilism as the entry point to a destructive intellectual and cultural crisis. Nietzsche (1967: 3) similarly expected that nihilism would eliminate a sense of shared purpose that could only lead to instability:

> What I relate is the history of the next two centuries. I describe what is coming, what can no longer come differently: *the advent of nihilism*. . . . For some time now our whole European culture has been moving as toward a catastrophe, with a tortured tension that is growing from decade to decade: restlessly, violently, headlong, like a river that wants to reach the end, that no longer reflects, that is afraid to reflect.

By the 1860s, socialism had also become a formidable alternative to conservatism and liberalism. The socialists, much like the liberals and nihilists, believed that the instinctive impulses of mankind could be transcended and viewed traditions with less affinity. While both the socialists and conservatives prioritised communitarian values, the socialists denounced communities such as the nation, monarchy, Orthodox Church and family as being institutions supporting capitalism. The socialist opposed serfdom and the autocracy and became increasingly radical as they shifted towards advocating revolution.

The Narodniki movement, a socialist populist movement, emerged in Russia in the 1860s. Narodnichestvo denoted agrarian socialism, a unique strand of socialism that based its legitimacy on traditions. The Narodniki intellectuals consisted of people from the middle class who styled themselves as left-wing conservatives celebrating the Russian peasantry as the embodiment of true Russia. While a key purpose of the movement was to serve the peasantry, the Narodniki initially did not have much support from the peasantry where the dark side of modernity had not been felt. The main audience and followers of the Narodniki were the cosmopolitan centres where people looked towards the countryside as a source of traditions that evaded the spiritual decay that accompanies modernity. The belief was that the tradition of peasant communes would enable Russia to skip the capitalist stage of development and transition immediately to socialism (Pipes 1964). However, by the 1870s, the Narodniki movement had penetrated rural regions with revolutionary propaganda.

Conservatism itself also developed internal division in terms of how to manage change. The first group believed that a strong state was necessary to withstand the storm caused by the revolutionary fervour following the abolishment of serfdom. Reliance on common faith, community and abstract ideas such as Jung's archetypes were deemed to be insufficient due to the extent of socio-economic disruptions. The people were expected to be ruled through obedience to historical traditions to ensure the collective good (Katz 2017). Mikhail Katkov, a liberal turned conservative, believed that the chaotic changes of the 1860s had to be stabilised with a strong autocracy and nationalism. The second group, which included Slavophile thinkers, expressed greater belief in the people and the nation to organise society if they could be guided by a shared consciousness based on a common past. While they had supported and were optimistic about the emancipation of the serfs, they believed that education, faith and romantic nationalism would reduce the reliance on crude obedience to a strong state. Thus, relying on internal compulsion would not require the political subjugation to the Orthodox Church. The monarchy was still to be a powerful centre of power, although it was believed it should lead through inspiration and spirituality rather than strong-arm the ignorant. This second path of conservatism had more in common Herder's conservatism, which endeavoured to preserve and defend the nation rather than the state. With the rapidly changing state structures, conservatism was reformed as it became less focused on the state and more focused on the preservation of the nation.

RAPID INDUSTRIALISATION AND URBANISATION

Dissatisfied with the slow progress with reforms, a left-wing terrorist group assassinated Alexander II in St. Petersburg in 1881. The new Tsar, Alexander III would rule Russia from 1881 to 1894. Conservatives after 1881 were largely convinced that the authority of the state had to be elevated

(Pipes 1971: 128). Alexander III intensified the industrialisation process and the minister of finance Sergei Witte oversaw the industries policies. Nicholas II succeeded Alexander III in 1894 and continued rapid industrialisation. With diminishing conditions for labour, a political vacuum opened for the socialists, and Nicholas became the last Tsar of Russia.

The hasty path to modernisation created profound socio-economic difficulties that were not properly addressed, and radical alternatives subsequently emerged to fill the vacuum. Rapid industrialisation and urbanisation created difficult conditions in both the cities and rural regions. Russia's major cities did not have the capacity or institutions to accommodate the large influx of workers, and the new wealth rapidly concentrated itself in the hands of a few industrialists and bankers. The influx of labourers from rural regions doubled the population of Moscow and St. Petersburg. The poor peasants flooded to the cities where they met poor living conditions, and an exploitative working environment due to the lack of legal protection and labour unions. The cities were densely populated and had a social culture that was foreign to the newly urbanised peasantry. Traditional sources of stability and security, such as the local communities and the church, were no longer able to able to provide comfort and assurance to the urbanised masses. In the vacuum, ideologues and populists could thrive in an environment where the difference between the elites and the people only became more profound.

Rapid industrialisation, aided by protective measures and foreign capital, created several opponents and enemies of Sergei Witte's reforms. The gentry was angered by the agrarian crisis caused by Witte's industrialisation (Pearson 2004: 206). While recognising that Russia had to use tariffs to develop its industries, the tariffs reduced domestic demand as prices increased (Witte 1954: 67). The Narodniks, the liberal Zemstvo men and agricultural exporters opposed tariffs. Some conservatives and nationalists opposed the reliance on foreign capital (Von Laue 1954: 61). Slavophile conservatives were attacking the industrialisation of Russia. Liberals were seeking greater political freedoms and representation to accompany economic development. Concurrently, socialists were abhorrent about the exploitation of the working class as economic disparity grew.

The administrative tools of the Russian state developed to manage relations with the social elites, merchants and industrialists. However, the decentralised administrative structured intended to maintain the state's control began to take on a life of their own by displaying autonomy. Furthermore, an educated public had begun to debate politics and modernisation independent of the state. The former conservative assertion that the Russian people were apolitical was no longer valid.

However, the cultural foundation also strengthened itself. Conservatives are notoriously concerned about that industrialisation would signify civilisation outgrowing its own culture, which would usher in the age of decay and eventual collapse. Optimism was therefore warranted as Russia also thrived in literature and culture during its Silver Age of literature (1890–1920). The last decade of the nineteenth century and the first decades of the twentieth century were characterised by the outburst of cultural energy with the emerging work of Leo Tolstoy, Fyodor Dostoyevsky, Ivan Turgenev, Pyotr Tchaikovsky and others. A common topic in the Silver Age was the idea that grand socio-economic and political changes reshape the external and diminish internal compulsions. Thus, society decays when it seems to be prospering, which is a key theme in conservatism. Conservatives recognise that art is a central contributor to culture and strengthens the foundation and stability of society. Dostoyevsky believed in internal freedom through faith. Christianity created internal compulsions and limited the need for external restrictions as the principal attack on freedom. Tolstoy believed that art should be a supplement to religion in terms of instilling morality in society. For example, Tolstoy's masterpiece, *War and Peace* from 1869, communicates the Christian concept of brotherly love. The reader learns to hate the sins of the lead character Natasha, yet the sinner is loved by exploring the weaknesses of the human condition. The main thesis of Tostoy's main novels was that change should be advanced by improving the internal rather than grand political reforms.

RESPONDING TO DISRUPTIONS AND INSTABILITY

The instability from rapid and deep socio-economic and institutional reforms could no longer be managed, and the autocracy began putting the brakes on reforms. The nobility and the Orthodox Church sought to scale back reforms, while revolutionaries movements had been emboldened and wanted more reforms faster. In response to the rebellion, Alexander began to strengthen the hand of the state.

The Zemstvo had its power reduced, the Western influence over the education system was scaled back, and the role of church in society strengthened. Furthermore, a strong national identity was recognised as a necessity to ensure stability during disruptive changes. In 1884, new reforms scaled back on the autonomy of universities, and an 1889 law centralised power with state-appointed officials for regional administration. The autonomy of Zemstvo was reduced in 1890 as the nobility had an increased voice.

Conservatives were also compelled to respond to the disruptions throughout society. Dostoyevsky believed that the divisions in society had themselves become the principal threat to Russia. Social strains between the elites and the people, between then Westernisers and the Slavophiles, had to be bridged for Russia to come together during these disruptive times. The elites were advised to return to the "native soil" to initiate a two-way dialogue by sharing the knowledge and skills they had accrued and also learning about the traditions and customs that modern society rested upon. Dostoyevsky thus called for a reform to conservative thought as the preservation of the collective had to prioritise national reconciliation:

> We are not talking about the Slavophiles or Westernisers. Our era is completely indifferent to their domestic quarrels. We are talking about the reconciliation of civilisation with the national principle. We believe that both sides must finally come to an understanding of one another, must clear up all the misunderstandings that had amassed in such incredible numbers between them and then advance in concord, with uncompromisingly combined forces, along a new, broad, and glorious path. Union at all costs, in spite of all sacrifices and as quickly as possible – that is our motivating idea, that is our motto. (quoted in Steiner 2011: 136)

Konstantin Pobedonostsev was an influential conservative and jurist who advised three Tsars. As a strong conservative critic of serfdom and the judicial system, Pobedonostsev had been an active participant in the Great Reforms. Albeit, the reforms became chaotic, and he became an opponent of further changes as it Russia's institutions could not absorb the shock, and it emboldened radicals seeking revolutionary change. The destabilisation of society was resolved by strengthening the autocracy, as conservatives had also advocated in the past. Pobedonostsev was a great admirer of Western Europe, especially England, although he had great scepticism and apprehensions towards western influence on Russia (Byrnes 1968). Katkov similarly considered Russia to be a part of European civilisation, although dialogue and partnership did not require Russia to accept a cultural, intellectual and political submission. The diversity of Europe's culture and intellect was the source of its vitality, and Russia's value and contribution to Europe depend on preserving distinctiveness.

THE REVIVAL OF PAN-SLAVISM AND EXPANSION IN THE BLACK SEA

Following the disruptive Great Reforms of the 1860s, conservatives began to gravitate towards Pan-Slavist ideas in the search for collective ideas. Pan-Slavism had become a formidable ideology by the 1860s as an imperial mission by claiming responsibility for the Slavs in other states and empires (Offord 2006: 227). Pan-Slavism evolved into a conservative movement as ethnicity and language were defined as central characteristics of the collective.

The growth in nationalism contributed to Russify the non-Russians within the Russian Empire through language and culture, which was deemed to be a challenge and a necessity due to the weak Russian ethno-cultural core within the Russian Empire (Boterbloem 2018: 134). Nationalism had similarly been central in Bismarck's Germany to unify the state. Rather than relying solely on loyalty to the tsar, the state relied more on developing a nation by turning non-Russians into Russians. The process of Russification entailed a shared language and faith for the citizens of the Russian Empire, which would increasingly be defined as a nation (Zevelev 2009). By the end of the nineteenth century, Russian conservatism had become more nationalistic and anti-Semitic (Andrew 1982).

Pan-Slavism grew in influence as Russia leaned towards liberating the southern Slavs (*Yugoslavs*) from the rule of the Ottoman and Austrians. Pan-Slavs had strengthened their position by the Second Slav Congress in 1867 in Moscow, and the movement only strengthened as a currency following German unification in 1871. The organisation of Pan-Slavism under Russian leadership created both supporters and opponents among the other Slavs in Europe. The homogenising and nation-building of Pan-Slavism meant that the Russian hosts at the Second Slav Congress demanded: "The acceptance by all the Slavs of Orthodoxy, of the Cyrillic alphabet and of the Russian language" (Kohn 1953: 139). Reformed conservative ideas became prominent Russian foreign policy. Danilevsky (2013) recognised that Russia was too strong and different to fit within the European family of states, and thus advocated an alternative and independent political system.

When war broke out between Russia and the Ottoman Empire in 1877, Dostoyevsky (1997: 889) wrote that "Sooner or later Constantinople must be ours". Dostoyevsky believed taking Constantinople would elevate Russian power and unite the Orthodox faith:

> Yes, the city must be ours, not only because it is an illustrious port, because of the straits, because it is the "focus of the universe", "the earth's navel"; not because of the long-acknowledged need for such an enormous giant as Russia to emerge at last from his locked room in which he has already grown to reach the ceiling – to emerge into open spaces where he can breathe the free air of the seas and oceans. (Dostoyevsky 1997: 891–892)

Rather, the principal reason for taking Constantinople would be to resolve the Eastern Question and the issue of nationality. In the absence of unity among the Slavs, the East would remain divided and in conflict as "England need's the Eastern Slavs to hate us with all the strength of the hatred she herself bears towards us" (Dostoyevsky 1997: 898). The Eastern Questions "contains, as it were, all our goals and, mainly our only way to move out into the fullness of history. It contains as well our final collision with Europe and out final uniting with her" (Dostoyevsky 1997: 900).

The Congress of Berlin in 1878 liberated Slavs from the rule of non-Slavic states, which thus resulted in the independence of Romania, Serbia, Montenegro (and later Bulgaria). However, as weak states in a vital geostrategic region, their independence would soon be infringed upon by great powers.

A new generation of conservatism emerged with Nikolai Danilevsky, Fyodor Dostoyevsky, Konstantin Leontiev, Apollon Grigoriev and others who shifted focus from interests to ideas (Pipes 1971: 124). Leontiev became a leading figure in terms of calling for the reversal of the liberal Westernisation of Russia that had commenced under Peter the Great. Russia had to find its particular path to modernity as the egalitarian-liberal posed a threat to culture, creativity and spirituality (Leontiev 1885: 144). Dostoyevsky similarly cautioned that Russia's obsession with the West's modernisation was counterproductive as it obstructed Russia from finding its national path to development:

> Embarrassed and afraid that we have fallen so far behind Europe in our intellectual and scientific development, we have forgotten that we ourselves, in the depth and tasks of the Russian soul, contain in ourselves as Russians the capacity perhaps to bring new light to the world, on the condition that our development is independent. . . . We have forgotten that all great nations displayed their great powers only to the extent that they were arrogant in their assessment of themselves, and precisely in this way they have benefited the world, and each of them has brought something into it, be it only a single ray of light, because they have remained themselves, proud and steady, arrogantly independent. (Dostoyevsky 1986: 260)

THE EXPANSION TO SOUTHERN EURASIA – INDIA

While Russia's defeat in the Crimean War had slowed down Russia's expansion into Central Asia, it continued again in the 1860s with the support of railway to cement new territories to the empire. The vast geographical expanse of Russia was gradually connected with a network of railroads. The first railroads built immediately after the Crimean War was designed as a quasi-colonial economy as they were financed by British, French and German corporations to extract Russian natural resources. The economic depressions in Europe from the 1870s to the 1890s, also known as *The Great Deflation*, severely slowed down the construction of railroads in Russia.

By 1879, railroads became instrumental to expand into Central Asia following new conquests in modern Turkmenistan (Cheshire 1934). The lessons from the Crimean War had been learned, which was that physical connectivity was imperative to consolidate control over the periphery of the empire. Once Russia conquered a new territory in Central Asia, new rail and road were constructed to defend the new lands from new threats. In other words, the centuries-old lesson of defence through expansion was supported by infrastructure. The infrastructure projects initially had a military function, albeit the economic significance soon became evident. The enhanced connectivity with Central Asia provided Russia with cheap imports of natural resources such as cotton.

While in the previous decades, Britain had been concerned about Russia's expansion towards the Ottoman Empire, now Russia was nearly bordering British India. In the nineteenth century, the Europeans divided up Africa between themselves, while the Russians also moved south and conquered the Northern Caucasus, Georgia, Armenia, Central Asia and finally reaching the Hindu Kush mountain range – with British India on the other side. In what became known as the Great Game, Russia and Britain fought in Afghanistan as the border between the Russian Empire and British India.

The expansion also fuelled the Anglo-Russian rivalry in Central Asia, especially as the Trans-Caspian railway began to be built towards Herat in Afghanistan (Cheshire 1934: 96). The conflict between Britain and Russia became known as the Great Game of the nineteenth century and can be said to have been concluded by 1895 with the signing of the Pamir Boundary Commission protocols.

THE DEFEAT TO JAPAN AS A SECOND CRIMEAN WAR

A few years after the Crimean War, Russian expansion had also reached the eastern coastline of the Eurasian continent. The British were alarmed that Russia as a Eurasian land-power had reached the eastern coastline of the supercontinent and thus challenging its power (Berryman 2002). Yet, a window of opportunity existed for Britain and Japan as maritime powers as Russia had acquired a huge territory that it had not consolidated control over. Much like the Crimean War, Russia was therefore vulnerable to be defeated at sea.

Following China's weakening as a result of its defeat in the Opium Wars against Britain, Russia acquired large territories from the declining Qing Dynasty through the Treaty of Aigun in 1858 and Treaty of Peking in 1860. The establishment of Vladivostok on the coast of the Pacific Ocean gave Russia the potential of scaling back British maritime power. In 1891, Russia commenced work on the Trans-Siberian Railroad to consolidate control over the new territory along the Pacific coast. The railway had mostly a geopolitical rather than a geoeconomic purpose, as evident by the location of the route, which was aimed to avoid exposure to possible Japanese and Chinese hostilities.

Before consolidating control over existing territory on the Pacific coast with sufficient railway infrastructure, Russia continued expansion to the south. In 1898, Russia leased Port Arthur on China's Yellow Sea, which was to be connected with the Russian railway. The warm-water port empowered Russia's navy and its commercial activity in Asia. With new power, Russia also faced new adversaries. In 1902, Britain established a naval alliance with Japan to balance against both Russia and France in the region. Japan had also grown weary as it wanted to dominate both Korea and Manchuria. During China's Boxer Rebellion (1899–1901), Russian troops moved into Manchuria to protect Port Arthur, which further stoked Japanese fears of an expanding Russian presence.

In 1904, Japan launched an attack on Port Arthur, which was intended to cut Russia down in size before its power grew further in the region and consolidated control with infrastructure. Russian territorial expansion had surpassed its own strength due to a backwards economy and technology. It had also displayed poor diplomacy by not mitigating Japanese concerns. Russia had to admit a humiliating defeat in 1905, as a European great power was defeated by an Asiatic power. The failure in the war was coupled with financial instability due to Russia's excessive reliance on foreign capital.

THE 1905 DEMOCRATIC REVOLUTION

By the early twentieth century, Russia was facing a variety of new challenges. Some conservatives drifted towards the far-Right with anti-Polish sentiments and anti-Semitism; the socialists threatened with revolution; the liberals considered the monarchy and tradition as slowing down progress; separatist movements threatened the territorial integrity; and foreign armies were modernising rapidly. At the end of the nineteenth century, the liberal-conservative Peter Struve had cautioned that the individual had to be elevated for Russia to prosper. Furthermore, Struve argued that the autocracy had to identify with society rather than the bureaucracy (Pipes 2005: 167).

The military defeat to the Japanese in 1905 had weakened the position of the state, and revolts began to emerge that resulted in the October Manifesto. The 1905 Democratic Revolution became a consequence of the war. The Russian-Japanese war stoked unrest, and the Bloody Sunday of January 1905 instigated strikes across Russia. Nicholas II responded by accepting liberal reforms. Political protests had shaken St. Petersburg, which was suppressed by the Tsar in what became known as Bloody Sunday.

Nicholas II was worried that an internal revolt would topple the monarchy and then embolden foreign invaders – a repeat of the Time of Troubles in the early seventeenth century. These concerns were justified, as in the winter of

1905 and 1906 the Baltic Germans had been informed that the German army would support them if the Russian monarchy collapsed.

In response to the growing protests, Nicholas II passed the October Manifesto that had been drafted by Witte. The October Manifesto of 1905 promised Russians political freedom and the creation of a legislative Duma. In 1906, Russia drafted a constitution and for the first time in its history, the Tsar had to share power with an elected Duma. Russia established itself as a constitutional monarchy, and a united cabinet was formed for the first time in its history. Censorship was essentially abolished. That same year, Witte was replaced by Pyotr Stolypin.

Stolypin directed his attention towards agrarian reforms to enhance productivity and the rights of the peasantry. The vast majority of Russians continued to live in rural regions, and agriculture was still in dire need of reforms following the emancipation of the serfs. Agriculture had fallen behind on industry in terms of modernisation, and a ghastly famine in 1891 had made reforms more important. Conservatism therefore had to make a shift from ideas and ideals to specific economic policies.

Furthermore, radicalism had been fueled, and the socialists were rising as formidable opposition. In 1907, Stolypin confronted socialists in the Russian Duma, arguing they "would like to choose the path of radicalism, a path alien to Russia's historical past, alien to its cultural traditions. They need great upheavals, we need a great Russia!" (Ascher 2002: 195).

The liberal-conservative Vehki (Landmarks or Milestones) was written in 1909 and featured seven important authors: Nikolai Berdyaev, Petr Struve, Sergei Bulgakov, Semen Frank, Mikhail Gershenzon, Aleksandr Izgoev and Bogdan Kistiakovskii. Vehki was written in the aftermath of the 1905 Revolution and addressed the intricate problems of idealism and the moral and legal relativism of the Marxist opposition. Russian political and cultural life after 1905 had been liberalised, and the Vehki authors feared that the elites were drifting towards excessive materialism and unsophisticated rationality. Under the initiative of Sergei Witte, the connection between the monarchy and the Orthodox Church had been decoupled, which deprived the state of ideology to lay the foundation for a unifying national idea and common political language. The book became of the most important, if not the most important, conservative writings that would a century later also be hailed by President Putin.

Communes were eventually broken up in 1910, despite widespread opposition by the peasantry who had relied on the communes as a social institution providing collective security. Traditional communities were further torn apart as Russia's rapidly growing population was incentivised to and resettle along the path of the Trans-Siberian Railroad.

Private ownership and the establishment of the agrarian bank had the intention of developing a large and prosperous middle class of private landowners to increase efficiency. The policies were largely successful as within a decade, from 1905 to 1915, land ownership among the peasantry grew from 20 to 50 per cent. However, the concentration of power within the agriculture sector caused growing tensions between the peasantry and the landowners. The socialists directed their contempt towards the kulaks as the source of exploitation. Stolypin recognised the need for bringing together the government and society. However, he was unable to push through the needed socio-political reforms and subsequently relied on emergency laws to advance his agrarian reforms.

Before his assassination, Stolypin had argued that if Russia could enjoy two decades of domestic stability and international peace, it would be completely transformed. Instead of stability, Russia was drawn into the First World War, followed by a century of internal and external calamity.

THE FIRST WORLD WAR AND REVOLUTION

Russia's support for Serbia leading up to the First World War had its pan-Slavic origin as both peoples were Slavic and Orthodox with a historical struggle against Turkic/Tatar oppressors. Following Russia's military victory over the Ottoman Empire in 1877–1878, Russia supported the independence and liberty of Serbia at the Congress of Berlin in 1878. The incursion of Austria-Hungary into Serbia and subjugation of Slavs undermined the Balkans as a buffer and pan-Slavic unity with Russia. The mobilisation of Russian forces to deter Austria-Hungary to invade Serbia thus became a contributor to the chain of events that caused the First World War.

The war initially mounted tremendous support for Nicholas II as the rising nationalist mood even culminated in renaming St. Petersburg to Petrograd as a more Russian-sounding name. However, as the war became more devastating the human and economic toll shifted the mood. Protests compelled Nicholas II to abdicate. When his brother refused to take the Throne, a provisional government subsequently took over governance of Russia – which transitioned Russia from a monarchy to a republic. Much like the end of the Rurik dynasty led to the horrors during the Time of Troubles, the disruption to the rule of the autocracy under the Romanovs would bring chaos and the destruction of the Russian state.

Conservatives were mostly open to cooperating with the provisional government. Some sympathies also existed with the revolt against the Europeanised elites. While conservatives were supportive of the monarchy, few sought to restore after the overthrow of Nicholas II.

However, the provisional government was not capable of acting decisively, and the failure to address challenges opened up a vacuum for governance. People began to arbitrarily elect their own councils separate from the central authorities to advice, which were called Soviets (advisors). The power of the Petrograd Soviet grew rapidly to the extent it could rival the authority of the provisional government. As the Bolsheviks became an increasingly formidable force, Germany sent Lenin into Russia to disrupt Russia's role in the war. The German operation was successful as Lenin drew great support for his ideas of withdrawing from the war and redistributing the land, a key problem that had persisted since the emancipation of the Serfs. In October 1917, the Bolsheviks launched a successful coup and seized power.

The Democratic Revolution of 1905 established a very weak foundation for democracy as it had not developed gradually or organically as a result of economic freedoms or legal evolution. Instead, democracy had been imposed rapidly and reluctantly to avoid a violent revolution. The freedoms awarded in 1905 with the stroke of a pen, were just as easily revoked again in the Bolshevik Revolution as it had no deep roots in the political culture (Pipes 2010). The fragility of Russian democracy makes a strong case for conservatism as freedoms must grow gradually and organically from the distinctiveness of culture to ensure it cements itself. While the Bolsheviks had risen to power on the opposition to Tsarist restrictions on political freedoms, the oppression by the Bolsheviks dictatorship would by far overshadow the former repressions. The Bolsheviks purged both the liberals and the conservatives as they sought to completely transform Russia.

Three different forms of crises historically emerge in Russia as a result of the failure to advance gradual change as a middle road between stagnation and disruptive leaps forward: The threat of domestic unrest as order; the failure of its economy and institutions; and vulnerability to aggression by foreign powers. As one of these three crises emerge, it affects the other two. In the early twentieth century, all three crises hot Russia at the same time.

It is reasonable to argue that the Bolshevik Revolution would not have been possible without the unique international situation of 1917. In 1905, Germany would likely have forcefully intervened if the Russian monarchy collapsed, and other European powers would under other circumstances not have accepted the emergence of a communist government that threatened the European and international order. The First World War put the situation on its head as Germany had directly contributed to the revolution as Russia's withdrawal from the war was the main priority.

In 1917, the Bolsheviks had the breathing space to consolidate their revolution. By the time foreign powers intervened, it had a contradictory impact as Russians consolidated around the Bolsheviks against the foreign invaders. The US invasion of the Soviet Union in 1918, from Vladivostok to Siberia, had the effect of strengthening the Bolsheviks in regions they previously had little support (Richard 2012). The British invasion of Arkhangelsk with the brutal use of chemical weapons and establishment of an infamous concentration camp also undermined the Whites and strengthened the Reds.

The second half of the nineteenth century demonstrated that defeat in wars diminishes political legitimacy and triggers revolutionary forces. The defeat in the Crimean War in 1856 necessitated the Great Reforms, and the defeat to the Japanese in 1905 was followed by a democratic revolution, and the losses in the First World War enabled the socialists to take over Russia.

CONCLUSION

The defeat in the Crimean War demonstrated the socio-economic and political backwardness of Russia, and its inability to counter maritime powers at the coastline of Eurasia. The defeat compelled Russia to embark on revolutionary change. The Great Reforms changed Russia domestically, while the focus on transportation infrastructure fuelled renewed efforts to strengthen control over the Eurasian coastlines.

The Great Reforms transformed Russia by moving away from an estate-based society with autocracy and serfdom at its core, and instead embrace modern civil society, the rule of law, industrialisation and urbanisation. The great leap forward was not sufficiently supported by the bureaucracy and was largely detached from previous customs. The rapidly urbanised population were detached from traditional life and community, and had to deal with alien institutions, poor working condition and growing economic inequality. Disruptions polarised society and fuelled radical movements. Conservatism is averse to such rapid changes without roots in domestic traditions, and conservatives had to reinvent themselves to address the fall-out. However, such great leaps forward became a necessity due to the failures of managing change in the past. Furthermore, the rapid and deep-seated reforms initiated by the state placed conservatives in an awkward position, as they had to support the state although contesting the great leaps forward as it opposed the concept of gradual and organic change.

The lack of efficient transportation infrastructure was central in Russia's defeat in Crimea as it had to fight modern maritime powers. Following the war, Russia drastically increased its efforts to consolidate control over the empire with railways. The effort responded to a key factor that had throughout history shaped Russian conservatism – the lack of access to the arteries of international trade. New connectivity between Russian regions also supported expansion towards the maritime borders of the Eurasian continent. The expansion was largely supporting geopolitical objectives rather than enhancing economic connectivity, which represents a historical continuity with significant implication for conservatism.

Chapter 5

Reforming the Concept of a Conservative Political Economy

INTRODUCTION

Conservatism around the world and in Russia was initially inclined towards resisting rather than managing change. In terms of economics, this entailed defending the community and traditional values from the corruptive impacts of economic activity. Yet, conservatism had to reform itself as industrialisation created asymmetrical interdependence between states that were converted into political and cultural influence. British geoeconomic leadership, defined by its control over strategic industries, transportation corridors and financial instruments, produced core-periphery relations with Europe and the world.

The conservative political economy had to shift towards managing change. Conservatives recognised that industrialisation was a central component of nation-building, and a strong nation was necessary to uphold cultural sovereignty and managing change. In Russia, Sergei Witte adopted the policies of Friedrich List that had also transformed the United States and Germany. By the last decade of the nineteenth century, Russia was the fastest-growing among all major economies. The strength of Russia's political economy was the Eurasian component that enabled a path towards organic change and used its unique geography as an advantage rather than a disadvantage.

This chapter first theorises the idea of a conservative political economy. Conservatism is confronted with a dilemma between economic activities of industrialisation and free-market capitalism that disrupts traditional communities and institutions, versus the stagnation and vulnerability to foreign influence caused by the failure to modernise. Second, the emergence of economic nationalism as a conservative political economy is assessed. The geoeconomic hegemony of Britain, and later the United States, incentivised the promotion of a liberal international economic system. Last, the advent of a Russian conservative political economy devoted to industrialisation emerged in the late nineteenth century. Russia's struggle towards a unique path for development has been linked to its geography at the periphery of Europe, as a land power endlessly attempting to catch-up with leading maritime European powers. The new political economy also laid the foundation for establishing a balance of dependence in the international economy by challenging the primacy of maritime powers.

THEORISING CONSERVATIVE POLITICAL ECONOMY

The industrial revolution and subsequent introduction of capitalism caused a schism in the organisation of society. Industrial society and the free market was not a natural order as it had to be imposed. People instinctively resisted and "the history of nineteenth-century civilization consisted largely in attempts to protect society against the ravages of such mechanism" (Polanyi 1944: 42). Conservatism inevitably had to take on an economic component as the industrial revolution imposed revolutionary change:

> The fabric of society was being disrupted; desolate villages and the ruins of human dwellings testified to the fierceness with which the revolution raged, endangering the defences of the country, wasting its towns, decimating its population, turning its overburdened soil into dust, harassing its people and turning them from decent husbandmen into a mob of beggars and thieves. (Polanyi 1944: 37)

Industrialisation fragments society as the individual is severed from the social group. It is therefore no coincidence that most religions condemn materialism as a corrupting influence on spirituality. The Reformation became a modern reform to Christianity by making a moral argument for work ethics and worldly success in terms of affluence. Max Weber (1958) therefore theorised that Protestant ethics was the source of why some societies were more capable of developing wealth. Émile Durkheim (2005), a late nineteenth-century French sociologist, explored the relationship between the rise of French industrial market economy and the drastic rise in suicides. Durkheim (2005) observed that the suicides among Catholics were lower than with the Protestants, as Catholics imposed greater social control with collective norms and values that limit the excesses of individualism and materialism.

Societies with high industrial capacity and positioned along transportation corridors for trade are likely to develop cosmopolitan values. Adams (1897) argued in *The Law of Civilization and Decay* that people tend to voluntarily flock towards population centres with a productive commercial climate. However, as cosmopolitan regions become increasingly affluent, communitarian institutions and values are dismantled to increase economic efficiency. The founding spiritual ethos is consumed by materialism, and decadence ensues. Thus, in its success, the cosmopolitan society dies (Adams 1897). The political economy of conservatism, therefore, aims to manage change by industrialising while minimising the adverse impact on the collective.

Even the intellectual godfather of free-market capitalism, Adam Smith (2006: 58), had cautioned against the "corruption of our moral sentiments" by private property and market activities due to "the disposition to admire, and almost worship, the rich and powerful". The legacy of Adam Smith in modern times is depicted as advocacy for neoliberal economics and unfettered market power due to his thesis on the "hidden hand". However, Adam Smith expressed nuance. Smith recognised the market reduced the need for central planning, albeit he did not advocate completely self-regulating markets as they do not always deliver social goods (Norman 2018).

Conservatism recognises the state as a central representative of the collective, and the principal instrument to achieve national goals. The state assists in protecting family values, faith and traditional communities from unfettered market forces. A central role for the government in the national economy, such as the Bismarkian economy, could address the imbalances between capital and labour to ensure the well-being of all its citizens, and thereby reduce the appeal of socialism.

Merely resisting industrialisation and change is not an option. The failure to develop results in stagnation and vulnerability in the international system. The complexity of human nature is at the core of conservative political economics, and economic development is a driving force for change. Tocqueville argued in *The Old Regime and the Revolution* that the restrictions on the economy and society contributed to the liberal French Revolution in 1789. It is also evident that a large middle class becomes an entrusted stakeholder in the status quo that benefits from preserving key institutions. These rational objectives must nonetheless be harmonised with the instinctive impulses in human nature.

State-led industrialisation is a conservative principle to ensure that the state is positioned between stasis and transformation. Conservatism began an internal reform due to the need for greater state intervention in the economy to industrialise and to mitigate the social and economic consequences from creative destruction to protect the collective such as the nation, community and family. The homogenising process for nation-building in Europe also relied heavily on constructing a national economy/industry, national education, military service and railways to assimilate the peoples of the state and augment loyalty to the state (Mann 2005: 49).

In agrarian societies, traditional values and spirituality are preserved, and the community tends to stand stronger. In the early nineteenth century, both the United States and Russia were apprehensive about following the path of Western European industrial societies. Thomas Jefferson aspired to develop an agrarian democracy to avoid the moral decadence of Western Europe. Conservative policies are inclined to preserve small family farms and small businesses as the source of virtue.

Industrial power is imperative to manage change as it encapsulates modernity and reason. Friedrich List suggested that "Industry is the mother and father of all science, literature, the arts, enlightenment, freedom, useful institutions, national power and independence" (List 2016). Kennan (2014: 520): even proclaimed he was "a believer in autarky. Not only do I believe that the healthy national society would rigidly eschew the importation of foreign labour . . . but I consider that it should restrict to a minimum economic and financial involvements with other peoples".

Economic stagnation and failure to modernise eventually results in excessive economic dependence on foreign powers and the loss of an organic path to change. Subsequently, a conservative political economy emerged that sought to industrialise while preserving the community and traditional values. The concept of economic nationalism from the nineteenth century recognised that industrialisation was required to cement national sovereignty by reducing excessive reliance on foreign powers. Before the conservative revolution of the 1980s under Reaganism and Thatcherism that paradoxically made economic liberalism a central tenet of conservatism, classical conservatives had sought to limit unfettered market forces to defend traditional communities and family values. The state, therefore, had an important role in terms of mitigating creative destruction from new technologies and unfettered market forces (Luttwak 1993).

The Russians were prosperous in Kievan Rus as their location on the Dnieper River connected it to trade. Once Kievan Rus began fragmenting in the twelfth century and then invaded by the Mongols in the thirteenth century, Russians began migrating towards regions disconnected from the arteries of international trade. The view of capitalism as corrupting the community spirit, the lack of private property, and reliance on internal trade influenced a unique path for Russia. Conservatives such as Nikolai Berdyaev (1947: 2) posited: "The various lines of social demarcation did not exist in Russia; there were no pronounced classes. Russia was never an aristocratic country in the Western sense, and equally, there was no bourgeoisie". Traditions and spirituality were preserved, albeit economic prosperity was undermined to the extent Russia became vulnerable to European powers. Connecting with major maritime transportation corridors or land-based transportation infrastructure consistently placed Russia in confrontation with great powers. Periods of rapid industrialisation to catch up has been immensely disruptive to society and fuelled political radicalism.

GEOECONOMIC POWER AND THE "BALANCE OF DEPENDENCE"

Economic interdependence between states is about relative gain. Economic interdependence has the positive effect of enhanced influence and the negative impact of reduced autonomy. States subsequently intervene in the economy to establish asymmetrical interdependence to maximise both autonomy and influence (Heckscher 1935; Hirschman 1945). Asymmetrical economic interdependence can then be converted into political and cultural influence. Hence, political economy replicates the theoretical assumptions of political realism as states seek a favourable "balance of dependence" by reducing one's own reliance on others and increasing the dependence of others (Diesen 2017).

The international system has systemic incentives to move towards a "balance of dependence". The stronger and less dependent state have systemic incentives to liberalise economic activities and cosmopolitan ideals to cement its comparative advantage. By contrast, the weaker side has systemic incentives to reduce its excessive dependence on a more powerful state by either establish economic self-reliance or diversifying its economic connectivity. Geoeconomic power is not merely about trade volumes as enhancing domestic capabilities and simple diversification of trade can mitigate asymmetrical interdependence. Rather, geoeconomic power derives from scarcity – economic activities that cannot easily be replicated or diversified.

Geoeconomic power that creates dependence can be divided into three main categories: strategic industry as an expression of technological sovereignty; transportation corridors to ensure reliable and effective commerce; and financial instruments in terms of a national bank and a strong trading currency.

ECONOMIC LIBERALISM UNDER A HEGEMON

The strategy of combining industrial superiority with free trade endowed liberal economics with an imperialistic inclination (List 1885). The UK was able to establish dominance over international commerce as it gained technological leadership during the industrial revolution, established dominance over the seas and controlled the main financial instruments in terms of banks and trade currency. Europe subsequently became a British-administered geoeconomic region throughout the Victorian era. British economic activity was principally about relative gain by intervening in the economy to create asymmetrical interdependence to maximise both autonomy and influence. This is relevant for conservatives as unfavourable symmetrical interdependence diminishes both autonomy and influence, which undermines both an organic approach to modernisation and cultural autonomy.

Britain's rise to geoeconomic dominance, much like the United States later, was based on state intervention and protectionism to develop asymmetrical interdependence (Chang 2002; Ashworth 2017). Once Britain dominated the three pillars on geoeconomic power: strategic industry, transportation corridors and financial instruments, London began to advocate free trade to cement its comparative advantage over adversaries. The uneven distribution of economic power enabled Britain to position itself as the dominant world trader, shipper and banker (Hobsbawm 1968).

Britain's repeal of the Corn Laws in 1843 denoted the transition to the free market. The objective of repealing the Corn Laws was to create core-periphery relations with continental Europe. Britain opened its agricultural sector to imports, and in return could exported manufactured goods to continental Europe and saturate their markets and prevent them from industrialising. Without free trade, Britain feared that Germany, the United States and other states would develop their own manufacturing and thereby undermine the comparative advantage of Britain – its technological leadership and manufacturing industry (Hilton 1977: 280; McKeown 1989). Britain "made it politically clear that she saw it as a primary goal to prevent other nations from following the path of industrialization" and used free trade as an ideology to legitimise its dominance (Reinert 2005: 48). While clothing his language in liberalism, David Ricardo was explicit about the geostrategic purpose of free trade in his concept of comparative advantage:

> Under a system of perfectly free trade each country naturally devotes its capital and labour to such employments as are most beneficial to each. . . . It is this principle which determines that wine shall be made in France and Portugal, that corn shall be grown in America and Poland, and that hardware and other goods shall be manufactured in England. (Ricardo 1821: 139)

In the British parliament, it was argued that under the auspices of free trade "foreign nations would become valuable Colonies to us, without imposing on us the responsibility of governing them" (Semmel 1970: 8). Any attempts to break the geoeconomic leadership of Britain would be confronted, and British prime minister William Pitt cautioned: "If the Americans should manufacture a lock of wool or a horseshoe, I would fill their ports with ships and their towns with troops" (Van Tyne 1927: 33). Similarly, challengers to British rule of the seas or banking power were confronted immediately. A liberal international economic system therefore tends to form under a hegemon that provides collective benefits, as competition between equal powers result in national authority placed above market forces:

> If economic capabilities are so concentrated that a hegemon exists, as in the case of Great Britain in the late nineteenth century and the USA after World War II, an "open" or "liberal" international economic order will come into being. In the organisation of a liberal order, pride of place is given to market rationality. This is not to say that authority is absent from such an order. It is to say that authority relations are constructed in such a way as to give maximum scope to market forces rather than to constrain them. (Ruggie 1982: 381)

ECONOMIC NATIONALISM AS NATION-BUILDING

A conservative political economy can and must accommodate industrialisation. A mutually beneficial relationship between conservative values and industrial power can be established as the state is a leading administrator of the community and traditions. National integration is a pre-requisite for economic growth, and economic activity is an important component of nation-building. History demonstrates that stats that control the leading industries, transportation corridors and financial instruments are more capable of preserving political and cultural sovereignty. Ivan Pososhkov (1987), an eighteenth-century conservative, recognised that the economic modernisation in Western Europe had been conducive to develop the nation-state.

The economic nationalism of Friedrich List, Alexander Hamilton and Sergei Witte was a conservative position as it built the economy around the nation as a collective. Friedrich List (1885: 27) repudiated Adam Smith's individualism and the cosmopolitanism of free trade as a failure to uphold a holistic and conservative view of society: "His doctrine at once sinks deeper and deeper into materialism, particularism, and individualism". However, industrialisation was recognised as a necessity to ensure political sovereignty in a world of nations competing with economic means.

Friedrich List cautioned against liberal laissez-faire economics as a strategy by the economic hegemon to cement its advantage. Under laissez-faire economics, the infant industries (high cost, low quality) of Europe and the United States could not compete and develop in direct competition with the mature industries (low cost, high quality) of Britain. Economic nationalism therefore advocates temporary subsidies and tariffs to protect infant industries from unfettered market forces to industrialise and thus ensure political independence. The use of tariffs and subsidies by conservatives also mitigates creative destruction and overall destructive influence of the free market on communities and traditional values. The advocacy of liberal economics by the geoeconomic hegemon was repudiated as an effort to "kick away the ladder":

> It is a very common clever device that when anyone has attained the summit of greatness, he kicks away the ladder by which he has climbed up, in order to deprive others of the means of climbing up after him. In this lies the secret of the cosmopolitical doctrine of Adam Smith, and of the cosmopolitical tendencies of his great contemporary. (List 1885: 295–296)

American conservatives also looked towards the state to conserve and as an agent of change by managing economic activities to strengthen the nation. The economic nationalism of Alexander Hamilton advocated that the United States establish an autonomous economic infrastructure to reduce excessive reliance on the British as a threat to preserving national sovereignty.

In the United States, a conservative political economy underwent reform as Hamilton convinced Jefferson to abandon his ambition for a morally superior agrarian democracy, as the United States would have to industrialise to cement its political independence from Britain. Two different conservative positions conflicted. The agrarian society envisioned by Thomas Jefferson was abandoned as it would prevent change, create stagnation and thus vulnerability to foreign powers. Jefferson was convinced by Alexander Hamilton that modernisation and industrialisation was a necessity to ensure political independence from Britain (Szlajfer 2012: 51). Hamilton's economic nationalism is debated as to whether it was truly conservative as it embraced industrialisation that undermined the agrarian community (Kirk 1953: 78).

Hamilton's (1791) conservative political economy has eventually been translated into the policy of the three-pillared American System, which would be central to development for more than a century. The three pillars of the American System to ensure geoeconomic power were a manufacturing base, transportation corridors and a national bank. Henry Clay was a leading conservative of his time and the principal advocate for the American System. In 1832, Clay denounced the liberal concept of free trade as an instrument for integrating and subordinating the United States under British colonial power:

> What was meant by free trade, was nothing more nor less than, by means of the great advantages we enjoyed, to get the monopoly of all their markets for our manufacturers, and to prevent them, one and all, from ever becoming manufacturing nations. (Williams 2011: 221)

Following Hamilton's economic nationalism, the United States pursued economic self-sufficiency for nation-building as economic dependence on Britain would undermine political independence (Mott 1997: 22). With strong support for infant industries with subsidies and tariffs, the United States industrialised rapidly and prevented Britain's attempt to convert the American Mid-West and Central America into informal dependencies (Gallagher and Robinson 1953: 10). For a century, the United States rose to greatness on economic nationalist principles such as the strategic use of tariffs (Hudson 2010).

The American System had previously taken on a failed format in France. The French-led Continental System in the early nineteenth century had the explicit purpose of blocking trade with Britain to replace its industries. However, the reliance on coercion to uphold the Napoleonic Continental System led to the disastrous invasion of Russia in 1812. Later, France also discovered that control over financial instruments is imperative to pursue change and modernity without unwarranted influence from other powers. Modernisation does not only require scientific discoveries, it also needs commercial applications. Following the path of the United States, France established Crédit Mobilier in 1852 to mobilise the savings from the middle class to develop industries, railways and other infrastructure. Besides restoring their autonomy by decoupling from British finance, Crédit Mobilier as also instrumental to expand influence as foreign lending was integrated into colonial projects. Crédit Mobilier was also imperative to establish core-periphery relations by exploiting the resources of underdeveloped states, including Russia (Henderson 1975: 125).

Germany adopted similar economic nationalist policies. As Germany had been an economic satellite of France, it was also vulnerable to an intrusive cultural influence. From the 1830s, Germany developed railways and an economic union as the "Siamese twins" of German nation-building (Earle 1943: 442). The German Zollverein, the Customs Union, was partly inspired by the Napoleonic Continental System and sought to insulate the region from the mature industries of external rivals. List (1885: 421) argued in favour of state intervention by European continental powers to restructure the international economy away from Britain as a maritime power:

> If we only consider the enormous interests which the nations of Europe have in common, as opposed to the English maritime supremacy, we shall be led to the conviction that nothing is so necessary to these nations as union, and nothing so ruinous to them as Continental wars.

A German banking revolution gathered steam in the 1850s, which had sought to emulate the success of Crédit Mobilier, as continued reliance on foreign banks to finance railway and industry was deemed to be irresponsible (Henderson 1975: 123). German efforts to establish transportation corridors, the Berlin-Baghdad railway or through naval power, all led to conflicts with rival powers.

The ideas of Alexander Hamilton and Friedrich List were also brought directly to East Asia in 1872. At the time, E. Pechine Smith, and advocate of the American System, was invited to serve as an advisor for Japan to assist with industrialisation following the Meiji Restoration (Hudson 2010). Under the patronage of the United States during the Cold War, the economies of Japan, South Korea and Taiwan developed on economic nationalist policies rather than free-market capitalism (Wade 2003). Large conglomerates, South Korean Chaebol and Japanese Keiretsu, developed with heavy state intervention that funnelled funds to large domestic corporations to climb up global value chains. Tariffs and non-tariff barriers were employed to keep foreign competitors out of the domestic market, and concurrently subsidising domestic companies to support an export-based development strategy.

The rise of Germany and Japan in the 1980s as rivals to American dominance was largely based on economic nationalism. While Japan sought to catch-up with the West, Germany employed economic statecraft as an instrument of social control to ensure national unity (Streeck and Yamamura 2005: 3).

RUSSIAN ECONOMIC NATIONALISM

As a late entrant to industrialisation, Russia was in high risk of being drawn into a core-periphery relationship. By exporting natural resources and importing manufactured goods, Russia's ability industrialise was marginal.

Economic backwardness is commonly perpetuated if a state becomes dependent on exports of natural resources to pay for imports of manufactured goods. Economically backwardness due to late industrialisation greatly influences political institutions and the role of the state in the economy (Gerschenkron 1962). The economically backward have more incentives for state-led modernisation intervention to support and channel capital to infant industries. However, subsidies and tariffs reduce domestic consumption and demand, or it is financed by foreign loans. Key challenges entail for the state to develop "national champions" capable of competing in international markets internationally, and serving national interests domestically. The benefit of economic backwardness is the proclivity for maintaining conservative values, as economically advanced states are more disposed towards economic liberalism to cement their comparative advantage internationally.

Sergei Witte became the finance minister in 1892 and embraced the conservative economic policies of Friedrich List, which acknowledged that nation-building and national power in the modern world depended on industrialisation. The economic nationalism of Friedrich List and Alexander Hamilton envisioned a central economic mission for the state, which fit the Russian tradition of a strong state. Witte even translated the ideas of List into Russian and had the pamphlets distributed. List (1885: 269) had cautioned against becoming an economic colony by not shielding domestic industry:

> The mother nation supplies the colonies with manufactured goods, and obtains in return their surplus produce of agricultural products and raw materials. . . . The superior power of the mother country in population, capital, and enterprising spirit, obtains through colonisation an advantageous outlet.

In a secret memorandum to Nicholas II, Sergei Witte outlined arguments with striking similarities to the recommended policies of Friedrich List and Alexander Hamilton. Witte argued in favour of an entrepreneurial role for the Russian state. Russia had become dependent on exporting raw materials to import manufactured goods, thus "the economic relations of Russia with Western Europe are fully comparable to the relations of colonial countries with their metropolises" (Witte 1954: 66).

Witte advocated in favour of a conservative development strategy and for the transition to a more efficient autocracy with top-down industrialisation. Under the policies of Witte, Russia rapidly developed industrial power, physical connectivity with railroads and financial power. Pobedonostsev similarly favoured a state-led development in Russia to ensure material modernisation, while preserving the paternalistic and autocratic government, centrality of the Orthodox Church, and Russifying national minorities (Byrnes 1968).

Economic nationalist policies were used to develop domestic industries that had lagged behind the Europeans, and construct large infrastructure projects such as railways to connect the Russian regions. The reliance on foreign capital, neglect of the rural regions and moral corruption from capitalism remained lingering concerns. A dramatic industrial expansion commenced in Russia in 1893. The Tariff Act of 1891 provided support for domestic infant industries in the effort to mature by shielding them from the more mature industries in international markets. Import substitution was largely successful, and Russian began to rapidly develop industrial machinery, cotton, iron and other industries. While Witte supported tariff protection for Russian producers to continue their ascendancy, he criticised calls for excessive protection as it would merely make Russian industries less competitive:

The influx of foreign capital is disadvantageous primarily to entrepreneurs who are harmed by any kind of competition. Not only our own, but also foreign, capitalists who have already obtained an advantageous place in Russian industry join in these heart-rending complaints and thus try to guard their monopolistic profits. (Witte 1954: 69)

When Witte came to power, the railroads developed at an unprecedented rate. Russia had 31,000 km of railway tracks in 1891, 53,000 km in 1900, and 70,000 km by 1913. The new railways to some extent "de-colonised" Russia as they were not merely designed to extract natural resources for Western power, or structured solely to feed maritime-led trade. Instead, much of the new railways increased physical connectivity between Russian regions. Russia's new territories became accessible for economic activity, although the wealth concentrated in the cities as the peasants in rural regions benefitted less.

Witte's development strategy also had a strong Eurasian component. The largest infrastructure project was the Trans-Siberian Railroad, constructed to ensure internal cohesion of the Russian Empire and to project power in Asia. With Russian agricultural settlements expanding to the east, Russia was increasingly replacing the ancient nomads who had previously controlled and connected Eurasia. The Asian vector was also intended to balance out Russia's unfavourable financial position in Europe. The key weakness for Russia, the reliance on foreign capital, was envisioned to be for by the profits from trade with Asia (Witte 1954: 71).

Russia's Eurasian economic structure gave birth to Mackinder's Heartland Theory, a geostrategic theory that juxtaposed maritime power and land power. Control over the world was argued to require control of the Eurasian supercontinent as the source of world domination. Britain as a maritime power could dominate the world by dominating the periphery of the Eurasian continent as the main trading corridors, while Russia was the main land power that could seize control over Eurasia by expanding towards the periphery. The industrial revolution had initially strengthened Britain's hegemony over the seas and thus global commerce, albeit physical connectivity across the Eurasian landmass was feared to rewire the global economic infrastructure. Mackinder (1904: 434) cautioned that Russia's use of railways to connect the Eurasian continent would undermine the entire power foundation of Britain as a maritime power:

Steam and the Suez Canal appeared to have increased the mobility of sea-power relatively to land-power. Railways acted chiefly as feeders to ocean-going commerce. But transcontinental railways are now transmuting the conditions of land-power and nowhere can they have such effect as in the closed heartland of Euro-Asia.

The supremacy of maritime power required Britain to keep Eurasia divided to prevent connectivity on the supercontinent. Britain's advocacy of division and animosity among the Slavs was expanded to encompass the wider Eurasian continent.

Russia's financial dependence became a growing concern, which was the price for rapid industrialisation. Witte aptly recognised that opening Russia for foreign investments was required for industrial advancements: "Any obstructions to the influx of foreign capital will only delay the establishment of a mature and all-powerful industry" (Witte 1954: 73). However, Russia's dependence on foreign capital created one weak pillar in the conservative economic model. Russia had a burgeoning industry and railway network, albeit foreign powers had too much influence over its finance. In 1895, Russia developed the gold standard to impose fiscal discipline and stabilise its currency.

By the last decade of the nineteenth century, Russia had become the fastest-growing major economy in the world. The contradiction of Russia became evident as a country with backward agriculture, poor and disconnected villages and low domestic demand suddenly develop a state-led all-powerful heavy industry. Conservatives had to concede that rapid industrialisation was a necessity, and the discussion shifted to managing change to uphold the collective ethos of society.

CONCLUSION

Conservative philosophy is commonly divided into cultural and political conservatism, yet the conceptualisation of a conservative political economy is imperative. Industrialisation and capitalism organised society according to rational and calculative behaviour that deviates from the traditional organisation of human activity, which therefore also sparked ideological alternatives. While early conservatives were predisposed towards avoiding change by shunning industrialisation and capitalism, the conservatives of the nineteenth century had to adapt to new realities and manage change.

Economic nationalism can be conceptualised as a conservative political economy as industrialisation is recognised as instrumental for nation-building. Economic statecraft denotes the state using economic instruments to advance interests, which includes protecting communities and traditional values domestically and avoiding excessive dependence on foreign powers. Three geoeconomic pillars influence the balance of dependence in the world: strategic industries, transportation corridors and financial instruments. While the geoeconomic hegemon has incentives to promote liberal economics, the balancing powers are incentivised to advance conservatism.

A Russian conservative political economy has natural Eurasian inclination. As a Eurasian power, the balance of dependence shifts in Russia's favour by reducing reliance on the maritime corridors under the control of Western powers, and instead, increases dependence on Russia by connecting the Eurasian supercontinent by land. The late nineteenth century demonstrated the prospect of using Russia's unique Eurasian history and geography to establish an organic political economy.

Chapter 6

Conservatism under Communism and the Advent of Eurasianism

INTRODUCTION

The Russian state seized to exist, and the Soviet Union took its place. The Bolsheviks aimed to uproot institutions and culture that have grown organically for more than a thousand years, as Russian history and traditions were considered corrupt remnants of a bygone capitalist era. The revolutionary mission of the Bolsheviks entailed dismantling the social institutions that upheld the capitalist system, which included the nation, monarchy, church and the family. Communist ideology denounced these institutions for perpetuating oppression and exploitation as they organise the collective in hierarchical structures and roots legitimacy in tradition. Dismantling the key societal institutions was intended to eradicate the flawed past of mankind that had been tainted by capitalism, and only leave the communist state as the unrivalled representative of the collective.

The revolutionary effort to create Communist Man, liberated from his past, transgressed all principles held sacred by conservatism. As Nietzsche had argued in his deliberations about creative destruction, construction of the new required first the destruction of the old. Mozhaev's character of a former Red Army commander lambasted the socialists for betraying Russian culture, traditions, spirituality and nationhood:

> Everything connected with the people, its way of life, its faith and religion, all of this is alien to our left-wingers. Not only do they not accept the faith of the people, but they are also hostile to the most sublime manifestations of the people's national spirit. To them Tolstoi is a religious fool, Dostoevskii an obscurantist, even Pushkin expresses the culture of the nobility. And this is without even mentioning their hatred for all Russian philosophers, from

Khomiakov to Bulgakov. For them the Russian historical experience is merely
foul soil which has to be cleared away, and that's where their historical intolerance, lack of moderation, and desire to create a social miracle comes from.
(Gillespie 1989: 202)

The conservative lesson from communism as a grand social experiment is
that the natural condition of human beings without these hierarchical social
institutions is not freedom, but nihilism, anarchy and eventually tyranny
as only a powerful and intrusive ruler can ensure order. The socialists had
opposed the authoritarian power of the monarchy and positioned themselves
as the representatives and defenders of the peasantry since the 1860s. Yet,
the Bolsheviks exercised less restraint on power and practically reintroduced
serfdom with the Soviet collective farm. In the absence of a society organised
according to traditional structures and the vote of past (deceased) generations
as the source of legitimacy for legitimacy, the Bolsheviks relied on brutality
by imposing an abhorrent system dependent on totalitarian instruments of
power that intruded in all aspects of life. Furthermore, the Communist Party
became dependent on using Tsarist imagery for legitimacy and to mobilise
patriotic sentiments (Brandenberger and Dubrovsky 1998).

Conservatism took on a very different direction under the communist rule
of the Soviets. Within the Soviet Union, the conservative ethos was rediscovered in the large and failed social experiment of communism. The communist
authorities gradually experienced that the institutions they had zealously
dismantled were founded on imperishable human instincts and could therefore not be overcome. Conservative impulses strengthen from the experience
of loss because without loss there would not be an acute recognition of the
imperative to preserve.

This chapter first explores the endeavour to dismantle the nation, the
Orthodox Church, the family and autocracy as the pillars of Russian conservatism. Within the Soviet Union, it was recognised that society could not
transition conservative ideals in an instant revolution, and Marxist-Leninist
doctrines became instead envisioned as a long-term transition. The Soviet
Union largely abandoned its internationalism and took the form as an
ethno-federal state; the Christian faith was evoked in these troubled times to
mobilise the people; the effort to deconstruct the family was reversed; and
the autocracy could not be abandoned without undermining the territorial
integrity of the state.

Second, this chapter addresses the conservative émigrés that had fled or
been exiled who continued to develop the conservative philosophy of Russia.
The émigrés were divided on several issues that failed to establish a unified
political movement. The common task, however, was to preserve conservatism throughout the revolution and develop ideas about what conservatism

would look like after the demise of communism. Conservative thought developed among Russian émigrés who deliberated on all that was wrong with communism and how society might heal itself after the communist system inevitably would collapse. Rather than merely holding on to the lessons and traditions of the past, conservatives also had to incorporate the revolutionary and historical changes in Russia that could not be reversed.

Last, the Eurasianism developed a conservative strand as an alternative to communism. The Eurasianists recognised that the Soviet experience fundamentally changed Russia and thus cautioned against turning back the clock. Eurasianism was a conservative departure from Slavophilism as Turkic and Ugro-Finnic components of Russian identity were recognised. Organic change would not be possible if Russia merely defined itself as an Eastern European state and thus neglected the history and traditions of Eurasia.

It is concluded that Soviet communism was an immense social experiment confirming the importance of conservative values. The destructiveness and reversal of Soviet policies demonstrated the inability to transcend traditional social groups.

CONSERVATISM IN A REVOLUTIONARY STATE

The Soviet Union was commonly believed to be impervious to reform, yet the revolutionary policies were pushed back against by human nature and Russian conservative traditions. A common mistake in the West during the Cold War was to expect reforms to be a step towards liberalisation and democratisation. Instead, the main opposition against communism was conservatism.

The Soviet authorities were widely resented for demoting the heroes and achievements of pre-Soviet Russia, which created a present isolated from the past. Yet, the Soviet authorities would also discover the need to preserve the past as the Kremlin had to reverse radical revolutionary policies and also deal with the early Soviet past.

Khrushchev's denunciation of Stalin in 1956 and the subsequent de-Stalinisation of the Soviet Union became a revolutionary moment, which subsequently sparked a conservative response. The cult of Stalin as the greatest leader and father of the nation had permeated throughout Soviet society for almost three decades. The de-Stalinising society included returning millions of political prisoners to society. The conservative impulse to salvage something from the Stalinist era, to avoid starting history from nothing again, resulted in crediting Stalin for leading the nation to victory against Nazi Germany, while still denouncing his crimes and mismanagement of the state. However, Marxism itself was a problem as it remained a foreign revolutionary ideology that could not be reconciled with conservatism.

While both Stalin and Khrushchev had to reverse key positions on the nation, tradition, family and the Orthodox Church, Brezhnev bore a resemblance to a conservative with a nationalist ethos. The political disagreements about Russia as a historical society reached heights in the 1960s, which resembled the disputes between the Slavophiles and Westernisers in the nineteenth century (Cohen 1984: 92). The reversal of key Bolshevik policies demonstrated that human instincts cannot be transcended and that Russian conservative roots went deep:

> It may be argued that a system born in revolution and still professing revolutionary ideas cannot be called conservative, but history has witnessed other such transformations as well as the inner deradicalization of revolutionary ideologies. Indeed, the conservative aftermath of a great social revolution may be a kind of historical law. (Cohen 1984: 95)

By the 1960s and 1970s, there seemed to be a common cause forming between moderate reformers and conservatives who were frustrated by stagnation, mismanagement and censorship. Russian conservatives within the Soviet Union were emboldened to speak up even though they were punished, with Solzhenitsyn being a prominent example. Society changed drastically towards the mid-1970s as a barter economy evolved, resulting in the market and society drifting further away from Marxist ideology. By the 1980s, Gorbachev initiated reforms to open and restructure the state in response to the internal contradictions.

THE NATION

Tsarist Russia as a multi-ethnic empire had struggled throughout the nineteenth century with the complex issue of nationality. The Bolsheviks became the most vocal party to address the nationality question by denouncing the cultural imperialism of the Russian Empire over other nations. Following the revolution, the Soviet Union aimed to abolish the nation as an alleged capitalist construct. The initial internationalist mission of transcending the nation very soon transitioned into Soviet national-building project with centralised power.

The socialist parties had advocated in favour of substantial national autonomy and self-determination of the peoples within the Russian Empire. The socialists' support for cultural and linguistic autonomy did not include the right to separate territory; rather, it had been in opposition to the policies of Russification of national minorities. Until 1917, Lenin had opposed an ethno-federal structure for the Soviet Union as it would decentralise power. Both

Lenin and Stalin initially considered the nation to be the product of historical development that belonged to the capitalist era and would gradually disappear with the transition into socialism. Nonetheless, the nation could not merely be wished away. Non-Russian ethnic groups were endowed with autonomous territories to ensure their support for the Bolsheviks, and the world revolution that would transcend the nation was demoted from an imminent objective to a long-term goal.

The internationalism or globalism of the Bolsheviks was genuine, and it was deemed to be a mere historical accident that the Soviet Union had become the birthplace of world revolution. Internationalism was prioritised as the interests of the Bolshevik Party was subordinate to the interests of the world-proletariat (Herz 1950: 170). In 1918 and 1919, it was expected that an imminent world revolution was merely months or weeks away. Already in the early 1920s, it was evident that the revolution would not spread across the world. Communist internationalism subsequently took on a national cause, and nation-building was prioritised above exporting revolution.

In 1929, Stalin revised his previous opposition to the nation by instead distinguishing between "bourgeois nations" and "socialist nations":

> On the ruins of the old, bourgeois nations new, socialist nations are arising and developing, and they are far more solidly united than any bourgeois nation, because they are exempt from the irreconcilable class contradictions which corrode the bourgeois nations, and far more representative of the whole people than any bourgeois nation. (Stalin 1981: 356)

The socialists had also initially denounced pan-Slavism as Russian imperialism. Albeit, the Soviet authorities found pan-Slavism useful in its foreign policy from the 1930s by rebranding it in the form of communist internationalism, although it diminished against in the late 1940s following the break with Yugoslavia (Kohn 1953). The internationalism of Soviet communism gradually became subservient to a national cause, which only intensified after the Second World War that relied on national-patriotism. The emergence of Soviet patriotism thus became an amalgam of socialism and the Great Russian nation as the largest nation within the Soviet Union (Meissner 1977: 62).

The Soviet Union gradually became a nation-building project under Stalin as the Russian ethno-cultural core set the standard for homogenising the entire state. Russia became the domineering language that would be adopted by all peoples within the Soviet Union. Furthermore, Stalin's deportation of ethnic groups deemed untrustworthy had a certain resemblance to the homogenising process of nation-building in Europe where non-conforming citizens were penalised.

Khrushchev aimed to advance the communist objective by transitioning from a Russian-centric state to the post-national Soviet Union by, for example, returning the ethnic minorities deported by Stalin and elevating the position of Ukrainians. In 1954, Khrushchev even placed Crimea, with a large Russian majority, within the administrative borders of Ukraine to commemorate the Treaty of Pereyaslav of 1654. However, by the end of the decade, Khrushchev paradoxically returned to Russification as increased centralisation was necessary to continue to the advancement of the communist project. Internationalism would continue under the Russian language, which was elevated to the status of an international language. Homogenisation was expected to create a larger and more unified social group, which is largely consistent with the conservative ethos. The merger of other ethnic groups with the Russians was largely consistent with Russia's historical role as a melting pot from the establishment of ancient Kievan Rus to the conquest of Tatar kingdoms in the sixteenth century.

Under Brezhnev in the early 1970s, the nation-building project had become official. Stalin's notion of socialist nations living in unity had been replaced with the concept of a Soviet nation. However, both Stalin and Brezhnev had used the emotional appeal of nationalism to mobilise popular support for their policies (Mitrokhin 2003). Brezhnev (1980: 34) advocated "socialist internationalism, intolerance of nationalism", yet constructed a new people united by civic virtues and ideology rather than a shared ethno-cultural core:

A new historical community of people, the Soviet people, took shape in our country during the years of social construction. New, harmonious relations, relations of friendship and co-operation, were formed between the classes and social groups, nations and nationalities in joint labour in the struggle for socialism and in the battles fought in defence of socialism. Our people are welded together by a common Marxist-Leninist ideology.

The ethno-federal structure of the Soviet Union was balanced and sustained with centralised power in the Communist Party. However, when Gorbachev's reforms weakened the central authority, the ethno-cultural republics within the Soviet Union began to break loose. Paradoxically, the Soviet Union through its ethno-federal structures eventually achieved what had never before existed in Eastern Europe or within the Russian Empire – clearly delineated and internationally recognised borders based on ethno-cultural distinctiveness.

THE FAMILY

The family is the most important autonomous group with social membership and strong loyalty based on biology. The family is the principal source for belonging, meaning, mutual security and even a sense of immortality by reproducing the group. The family is not only an institution to reproduce, but an instrument for socialisation as organic growth and traditions are passed down from father to son. The family is also a source of liberty with its private space guarded by natural biologic inside/outside borders as a refuge from the disruptive.

Conservatism scorns the socialist and liberal policies of liberating the individual from dependence on the family since it destroys social membership in mankind's most important institution. Modern research empirically demonstrates that broken families are likely the leading source of societal decay (US Senate 1983). There is a strong correlation between children raised in single-parent households and anti-social behaviour such as drug abuse, alcoholism, violence and rape (Fagan 1995; Kendall and Tamura 2010).

Socialism, even when necessary and well-intended, has an inherently adverse impact on the family to the extent it becomes a rival institution. Even in modern democratic Scandinavian socialist states, the rise of a supportive state to solve problems replaces the role of the family. For example, the altruistic policy of providing single-mothers with financial support reduces the economic necessity to keep the family together. From the cradle to the grave, the function of the family as an institution diminishes as the atomised individual thus shifts reliance towards the state. Furthermore, such social programmes can be funded with, for example, an inheritance tax, which is an invasive state intrusion into the family that delegitimises biological ties to seize the money.

The initial Bolshevik approach to the family was extremely radical. The family was denounced as a socio-economic institution that perpetuated the ideological functions of capitalism. The state would take over the role of the family. The argument was that equality between genders could not be achieved within the family; rather, it required the abolition of the family. The totalitarian Soviet state distrusted the family as a high-loyalty community to organise the collective that diverted power away from the state. The family had a rival role as an institution of the collective, and even marriage was expected to become an outdated institution as it no longer served economic or social function.

The family was opened up to the administration of the state to ensure that the family serve the interests of the wider community, as opposed to providing a sphere immunised from state intervention and the revolution: "Our family is not a closed-in collective body, like the bourgeois family. It is an organic part of Soviet society, and any attempt it makes to build up its own experience independently of the moral demands of society is bound to result in a disproportion, discordant as an alarm bell" (Makarenko 1967). Old bonds and social institutions that had for centuries organised society were seen as upholding inequality, which was resolved by transferring responsibility to the state as the guardian from the cradle to the grave. Freedom for divorce and abortions accelerated the collapse of cultural values in the family (Imbrogno 1986).

Feminism for the Bolsheviks entailed liberating the woman from household work by transferring these responsibilities to the state. Marriage was revolutionised by liberating each of the genders from their respective contractual obligations. Friedrich Engels had argued in 1883: "It is a curious fact that with every great revolutionary movement the question of 'free love' comes into the foreground" (Hill 1972: 306). The extensive causality of men during the Second World War also incentivised the state to reduce the social taboo of illegitimate children as single-motherhood was imperative to restore the population. Communal dining rooms, nurseries and childcare centres would free women from caring for the family. The state would feed, care for, bring up and educate the children. Lenin argued housework needed to be socialised as it is "the most unproductive, the most savage, and the most arduous work a woman can do" (Goldman 1993: 5). Feminism was not solely altruistic by supporting women, but it also had the purpose of freeing up more labour that could be mobilised.

Parenting was no longer the prerogative of the parents, but a task should be shared with the state. By removing the socio-economic functions of the family as an institution, it was expected to wither away (Goldman 1993: 1). A Soviet sociologist, Volfson, posited that the family "will be sent to a museum of antiquities so that it can rest next to the spinning wheel and the bronze axe, by the horsedrawn carriage, the steam engine, and the wired telephone" (Volfson 1929: 450). Socialist endeavours such as comprehensive childcare were provided, although both parents were compelled by law to work. Communal housing was advocated as an egalitarian policy as separate households perpetuated inequality. Communal housing and limited space put downward pressures on the number of children each family could sustain. Divorces became easy and abortion became an out-patient treatment (Hitchens 1999). Single-motherhood and abortions increased dramatically.

The heroes constructed by the Soviet state revealed that the ideal citizens would have their primary loyalty to the state rather than the family. For example, books, songs, poems and plays were written, and a statue was raised in the honour of Pavlik Morozov, a peasant boy who was hailed by Soviet press as a martyr. Pavlik had allegedly denounced his father to the government for hoarding grain under the farm collectivisation in the early 1930s, and Pavlik was thereafter killed by his grandfather (Hitchens 1999: 211).

The Soviet Union soon had to reverse its family policies as the outcome was detrimental. Birth rates had decreased rapidly, and the break-up of the family had profound social implications (Coser 1951). The state subsequently began supporting family values as a vital institution as stable marriages and large families fuelled population growth and was imperative to transfer skills between the generations. In the 1930s, the state illegalised abortions made divorces more expensive and difficult, promiscuity was shamed, and homosexuality was banned. The introduction of the Order of Maternal Glory in 1944 was awarded to mothers with seven or more children.

State support for the family was nonetheless contradictory as it removed their autonomy and central socio-economic function in society. Yet, the full reversal from deconstructing the family to promoting family values revealed the ideological flaws in Marxism about human nature.

THE ORTHODOX CHURCH

Since Prince Vladimir baptised the Russian people in 988, Orthodoxy has had a dominant role in Russian culture, history and nation-building. Lenin famously dismissed religion as opium for the people in 1905, which was a reference to similar statements from Karl Marx. Marx was inexorably hostile to religion as it diminished mankind's ability to apply reason. Although Marx did not express a need to actively destroy religion, it was believed to dissipate with the abolishment of capitalism. Marx (1977: 131) viewed religion as an instrument for oppressed peoples: "Religion is the sigh of the oppressed creature, the heart of a heartless world, and the soul of soulless conditions. It is the opium of the people". It was believed that people could not be expected to forego their religious illusions under capitalism, as it was a necessity to address the injustices. Once liberated from capitalism, mankind would no longer require religion as a crutch. Dostoyevsky (2017: 254) cautioned:

> Socialism is from its very nature bound to be atheism, seeing that it has from the very first proclaimed that it is an atheistic organisation of society, and that it intends to establish itself exclusively on the elements of science and reason. Science and reason have, from the beginning of time, played a secondary and subordinate part in the life of nations; so it will be till the end of time.

Lenin believed, much like Marx, that religion would fade following a revolution. However, Lenin was extremely hostile in terms of arguing for the state to take an active role in abolishing religion. The difference could be explained by the difference between Marxist theory and Leninist implementation of theory as the church was seen as a rival authority. In Marx's Germany, the Lutheran Church was deemed to be in decline and was largely allied with the bourgeoisie. Thus, it was reasonable to expect the church to naturally fade away the following the coming proletariat revolution. In Lenin's Russia, the church had a much stronger societal role and institutional power, and enjoyed profound support among the peasantry (Wynot 2004: 37). Rather than waiting for religion to wither away, Lenin was convinced that the communist state could only be realised with the destruction of the Orthodox faith.

The first assault on the church was the *Decree on Land Nationalisation* on 8 November 1917. The lands, buildings and livestock of the Orthodox Church thus became the property of the state. By state decree, the word "God" (Bog) could no longer be written with a capital letter. From 1917 to 1940, the mass closure of churches resulted in the number of active churches in Russia being reduced from 39,530 to 950 (Dickinson 2000: 330).

The nation and religion is something that people are willing to kill for, but also worth dying for. Due to the spiritual shallowness of communist ideology, even Stalin had to call on the Orthodox Church to rally support, and he tapped into a deep reserve of Russian patriotism and love for the nation to fight the Nazi invasion. The Soviet state was responsible for both the decline of the Orthodox Church in the inter-war period and its revival during the Second World War as Stalin found political use of the Orthodox Church between 1943 and 1953. When the Soviet Union was finally stabilising, Khrushchev intensified the persecution of Christianity – especially in the late 1950s and early 1960.

After Khrushchev, the effectiveness of his persecution of Christians was questioned. Instead of spreading atheism, it was argued to have pushed religion underground. Away from the watchful eyes of the state, religion could also develop as an institution of dissent. The philosophy of Slavophiles and Pan-Slavs began to re-emerge in the Soviet Union. Russian conservatives considered social problems such as alcoholism, the decline of the family and poor manners to be caused by the decline in morality and religion. Russian nationalists also viewed the Orthodox Church was also recognised to be indispensable to revive the Russian nation. In a country ruled by one political party, political opposition could look towards religion as a source of legitimacy.

RUSSIA AND EUROPE

Russia's relationship with Europe during the communist era strengthened existing divisions. While Europe and Russia had its deep divisions for centuries, this took on a more ideological and binary format as the capitalist, liberal and Christian West rivalled the communist, authoritarian and atheist Soviets across the world.

Following the victory over Napoleon, Russian military officers that returned to Russia had picked up interest and fondness for liberal ideals during their military campaign in Western Europe. This had spurred the Decembrist revolt and subsequent liberal movements in Russia throughout the nineteenth century. Stalin sought to avoid this mistake by purging his own military that had returned from the war in Europe. Unlike the conservative endeavour to manage a balance between preservation of tradition and embrace of change/ modernisation, the revolutionary communism of Stalin was seen purely to be in a zero-sum relationship with capitalism.

The rivalry with the West caused grave misery for the Soviet Union. After years under rapid industrialisation and the tyranny of Joseph Stalin, the Second World War caused untold destruction as an approximate twenty-seven million Soviet citizens died. Following the war, there was limited time to recover as the United States was armed with nuclear weapons and soon after established NATO. With a large portion of the men having been killed during the war and the need for reconstruction demanded extreme social adjustments.

ÉMIGRÉ COMMUNITIES

The émigré community was deeply divided and failed to establish a common political platform, and even the Orthodox Church was divided abroad. The émigrés were principally divided by how to respond to the Bolshevik's control over the country. For example, while Trubetskoi rejected the possibility of working with the Marxists, Suvchinsky believed that the Soviet Union could be reformed.

The concept of nationalism evolved among the émigrés, who increasingly defined the nation as a distinctive people rather than loyalty to the monarchy. The empire was thus increasingly defined as a civilisation state.

Ivan Ilyin was concerned about the depiction of Russia in the West as an artificial creation due to its multi-ethnic construction: "Russia is neither an accidental conglomeration of territories and tribes nor an artificially assembled 'mechanism' of regions (oblasts) but a live, historically grown and culturally justified organism which is not subject to voluntary partitioning" (Ilyin 1956: 245).

Ilyin has become immensely influential in post-Soviet Russia and is commonly vilified in the West for his support of fascism in its early stages before the implementation of militarism and racism as a central platform. Much like his philosophical contemporary, Martin Heidegger, Ilyin celebrated connectedness with nature and was attracted to "healthy national-patriotic sentiment, without which no people can either reaffirm their existence or create their own culture" (Ilyin 1956: 70). The nationalism of Ilyin resembled more that of Herder in terms of rejected the xenophobic strand of nationalism. Ilyin wrote: "The true patriot not only is not blind to the spiritual achievements of other peoples, but he seeks to comprehend and assimilate them, to introduce them into the spiritual life of his own motherland, in order to enrich" (Robinson 2019: 135).

Ilyin cautioned that the West's hostility towards Russia was not merely caused by opposition to socialism; rather, it was also against Russian conservatism as the West despised the cultural distinctiveness and unity of Russia:

> We know that Western nationalities neither understand nor tolerate Russian distinctiveness. . . . They are planning to separate the united Russian broom into little twigs, to break these little twigs one by one, and to fuel with them the dying-out fire of their civilisation. They need to partition Russia in order to establish here Western equalisation and unleashing, thus destroying her – a plan of hatred and power lust. (Ilyin 1956: 246)

Politically weak as unity could not be kept abroad, although they became an intellectual force with great conservative minds that contemplated the inevitable implosion of communism and the subsequent task ahead of reviving Russian culture, traditions, spirituality and nationality. If Russian nationality was its spirituality and historical memory, then the belief was that this could be conserved and brought back once the communist project collapsed. Besides preserving the conservative ideas of nineteenth-century Russia, they also deliberated on the complex relationship with the Europeans as they sought to assimilate in their host nations. The conservative debate continued in terms of what the Russian identity and history represented in terms of faith philosophy and culture. One learns more about the distinctiveness of one's own country as an émigré standing on the outside. These thinkers have been central to inform the ideas of the political leadership in Russia after communism collapsed.

The reaction of émigrés to Bolshevism varied due to competing ideas about the cause and effect. Berdyaev believed that communism was the result of a spiritual illness that had festered in Russia through the previous decades. Russia's shift to the material at the expense of the spiritual had paved the way for the repugnant Bolsheviks, although Berdyaev posited that the collapse would lead to spiritual rebirth and rediscovery of what is sacred to Russia: "Our hour has yet not come" (Finkel 2010: 352). The armed struggle against Bolshevism was tantamount to fighting the symptom, and Berdyaev instead advocated taking on the disease:

> I consider my mission as much as I can to draw Russians abroad away from furious politics and petty political intrigues and to focus their awareness on spiritual life and spiritual interests. Russia's soul is gravely ill and can be saved only by means of a spiritual healing and strengthening, and not by external politics.

Russia's political recovery will come only by means of spiritual sources. Bolshevism is a secondary phenomenon, of the reflexes, and only a symptom of the spiritual illness of the people. (Finkel 2010: 356)

The importance of conservative values became all the more evident when tradition and culture are threatened:

We will need great tremors for the ground to shake beneath our feet. Only then will we realize that the people's historical experience is the only reliable foundation. Only then will we return to our national roots and bow down in due respect again at the feet of Mother Russia. . . . Despite all these sufferings, our people will not perish. It will emerge morally and spiritually stronger and begin a new, rational life. The only question is how long these trials will last. (Gillespie 1989: 205)

Peter Struve blamed the autocracy partly for the revolution as efforts to suppress powerful forces in society had set Russia on the path to a violent upheaval, which manifested itself as the Bolshevik Revolution. Much like Berdyaev, Struve believed that spiritual revival was more important than squabbling with other émigrés over political formats. The past informs the future, and émigrés should therefore devote their focus towards preserving the history, culture and faith of Russia. According to Struve, the task of an émigré was "almost exclusively spiritual and as such it will count in Russia in the future, when the political struggle in its contemporary forms will move to the background, and social relations will solidify" (Burbank 1986: 151).

Ilyin also believed that Bolshevism was principally a symptom of a spiritual crisis, and that the curse of communism could be a time for Russians to repent and rediscover the value of its spiritual traditions. Bolshevism merely destroyed one form of Petrinism and replaced it with another form. Albeit, Ilyin was also advocating armed struggle that would also restore honour in Russian society that was upheld by the Whites. While finding refuge in the West, Ilyin believed that after communism Russia would need to rediscover its past rather than see the Westernisation as the alternative to communism. Ilyin argued:

There is no single universally obligatory "Western culture" compared with which everything else is "darkness" or "barbarism". . . . The West has its own errors, ailments, weakness, and dangers. . . . Out salvation does not lie in Westernism. We have our own path and our own tasks. (Ilyin 1956: 317–318)

The conservative emphasis of morality as an internal compulsion as opposed state-imposed external compulsion was of more important than ever due to communism. Under the Soviet authorities, the sources of morality such as church and family had been decimated, and conduct had been imposed arbitrarily through totalitarian means by the communist state. The moral foundation and legal consciousness of Russia were therefore deeply wounded and not capable of supporting democracy. A transitional period of a patriotic autocracy would therefore be needed to restore the collective conscious-ness of Russia and stability. Ilyin cautioned that "any attempt to introduce a democratic order will lead either to mob rule (that is the masses, morally unbridled and deprived of any sense of self-worth, having no sense of respon-sibility, or of freely given loyalty), or to a new right-wing totalitarian tyranny. Democrats who don't think about this and can't foresee it, don't understand the essence of either democracy or totalitarianism" (Robinson 2019: 144).

EURASIANISM AS THE EVOLUTION
OF RUSSIAN CONSERVATISM

Eurasianism emerged as a conservative idea in the 1920s among émigrés in response to the Bolshevik Revolution. Nikolai Trubetskoi, Pyotr Savitsky, Andrei Lieven, Georgy Florovsky, Lev Karsavin, Ivan Ilyin and other émi-grés that had fled to Europe following the Bolshevik Revolution defined themselves as Eurasianists. The Eurasianists were diverse and included his-torians, philosophers, economists, writers, linguists and other strands of intel-lectuals. Yet, as Eurasianism branched into various forms and approaches, it did not result in a unified political movement.

Eurasian emerged among émigrés as a conservative philosophy con-tending that civilisations are greatly influenced by geography. For the Eurasianists, the vast open steppes of Eurasia have had a profound influence on the culture and traditions of Russia, which must lay the foundation for modernisation. Eurasia is depicted as a separate "third continent" with a geo-graphical and historical space distinctively different both Europe and Asia. Defining the concept of Eurasianism is problematic as the intellectual found-ers of Eurasianism in the 1920s were divided over the underlying assump-tions, which contributed to ending the Eurasianism as a unified movement in the 1930.

Eurasianism centred on the idea that Russia was not merely an Eastern European state. Following the Mongol invasion in the thirteenth century and Russia's conquest over Tatar kingdoms in the mid-sixteenth century, Russia had adopted a history and geography that was no longer European. Russia's future would need to be balanced by engaging more with Asia. Defining conservatism and organic growth according to Slavophile ideas that roman-ticised Russia before the Cultural Revolution of Peter the Great was deemed outdated. Yet Eurasianists drew on many of the traditions of Slavophiles, and especially the ideas of Pan-Slavist Danilevsky.

While Westernisers had been seeking Russia's return to Europe following the Mongol yoke and the Slavophiles had romanticised the Byzantine era, the Eurasianists were opposed to turning back the clock. Trubetskoi and Savitsky posited that the Mongols had protected the Orthodox Church and Russia from the decadence of the Roman-Germanic world (Mirsky 1927). Trubetskoi argued that Russia obtained spiritual maturity and unity under the Mongol experience – "A miracle happened and the Mongolian state idea was transformed into the Russian Orthodox state idea" (Badmaev 2015: 36).

However, the intellectual roots of Eurasianism can be said to have even deeper roots with links to the cultural Silver Age and the political economy of Sergei Witte in the late nineteenth century. Dostoyevsky (2001: 260) argued:

> Russians are as much Asiatics as European. The mistake of our policy for the past two centuries has been to make the people of Europe believe that we are true Europeans. We have served Europe too well, we have taken too great a part in her domestic quarrels. As the first cry for help we have sent our armies, and our poor soldiers have died for causes that meant nothing to them, and have been immediately forgotten by those they had served. We have bowed ourselves like slaves before the Europeans and have only gained their hatred and contempt. It is time to turn away from ungrateful Europe. Our future is in Asia. True, Europe is our mother, but instead of mixing in her affairs we shall serve her better by working at our new orthodox idea, which will eventually bring happiness to the whole world. Meanwhile it will be better for us to seek alliances with the Asiatics. In Europe we have been mere intruders; in Asia we shall be masters.

Dostoyevsky (1997: 1373) advocated already back in 1881 for a Eurasian frontier to restore a sense of purpose was compared with the American frontier:

> When we turn to Asia, with our new view of her, something of the same sort may happen to us as happened to Europe when America was discovered. For, in truth, Asia for us is that same America which still have not been discovered. With our push towards Asia we will have a renewed upsurge of spirit and strength. Just as soon as we become more independent we'll at once find out what we have to do; but living with Europe for two centuries we've become unaccustomed to any kind of activity and have become windbags and idlers.

The Eurasianists of the early twentieth century also had predecessors from the late nineteenth century who were growing weary of Pan-Turkism (Wiederkehr 2007). While the Turks could point to cultural, ethnic and lingual ties to the East, the Russians could be depicted as imperial by merely being Slavs that had crossed the Volga into foreign lands. Russia's engagement with Central Asia through the nineteenth century was largely accepted due to economic progress and improved governance, yet culturally it entailed Russification and Christianisation (Landau 1995: 45). Reforms to Russian conservatism was warranted to reflect the Eurasian melting pot that Russia had become over the centuries.

Eurasianism makes a distinct break from previous forms of conservative thought. Former conservatives had envisioned a different Europe and as a member of the European family launched an internal civil war by reaching out to its Byzantine legacy, Kievan Rus and the Slavic world. Eurasianists liberated themselves from the resentment of being rejected from Europe, and instead embraced the notion of belonging to a distinctively different civilisation. However, Eurasianists were linked to the Slavophiles with their affinity towards the Orthodox Church, the Russian land and pre-Petrine traditions. Religion is central in the formation of civilisations, and the ability of the Russian Orthodox Church to engage with Eurasia's major religions in a conservative format for cooperation.

Eurasianism demands a break with the fixation on the West and the struggle to catch-up as the source of Russia's revolutionary history. Eurasianism exists on a spectrum from a complete break with the West and organise a collective rebellion against Europe with non-Western peoples, to merely constructing a wider Eurasian cultural, economic and political structures that treat Europe as an equal as opposed to subservience to its cosmopolitan universalism.

Conservatism builds on the past, and the Soviet experience could not merely be ignored once the communist experiment would eventually fail. The Eurasianists expected that the character of the Russians would be altered after eventually shedding the Bolshevik yoke, much like the Mongol yoke had altered the nature of Russia (Glebov 2017). Russia could not return to the Slavophile orientation of previous conservatives, and the Euarsianists thus argued that the Russian identity also has to include Turkic, Ugro-Finnic and other non-Slavic elements into the collective consciousness of Russia. The Bolsheviks would eventually fail as the internal contradictions of communism imposed limitations, and it was the job of Eurasianists to ensure a conservative response to Soviet Eurasianism existed (Bova 2015: 72).

The Eurasianist position envisions Russia as a civilisation state. Unlike the European empires that ruled over foreign peoples, Russia had drawn other peoples into a great melting pot and thereby also altered the character of Russia. While Western critics of Eurasianism often depict Eurasianism as an ideology of imperialism, the Eurasianist concept is anti-imperial by redefining "us". By incorporating Tatars and other peoples into the national identity of Russia, there is no longer any rule over other people. Hence, Russia transitions from a Slavic empire to a Eurasian civilisation state.

Eurasianism subsequently became a conservative opposition to the communist Soviet Union on the radical political Left. Trubetskoi and Savitsky had expected Eurasianism to eventually replace communism. Towards this objective, the Eurasianists were positioned along a spectre between reforming the Soviet Union from within, to opposing it from outside. Some success can be identified with the former category as the ideas of Eurasianism made its way into Soviet thinking and concepts to address the issue of ethnicity that lingered (Rangsimaporn 2009: 27). These divisions resulted in the Eurasianist movement fading away in the 1930s as several Eurasianists positioned themselves as reformers of the Soviet Union rather than opponents.

Eurasianism had its intellectual heyday in the 1920s and 1930s. The origin of movement can be attributed to Trubetskoi's book *Europe and Mankind* in 1920, and the following "Turn to the East" in 1921 by a group of émigré intellectuals. Trubetskoi posted there were two opposing ways of addressing the challenge of nationalities – chauvinism and cosmopolitanism. Chauvinism supported the preservation of the distinctiveness of a people in the tradition of Herder. Cosmopolitanism denotes the endeavour to pursue universal civilisation. In more modern lingo, Trubetskoi suggested that the world was divided according to a national-patriotism versus cosmopolitan-globalism (Diesen 2019).

Eurasian conservatives appreciated the cultural distinctiveness of the West, yet scorned Western cosmopolitanism and universalism. Trubetskoi (1920) argued that civilisation in the cosmopolitan tradition entailed the Roman-Germanic culture. The concept of "civilised people" had been limited to Roman-Germanic people and those who accepted and adopted their culture. The West had systemic incentives to embrace cosmopolitanism and universalism as it entailed reconstructing the world in its own image. For the West, there was less distinction between cosmopolitanism and chauvinism as universalism meant the export of its own distinctive culture (Trubetskoi 1920).

However, Western cosmopolitanism and universalism was the source of decay. Defining Western culture as superior due to recent advancements also made the West view its own past as barbaric. From a conservative perspective, the impulse of distancing away from one's own tradition and history undermines the required foundation for organic growth.

Russia's plight resembled that of the other non-Western peoples, the path to cosmopolitanism and universalism entailed cultural submission to the West as the self-declared representatives of a shared human civilisation. Westernisation offered Russia and others a fast-paced track towards modernity, although in the process eviscerating the cultural foundation of a sovereign people and civilisation. Cultures that imitate others tend to develop a disdain for their own traditions and historical experience. Imitating cultures can develop more profound class divisions as educated, Westernised and "civilised" Russians became defined their higher class in society by the ability to shed commonality with the native culture. Those who denounced their own culture and people by being more Western and cosmopolitan would elevate above others, while the lower classes were defined by chauvinist loyalties. Russia's own Westernised intellectuals thus became convinced about the Europeans as the representatives of a universal civilisation. The distance between the elites and people thus grew further.

Imitating cultures following in the footsteps of others would perpetually struggle with internal divisions and more powerful adversaries. Herein lies the disruptive and destructive historical necessity of Russia to catch up with the West:

> These leaps break the entire process of historical development. In a trice a people must cover that ground which the Romanogermans had covered gradually in the course of a longer period of time. . . . The results of such leaping "evolution" are truly horrible. Each leap has to be followed inevitably by a period of apparent (from the European point of view) stagnation, necessary to put culture in order. . . . And during this "stagnation", naturally, the people is falling behind again and even more. History of Europeanized peoples consists precisely of this mixture of brief periods of rapid "progress" with more or less lengthy periods of "stagnation". . . . Leaping evolution wastes still further national strength already overexerted by the very fact of Europeanization. As a man who tries to keep in step with a faster companion and resorts for that purpose to the practice of periodic leaps will inevitably perish, having spent its national strength on no purpose. (Trubetskoi 1920: 68–69)

The Eurasianists were, however, equally dismissive of Marxism as a response to class struggle, which was denounced as a European ideology alien to Russia and a direct result of the fixation on the West. Tubetskoi argued:

> Bolshevism is as much a product of the two-century Romano-Germanic yoke as Muscovy was a product of the Tatar yoke. Bolshevism shows what Russia has learned from Europe during that period, how it understood the ideals of European civilisation, and how these ideals fare when translated into reality. It is in this light that we should judge whether the Romano-Germanic yoke was beneficial or harmful. And when you compare these two diplomas of the Tatar school and the Romano-Germanic school you cannot help but to reach the conclusion that the Tatar school is not so bad after all. (Badmaev 2015: 37)

The cultural superiority of the West was according to Trubetskoi premised on flawed assumptions. The West's definition of civilised people versus barbarians was based on its ability to defeat its less developed adversaries on the battlefield. The West had an economic and military leader, and Trubetskoi was adamant overtaking the West would not be possible if Russia and other non-Western powers merely seek to catch up in perpetuity. Trubetskoi's (1920: 81) call for "a revolution in the psychology of intelligentsia" to overcome the obsession with the West resembles Gramschi's ideas of challenging the cultural hegemony. In other words, Russia requires a national idea that breaks from the Western ideology that justifies the socio-economic and political structures as natural and unavoidable.

While Eurasianism emerged as an anti-hegemonic movement against the West, it nonetheless also had a strong hegemonic component as Russia was expected to immediately assert leadership in the movement. Eurasianism also has universal components as the civilisational space is not demarked by concise national borders. Furthermore, Eurasianism conceptualises Russia as a civilisational bridge between Europe and Asia.

GUMILEV AND THE EURASIAN TRANSITION AWAY FROM COMMUNISM

Lev Gumilev and Georgy Vernadsky emerged as leading thinker among the next generation of Eurasianists. Gumilev argued that Russia had been founded on a natural coalition between Slavs, Mongols and Turks. The attempts to reform the Soviet Union created an opportunity for conservative believing that conservative Eurasianism was the best path forward when communism finally failed. Gumilev's (1989) *The Ancient Rus and the Great Steppe* had a profound impact on Russian society following the demise of the Soviet Union.

Gumilev contributed greatly to developed Eurasian ideas that would enable Russia to transition from empire to a civilisation state. Gumilev argued that nomadic tribes of inner Eurasia had historically been victorious over societies that were more advanced in terms of science and reason. On the Eurasian steppes had equipped the peoples with a martial spirit, and the geography had historically endowed one power with dominance as the source of stability. The Huns, Turks and Mongols had in the past dominated this space, although now the Russians had adopted the nomadic ethos and were the leading power. Gumilev's theory offered an alternative to European nationalism and utopian internationalism. Instead, Eurasia was an amalgam between nationalism and internationalism.

The influence of Gumilev persists, and Putin even referred to him as "the great Eurasian of our time" (Podberezkin and Podberezkina 2015: 47). The establishment of Lev Gumilev University in Kazakhstan indicates the immense influence on new thinking. During his visit to the University, Putin argued that Gumilev's ideas were "beginning to move the masses". The collapse of the Soviet Union and the loss of the vast Eurasian territory was not necessarily a negative development for the Eurasianists. The new Eurasianism would require the establishment of a cooperative arrangement among Eurasian powers to align interests rather than seeking hegemonic control.

CONCLUSION

The principal idea of conservatism is that reason is restrained by instincts that evolved over thousands of years. The reliance on social groups is the most important and enduring instinct. The Bolshevik Revolution can be considered a great social experiment that tested the ability of mankind to transcend the reliance of traditional social groups organised as family, ethnicity, religion and culture. The need by Marxist revolutionaries to reverse their policies demonstrated that society was not merely a shallow social construction to uphold an exploitative system.

The Bolshevik Revolution changed Russia and subsequently the content of Russian conservatism. The Soviet experience convinced several conservatives that the collective "we" was not merely Slavic but Eurasian. The attempts to make Russia more European had undermined its instincts and reason as Russia can only prosper by embracing its Eurasian character.

Chapter 7

The Liberal Revolution of the 1990s

INTRODUCTION

Russia's failed communist revolution was replaced by a liberal revolution in the early 1990s. Marxism had lost its legitimacy due to economic failures and moral bankruptcy, and liberalism emerged as the dominant alternative due to the binary ideological division of the Cold War. The subsequent dual liberal revolution of both the domestic and the international system caused great disruption and hardship for Russia. At the domestic level, Russians had to adapt to a new state, borders, identity and ideology as the government and economy faltered. At the international level, the liberal international order facilitated Western hegemony and sovereign inequality.

The civilizational vision of the Yeltsin administration entailed reinventing Russia as a liberal European state. This objective appeared to repeat of the Cultural Revolution of Peter the Great, albeit without strengthening Russia's ability to project power through education, industry and maritime power. The "return to Europe" was not merely a political and economic pivot, but it also had a social and cultural dimension with profound metaphysical implications.

This chapter first explores the destructiveness of the liberal revolution for Russian society. Liberals, much like socialists, tend to believe in a linear progression as mankind sheds the instinctive, and presume that preserving traditions as a "vote of the dead" slows down progress. Conservatism recognises that by undermining the collective to advance personal liberties, society no longer becomes morally equipped to handle liberty. Second, the advancement of the liberal international order is assessed. The decade began with Russian foreign policy focusing almost solely on the objective of integrating with the West, and by the end of the decade, the West had returned as the principal security threat. It is concluded that the excesses of liberalism create incentives for Russia to revive conservative traditions.

SOCIO-ECONOMIC COLLAPSE

Liberalism appeared to be the only game in town following the collapse of communism. After more than seven decades of communism, Russia needed to restore its community in the form of a nation, faith and traditions. Instead of rejuvenating the collective identity and navigating towards organic growth, Moscow moved towards radical individualism and materialism to become more like the liberal West. Russian liberals shared many similarities with the Marxists and preserved Leninist ideas as liberalism was expected to result in "transcending classes" and "transcending the nation" (Lukin 2000: 194).

The 1990s became a revolution in Russia similar to America in the 1770s, France in 1789, and Russia itself in 1917 (Mau and Starodubrovskaya 2001). Adopting neoliberal policies was even more destructive in post-communist states that did not have a long tradition of individualism. Economic liberalism enabled Western powers to cement its hold over advanced high-tech industries in global value chains, while Russia rapidly de-industrialised and became an exporter of natural resources in the international division of labour.

Historical parallels can be drawn to the darkest periods of Russian history as the collapse of the state led to destruction due to domestic anarchy and foreign powers eying opportunities. When the Rurik dynasty fell it ushered in the Time of Troubles in the early seventeenth century, a third of the Russian population perished. The fall of the Romanovs led to the loss of territory, a brutal civil war and brutality under communist rule. The collapse of the Russian state, for the second time in the twentieth century, brought yet again untold misery.

An era of nihilism and degradation swept across Russian society, which was not equipped to restore unity and order due to decades of the moral and legal relativism of Marxism. The nation continued its disintegration as the nation and ideals had been broken, the economy collapsed, communities were dislodged and families broke apart. Economic liberalism, aided by US shock therapy, resulted in a criminal revolution. Chaos permeated, mass poverty spread, the financial system collapsed, crime and corruption became the new normal, and a rising oligarchic class plundered the country and formed dubious partnerships with foreign powers. Russian authorities feared a quasi-colonial status as the leading oligarch, Mikhail Khodorkovsky, was preparing to sell a major share of his oil empire to ExxonMobile and Chevron-Texaco (Tsygankov 2009: 146).

Sergei Glazyev (1998), who later became an advisor to President Putin, used the term "genocide" to describe the social decay and population loss of the 1990s. Glazyev argued that the destruction in Russia by Stalin's purges and the mass famine of the 1930s faded in comparison to the 1990s.

The expectation that the Russian Federation would disintegrate and share the fate of the Soviet Union was common and reasonable. The state no longer carried out key functions such as paying government employees providing security, upholding the financial system and currency, and other basic functions of the state. The state also did not have the authority to impose a common vision of society and moral codes in terms of what should be legal and illegal. The legitimacy of the Russian state was in question and various regions were moving towards secession.

George Kennan (2014) wrote in 1994 that there should be more sympathy for Russia as more than seven decades of communism had distorted and degraded one of the greatest civilisations in the world. Kennen (2014) recognised the conservative struggle for this "tragically injured and spiritually diminished country". Putin (2005) later recalled the turbulent birth of modern Russia:

> Let me remind you again of how modern Russian history began. First of all, it should be acknowledged, and I have spoken of this before, that the collapse of the Soviet Union was the greatest geopolitical catastrophe of the century. And for the Russian people, it was a real drama. Tens of millions of our citizens and fellow-countrymen found themselves outside the Russian Federation. Moreover, the epidemic of disintegration spread to Russia itself. Citizens' savings lost their value. The old ideals were destroyed. Many institutions were disbanded or simply hastily reformed. . . . With unrestricted control over information flows, groups of oligarchs served exclusively their own corporate interests. Mass poverty started to be accepted as the norm. All this evolved against a background of the most severe economic recession, unstable finances and paralysis in the social sphere. It seemed to many at the time that our young democracy was not the continuation of Russian statehood, but its final collapse, the prolonged death throes of the Soviet system.

From a conservative perspective, the radical socio-economic and political changes could not lead to stable democracy as they had no historical roots in Russian culture and traditions. Much like Peter the Great, the changes of Yeltsin were tyrannical to the extent they had to be enforced with a strong hand instead of relying on tradition. Oligarchs became the new nobility, Russia weakened, anarchy took hold and foreign influence expanded within the country.

Unlike its Western counterparts, liberals in Russia throughout history have been deeply distrusted due to fears that their ideological inclinations result in support for foreign powers. Many liberals have commonly argued against the Russian victory over Napoleon's invasion as a set-back in Russia's liberalisation and development. This liberal sentiment was depicted in Dostoyevsky's novel, *The Karamazov Brothers*, with the brother Smerdyakov who argued it would have been better if Napoleon would have defeated Russia as "A clever nation would have conquered a very stupid one and annexed it" (Dostoyevsky 2016: 246). Following Russia's humiliating defeat to the Japanese in 1905, Russian liberals sent telegrams to the Japanese emperor to congratulate him on the victory over the Russian army (Chebankova 2016). Duma liberals also used the hardship during the First World War to delegitimise the authority of Nicholas II to instigate revolutionary change, although the socialists first seized upon the subsequent chaos (Nikonov 2017).

Maintaining the dividing lines in Europe following the Cold War by excluding Russia from membership in the main institutions has revived the misgivings of Russian liberals. It is common for Russian liberals to express affinity and allegiance towards the West to the extent it is reasonable to question their patriotism. Furthermore, much like their counterparts in the West, Russian liberals often depict protests and civil disobedience buoyantly as a revolutionary movement to topple the government. The Western-backed colour revolutions and the toppling of President Yanukovich of Ukraine in 2014 were therefore supported by many liberals, as a precursor to a "democratic revolution" in Russia.

THE QUESTION OF NATION AND EMPIRE

The collapse of the Soviet Union represented the rejection of communism and centuries-long imperial history. The fatigue over subsidising less prosperous Soviet Republics, primarily Central Asia, was a leading motivation for Russia to dismantle the Soviet Union and walk away from its empire (Tsygankov 2006: 59). The collapse of the Soviet Union compelled Russia and the other fourteen former Soviet Republics to engage in nation-building, a process of defining the collective (who are "we") in terms of ethnicity, language, culture, religion and other aspects.

The collapse of the Soviet Union, as an ethno-federal state, made Russia resemble a traditional European nation-state, which has no precedent in Russia's national experience. The Russian Empire had officially been born in 1721 as a result of Peter the Great's victory in the Great Northern War, and the Soviet Union had inherited this empire. For the first time in almost three centuries, Russia was no longer an empire and made itself comfortable with a much smaller territory.

In post-imperial Russia, the question about the "nation" was no longer as complex. Ethnic Russians make up approximately 80 per cent of the population, which constitutes a strong homogenous ethno-cultural that defines Russia. With Russia suddenly having a more homogenous population than several European nation-states, a cogent argument was made by nationalists that the new demos could lay the foundation for democracy. Solzhenitsyn provided strong support for ethnic nationalism to cement Russian distinctiveness and escape the supranational inclinations the fuelled imperial impulses. Solzhenitsyn referred to northern Kazakhstan as Southern Siberia and Southern Urals due to the large ethnic Russian population there (Zevelev 2009).

Russian conservatives were divided on the issue of the nation as the lingering concerns were that an ethnic focus risked sowing internal divisions and clashing with foreign powers. After gaining its independence from the Mongols in the fifteenth century, Russia had to be cautious in defining its heritage: An identity linked to Kievan Rus could create conflicts with Lithuania; claiming the authority of the Byzantine Empire could compel Russia to reconquer Constantinople; and a successor role to the Golden Horde would demote Russia to an Asiatic power. After Russia gained its independence from the Soviet Union, defining the state could yet again fragment the state from within or challenge the borders of neighbours.

The reinvention of nation-states following the collapse of the Soviet Union creates tensions across the fifteen independent post-Soviet Republics. Approximately twenty-five million ethnic Russians were left outside Russia's borders when the Soviet Union collapsed in 1991. This included about two million ethnic Russians in Crimea, who officially became Ukrainians due to the alternations of the administrative borders under Khrushchev in 1954 – a process of de-russification in several former Soviet Republics. A civil war was sparked in Moldova as ethnic Russians and the Russian language were suppressed.

Some conservatives believe that preserving the ethno-cultural core should be a priority for the stability of Russia. The mass immigration of cheap labour for Central Asia is commonly depicted as a reversed colonisation, akin to the situation in Europe. This is a result of liberal policies by the elites who put profit above societal concerns. It is thus argued that Russia should attract and offer citizenship to the millions of Russians living in neighbouring states, which would strengthen the ethno-cultural core of Russia and tame its imperial impulses.

There are two main approaches in Russia to address the national question. The first seeks to resolve the question of Russians being the most divided people on the planet by state borders. The second group is more moderate by reaching out to "compatriots" in the Russian world (Zevelev 2009).

In his 1994 New Year's address to the nation, Yeltsin also spoke to the Russian diaspora: "Dear compatriots (sootechestvenniki), you are inseparable from us and we are inseparable from you. We were and we will be together" (Tolz 1998: 1009). However, in terms of defining the nation, Yeltsin was cautious to avoid ethnicity. Further, in 1995, Yeltsin cautioned against the European nation-state model as it could unravel Russia:

> We should not copy a Western path of state building. It is based on assimilation, which has always been carried out by force. We are unique, because 150 different nationalities live in our country, and they preserve their ethnicity, culture and languages. . . . For the people of the RF collective rights have priority over individual human rights. It is only in the distant future that the latter could take priority. In the West, the supremacy [of individual rights] is achieved through the destruction of entire populations. Thank God, the Russian nation has never been historically that cynical. (Tolz 1998: 1014)

Excessive reliance on ethno-nationalism also risks unravelling Russia due to its complex ethnic history. Unlike the Muslims of Europe, the Russian ethnic groups such as the Muslim Tatars are also native to Russia and have integrated with ethnic Russians for centuries. The saying "scratch a Russian you will find a Tatar" purportedly originated in nineteenth-century France with the derogatory intent of depicting Russians as barbaric Asians. In modern Russia, this phrase is commonly used, also by President Putin, but as a positive quality and expression of the kinship between ethnic Russians and Tatars. The affinity ensures that Russia is not an empire as it does not rule over "other peoples".

While ethnic Russians had a comfortable majority on the 80 per cent mark, the ethnic minorities are largely concentrated in specific regions. Nationalism thus threatened to continue the disintegration of the Russian Federation as secessionist movements emerged in the Urals, Tatarstan and most violently in Chechnya. Due to the chaos of the 1990s, a Russian general commented on the situation in the region of Tatarstan in Russia: "Half the population is building mosques, the other half is building churches. And the bosses are building big brick houses for themselves" (Mann 2005: 23–24).

THE LIBERAL INTERNATIONAL ORDER

During the final years of the Soviet Union, Gorbachev advocated for a *Common European Home* to replace bloc politics. The Cold War infrastructure had created two separate European systems in which the leadership of the United States and Soviet Union was predicated on perpetual tensions.

The Common European Home was conceptualised as a large house (shared institutions) with separate rooms to accommodate both capitalist and socialist states in a peaceful format. The United States developed a rival concept, a *Europe Whole and Free*, which would unite all of Europe under liberal principles, and thus US leadership as the champion of liberalism. The two concepts seemed similar at the surface, although the power structure underpinning the ideological leadership of the United States was the principal difference. The collapse of the Soviet Union gave way to the US idea of organising the world around liberalism principles and US leadership.

The West emerged from the Cold War with unprecedented power and a common liberal mission to unite them and direct the use of its power. The prevalent argument was that the United States had led a liberal international order in the West since the Second World War, which could after the Cold War finally be realised on a global scale. The expectations of the West was summarised in Fukuyama's (1989) "end of history" thesis that stipulated that the world would reorganise itself under liberalism and coalesce under US leadership.

Liberal hegemony assumed a mutually beneficial relationship between US hegemony and liberal values, which was to be achieved by advancing US primacy as the guardian of democracy and human rights (Walt 2018). Albeit, ideologies of internationalism rapidly descend into nationalist causes as opposed to advancing a multilateral, rules-based and benign order.

The triumph of liberalism in the Cold War provided the ideological foundation for a revolutionary age similar to what had followed the French Revolution. The French Revolution expected that by exporting the revolution abroad, a new international system would be born that broke with the international anarchy of the past. The French National Convention had declared in 1792 that France would "come to the aid of all peoples who are seeking to recover their liberty". The ideas of Kant's "Perpetual Peace" then manifested themselves in Woodrow Wilson's missionary duty for the United States to make the world "safe for democracy". Following the Cold War, the collective West under US leadership asserted the prerogative to advance liberalism in the world through intrusive democracy promotion and humanitarian internationalism. The internationalism of the French Revolution and Bolshevik Revolution was repeated by the West, which was best articulated by Tony Blair's (1999) advocacy of humanitarian internationalism: "We are witnessing the beginnings of a new doctrine of international community . . . we are all internationalists now, whether we like it or not".

The United States as the self-proclaimed leader and vanguard of liberalism embraced the concept of being the indispensable nation. In 1998, US secretary of state Madeleine Albright (1998) proclaimed: "If we have to use force, it is because we are America; we are the indispensable nation. We stand tall and we see further than other countries into the future, and we see the danger here to all of us." The statement on American exceptionalism was followed by more than two decades of prolonged war under liberal pretences, and with very little to point to as a success.

Liberal hegemony becomes a contradiction in terms as the advancement and preservation of hegemony undermine the liberal rules it was intended to uphold. This contradiction becomes even more evident when the relative power of the hegemon decreases. In the age of Trump, there is no more any pretence of adherence to liberal order as the objective of dominance takes an overtly military approach in what Posen (2018) defined as "illiberal hegemony". The leading defenders of liberal hegemony are therefore often the first to trample upon international law and advocate the use of military power.

Hegemony and liberal values unavoidably came into conflict, which expressed itself in military adventurism and containment of other large powers such as Russia and China (Mearsheimer 2018; Walt 2018). Liberal hegemony implied a system of sovereign inequality as the champions of liberalism would rule. An obvious weakness was that if justice and international law depended on the unity of the West, then non-Western centres of power such as Russia would always be in the wrong. The need for solidarity among the West would always trump the consistent application of international laws and rules (Diesen 2020a: 110–111). In the Long Telegram, Kennan (1947) cautioned that by linking Marxist ideology to an entity of power, the Soviet authorities would denounce any criticism of their rule as a "counter-revolutionary act":

> That is the infallibility of the Kremlin. The Soviet concept of power, which permits no focal points of organization outside the Party itself, requires that the Party leadership remain in theory the sole repository of truth. For if truth were to be found elsewhere, there would be justification for its expression in organized activity. But it is precisely that which the Kremlin cannot and will not permit. The leadership of the Communist Party is therefore always right.

In the post–Cold War era, the aforementioned description has a striking resemblance to the United States and the wider West, which denounces all opposition to its power as an unacceptable assault on liberal values that promise perpetual peace.

The function of liberalism is to advance rationalism, modernisation and individualism – although conservatism recognises that it must be balanced by the instinctive, tradition and the collective. The "liberal idea" became an absolutist ideological dogma, a liberal Messianism, which elevates liberalism to the sole solution for organising human activities. The liberal West became a crusader seeking to dispose of unfavourable governments around the world.

The universalism embedded in liberalism presents a great challenge. Civilisational diversity is imperative as it, much like biodiversity, makes the world more capable of absorbing shocks and handle crises: "Universalism, if realized, would result in a sharp decline of the complexity of the global society as a whole and the international system in particular. Reducing complexity, in turn, would dramatically increase the level of systemic risks and challenges" (Kortunov 2017). As Nikolai Danilevsky postulated more than 150 years ago:

> The danger consists not of the political domination of a single state, but of the cultural domination of one cultural-historical type. . . . The issue is not whether there will be a universal state, either a republic or a monarchy, but whether one civilization, one culture, will dominate, since this would deprive humanity of one of the necessary conditions for success and perfection – the element of diversity. (Robinson 2019: 83)

Russia's Foreign Minister Sergei Lavrov (2015) similarly opined that the effort to homogenise the world with liberal universalism was the source of the West's military conflicts:

> We firmly believe that the only practical formula for settling these issues has nothing to do with military interference or any other way of forcing a certain mode of behaviour, which may seem right to the enforcer, on others, but that this formula is based on respect for the right of nations to persona identity and the diversity of the modern world. Both in nature and in society, diversity is the key to prosperity and progress.

Through the eyes of Russian conservatives, the liberal West following the Cold War began to resemble Jacobinism by advocating a new Reign of Terror to advance liberal ideals. When political idealism fails to transform the world, it descends into radicalism and chaos. The promise of perpetual peace justifies aggressive means to implement the ideals that "separates the present evil world from the brave new world of the future" (Herz 1950: 164). Ideologies of advancing human freedoms

> paradoxically, has its time of greatness when its ideals are unfulfilled, when it is in opposition to out-dated political systems and the tide of the times swells it toward victory. It degenerates as soon as it attains its final goal; and in victory it dies. (Herz 1950: 159)

Aron (2017: 584) similarly cautions:

Idealistic diplomacy slips too often into fanaticism; it divides states into good and evil, into peace-loving and bellicose. It envisions a permanent peace by the punishment of the latter and the triumph of the former. The idealist, believing he has broken with power politics exaggerates its crimes.

The notion of the idealism of progressive ideologies legitimising destructive revolutionary acts has also been a key theme among Russian intellectuals. Dostoyevsky (2009b: 66–67) recognised that people were "inflamed by theories of future bliss" that "seemed to be sacred and moral in the highest degree and, most of all, they seemed to be universal – the future law of all humanity without exception". The belief that the current flawed world can be replaced with a utopian future legitimises the means as "even the purest of hearts and the most innocent of people can be drawn into committing such a monstrous offence. And therein lies the real horror: that in Russia one can commit the foulest and most villainous act without being in the least a villain!" (Dostoyevsky 2009b: 67).

THE EUROPEAN QUESTION

Russia in the early 1990s was led by Atlanticists. It was believed that Russia had always been a European power, but had been taken away from its natural home. Russia's Asian territory and Eurasian entanglements were believed to have corrupted its European past. Russia's traditional partners in Central Asia and East Asia were deliberately neglected as they were seen to weigh down and obstruct Russia's pivot to Europe.

Yeltsin had aspired to for the Russian Federation to be reborn as a normal European state and join the liberal democratic order led by the United States. The principal foreign policy objective was to create Greater Europe, a concept based on Gorbachev's Common European Home. Russia preferred developing a Greater Europe within the institutional framework of the inclusive Organisation for Security and Cooperation in Europe (OSCE).

However, the new Europe was defined by an expanding NATO and EU, which used liberal justifications to include all of Europe except Russia. The new liberal Europe represented a British-American continuity in terms of the rule of maritime powers, and Mackinder's objective to organise the German-Russian relationship in a zero-sum format to prevent the alignment of interests. The historical competition between Germany and Slavic lands continued along the same trajectory as in the past. The Brest-Litovsk Treaty of 1918 that was imposed on Russia during the First World War gave Eastern Europeans independence from Russia, yet in reality, it was structured to make them vassals of Germany. Winston Churchill (2013) argued, the

Brest-Litovsk Treaty drastically reduced the ability to contain Germany by sea by endowing Berlin with "the granaries of the Ukraine and Siberia, the oil of the Caspian, all resources of a vast continent". The preservation of dividing lines in Europe subsequently collapsed the entire liberal and pro-Western platform of Yeltsin.

The only major Russian political institution that remained an advocate of an Atlanticist orientation was Yabloko, a liberal opposition party. Yet, even a founder of Yabloko, Vladimir Lukin, who had regarded good relations with the United States as the main priority, had to walk back his Atlanticist visions for Russia. Lukin reiterated Eurasianist ideas as he argued Russia was a distinct civilisation that was not solely Europe. Lukin argued:

> Any attempts to force Russia solely into either Asia or Europe are ultimately futile and dangerous. Not only would they cause a serious geopolitical imbalance, but they would also undermine the historically established social and political equilibrium within Russian itself. (Mankoff 2009: 72)

Russia's abandonment of empire and embrace of painful liberal reforms had a key purpose – the ambition of "returning to Europe" and joining the collective West. The Cold War had been declared over in Malta in 1989 through compromise. The assumption among Russian liberals had been that Greater Europe was a more feasible prospect once the Soviet Union and Marxism had been dismantled, and Russia began adopting liberalism values such as free-market capitalism and democracy.

However, the collapse of the Soviet Union incentivised historical revisionism as the United States altered the narrative and proclaimed that the Cold War was won. The liberal leadership of President Bush (1992) was announced merely one month after the collapse of the Soviet Union:

> The cold war didn't end; it was won. . . . By the grace of God, America won the cold war, which was . . . There are those who say that now we can turn away from the world, that we have no special role, no special place. But we are the United States of America, the leader of the West that has become the leader of the world. And as long as I am President, I will continue to lead in support of freedom everywhere.

The last US ambassador to the Soviet Union, Jack Matlock (2010: x), cautioned that "too many American politicians looked at the end of the Cold War as if it were a quasi-military victory rather than a negotiated outcome that benefitted both sides". The implication was that a peaceful future did not rely on compromise, rather it depends on merging liberalism with US military might. George Kennan similarly criticised US senators for wanting to use

NATO as an instrument for continuing to contain Russia after the collapse of the Soviet Union:

> I was particularly bothered by the references to Russia as a country dying to attack Western Europe. Don't people understand? Our differences in the cold war were with the Soviet Communist regime. And now we are turning our backs on the very people who mounted the greatest bloodless revolution in history to remove that Soviet regime. (Friedman 1998)

The myth of US *victory* in the Cold War subsequently became a leading source of resentment as it denied Russia a seat at the table in the post–Cold War era (Sakwa 2017: 16). The so-called defeat in the Cold War had striking similarities to the actual defeat in the Crimean War in 1856, as the terms of surrender appeared to be pushing Russia out of Europe and into Asia.

The Cold War had offered a comfortable binary ideological division that reflected the international distribution of power. The West was capitalist, democratic and Christian, while the Soviets were communist, authoritarian and atheist. Liberalism has largely been instrumental to recreate new dividing lines by creating a Europe without Russia as a new liberal-authoritarian divided had to be constructed.

Cooperation with Russia under liberal hegemony was largely organised under the concept of *Europe Whole and Free*. Cooperation no longer entailed sovereign equality by making mutual compromises to reach agreements of common interest. Instead, under the auspices of the liberal idea, the West undertook a pedagogic role as Russia would adapt to the West through unilateral concessions. Russia was demoted to the object of security in a teacher-student relationship (Neumann 1999: 107–109; Haukkala 2005: 9). The EU-Russian "Partnership for Modernisation" initiative of 2010 failed for the same reason, as liberalism was used as a paternalistic civilising mission. Moscow invariably focused on the need for technological and economic development to create more equality. Brussels focused on political and social modernisation, which gave EU officials the right to decide who should represent Russia's civil society and demoted Russia to the role of a compliant student.

Relations between the United States and Russia similarly collapsed as they were organised along a subject-object format. Kissinger warned that Washington lecturing Moscow about democracy and free-markets was making liberalism an instrument for Russia "having come under a kind of colonial tutelage" (SMH 1999: 19). President Bill Clinton referred to cooperation with Russia as issuing orders to an inferior: "We keep telling Ol'Boris, 'Okay, now here's what you've got to do next – here's some more shit for your face'" (Talbott 2002: 202). Liberalism internationalism had much like Marxist internationalism spawned a Brezhnev doctrine of limited sovereignty (Narochnitskaya 2003: 508).

Through pedagogic behaviour modification, the West either "reward" good behaviour or "punish" undesirable behaviour, defined as an amalgam between liberal ideology and Western interests. Moscow was left with an ultimatum of accepting its role as an apprentice of the West, or become a "counter-civilisational force" by contesting the hegemony of NATO and the EU as the guardians of liberal values (Williams and Neumann 2000).

Containment was temporarily replaced with a civilising mission, which could then be reversed to containment if Russia would reject its role as an obedient student. NATO was therefore seen as an insurance policy against a resurgent Russia. However, as James Baker (2002) cautioned, organising NATO as an insurance policy would merely make the possible future conflict a self-fulfilling prophecy. George Kennan, the architect of containment policies, lambasted the ideological debates in the Senate as justification for NATO expansionism:

> It shows so little understanding of Russian history and Soviet history. Of course there is going to be a bad reaction from Russia, and then [the NATO expanders] will say that we always told you that is how the Russians are – but this is just wrong. (Friedman 1998)

Wider Europe the EU's main concept for organising Europe, which is a Brussels-centric project with concentric rings with weaker influence the longer they move away from the centre. The principal task is to ensure there is only one centre of power and to draw the periphery towards the EU (Wæver 2000). The obvious consequence is the inability to fit Russia within this format and the lack of legitimate Russian influence beyond its borders as an encroachment of the EU's backyard. As Russia was excluded from the institutions representing Europe, the concept of European integration became a contradiction. The zero-sum logic of bloc politics remained and European integration entailed that states decoupled from Russia (Diesen 2016).

The historical continuity of cutting Russia from economic corridors resumed. Much like the Treaty of Stolbovo in 1617 that aimed to ensure all Russian trade went through Swedish waterways, NATO expansionism in the Baltic Sea and the Black Sea cemented control over the remnants of Russia's maritime transportation corridors. Former US presidential advisor, Brzezinski (2017) opined that the "Russia must know that there would be a massive blockade of Russia's maritime access to the West" if there would be a conflict.

Moscow principal argument concerning the European security architecture was that if Western institutions were expanding they had to include Russia to avoid extending the zero-sum format of Cold War bloc politics. However, from the perspective of values, it became difficult for Russia to oppose the expansion of Western institutions if Russia truly identified with the cultural and liberal space of Europe (Mezhuyev 2017). Furthermore, Russia could not endeavour to mimic the liberal political system of the West if it wanted to have competitive soft power in the contested shared neighbourhood.

The West did not enhance its security with territorial gain; instead, the geographical expanse became a source of insecurity. Much like Tsarist and imperial Russia, the West no longer has any natural borders. Security is advanced by controlling its periphery and continuously expanding its borders. With each wave of expansion, NATO and the EU have a new immediate neighbourhood and need to address the security challenges of an even more distant front line.

As the liberal international order is defined by hegemony, the West under US leadership began to conflate "revisionism" with opposition to hegemony (Cooley and Nexon 2020). The West's revisionism of the European security architecture by continuously expanding NATO and the EU was depicted as the status quo of the order, while Russia's efforts to halt expansion and preserve the status quo was castigated as revisionism and attempt to restore the empire.

The Western-backed colour revolutions presented another historical comparison to the Napoleonic Wars. Moscow considers the domestic demands for democracy and fighting corruption to have been high-jacked by the West, which sought to transform the movements into the geostrategic platform of promoting anti-Russian government striving to join NATO and the EU. Gleb Pavlovsky, an advisor to Putin's administration, argued that the Orange Revolution "was a very useful catastrophe for Russia. We learnt a lot. . . . It very quickly became clear that they [the West] would try to export this to us and that we should prepare for this, and very quickly strengthen our political system" (Popescu and Wilson 2009: 29). Largely confirming Washington's effort to weaponise liberalism against adversaries, US senator John McCain tweeted on 5 December 2011 a direct threat to Moscow: "Dear Vlad, the Arab Spring is coming to a neighbourhood near you".

THE WEST'S ETHNO-NATIONALIST PARADOX

The West's position on ethno-nationalism has been inconsistent and paradoxical. The cohesion of the West after the Cold War has become heavily reliant on liberalism. Liberalism has pushed the west to juxtapose ethnocultural identities with a civic identity to define the collective. The liberal post-ethnic identity of the West is intended to overcome its own troubled history of nationalism, and it is deemed necessary to construct an EU that transcends the nation-state.

However, within the post-Soviet Space and Yugoslavia, the West has incentives to align itself with ethno-nationalists to advance democracy and marginalise multi-ethnic states such as Russia, Yugoslavia and even China. The West actively supported breaking up Yugoslavia along ethnic lines, and the United States aligned itself with the Croats during the ethnic cleansing of Serbs from Krajina. The West supported Bosnia's secession from Yugoslavia but denied the Serb regions of Bosnia (Republica Srpska) to remain in Yugoslavia or secede from Bosnia. Similarly, the West severed Kosovo from Serbia by force, although denied the Serbs in northern Kosovo to remain in Serbia or secede from Kosovo.

NATO's liberal "humanitarian" intervention in Kosovo in March 1999, less than two weeks after expansion, demonstrated the failure of the liberal international order. NATO pushed aside the UN as the arbiter of international law due to the "obstruction" by Russia and China, by not voting in favour of military means. The war in Kosovo changed the borders of Europe by military power for the first time since the Second World War. Henry Kissinger (1999) argued: "The Rambouillet text, which called on Serbia to admit NATO troops throughout Yugoslavia, was a provocation, an excuse to start bombing." John Norris (2005: xxiii), the director of Communications for US deputy secretary of state Strobe Talbott during the Kosovo crisis, similarly wrote: "It was Yugoslavia's resistance to the broader trends of political and economic reform – not the plight of Kosovar Albanians – that best explains NATO's war".

The West supported or remained silent concerning de-russification policies in former Soviet Republics to support former Soviet Republics to de-couple from Russia and pursue "European integration". Case in point, Russian-speakers in Estonia and Latvia are denied basic citizenship rights such as voting, which is supported indirectly by the EU.[1] The de-russification policies were also advanced in Georgia, Ukraine and other states pursuing "European integration".

The complex history and identities in Ukraine are commonly presented ideologically in the West as a move away from authoritarian Russia and towards the West – only to be prevented by the imperial hand of Russia. Trenin (2011: 92) refers to Ukraine as a "cleft state" that consists of a series of mutually exclusive identities resulting from centuries of imperial competition. The intertwined history between Russia and Ukraine has been a double-edged sword as what can be deemed a profound bond between brotherly people is also an impediment to full sovereignty. For Ukrainians who deem their country to be a bi-ethnic, bi-cultural and bilingual state, the greatest threat to the nation are Ukrainian ethno-nationalists vilifying and alienating the Russian component of their identity (Shulman 2004). Ukrainians who consider the ethnic, cultural and lingual Russian presence in Ukraine to be an imperial legacy, the principal threat to the nation are those seeking to legitimise and preserve the Russian component. The West again leans towards supporting the ethno-nationalists in Ukraine as a zero-sum choice was imposed upon Ukraine in 2004 and 2013 to choose either the West or Russia, which fuels domestic and foreign forces to pull the country apart (Diesen and Conor 2017). Similarly, Washington's tacit support splitting the Orthodox Church is intended to support Ukrainian nation-building as an anti-Russian project.

Within Russia, the West aligns itself with and promotes ethno-nationalists such as Navalny, who seeks to disassociate Russia from the post-Soviet space and advance the democratic nation-state. A strong nationalist component emerged among the Russian liberals seeking to advance democracy, which promoted xenophobia under the banner of democracy. Navalny was expelled from the liberal Yabloko party in 2007 due to his ethno-nationalist fervour and disparagement of the Muslim population. Yet, in the West, Navalny is commonly hailed as a liberal alternative to Putin.

It is a common belief in the West that Russia must give up its imperial ambitions and become a normal nation-state to develop a functioning democracy and no longer be a threat to the world. Russian liberal nationalists caution against immigration from former Soviet Republics, especially Muslim republics in Central Asia and Azerbaijan. The liberal nationalists become attractive partners for the West as the vast and ill-defined borders of Russia as a civilisation state provides uncertainty and temptations for restore empire, which is why the continued fragmentation of Russia along ethnic lines could serve Western interests.

Yet, the West walks a tightrope as it supports greater national autonomy or even independence for ethnic groups within Russia, although the shift in focus to ethnicity could instigate similar ethno-nationalism among ethnic Russians in former Soviet Republics. If ethno-nationalism becomes a powerful political force in Russia, it could become a pernicious force for redrawing borders due to a complex and the tens of millions of ethnic Russians who became minorities outside their homeland.

THE WEST LOSES ITS STATUS AS A ROLE MODEL

The success and attractiveness of the West were based on liberal-conservatism, which used the ethno-cultural nation-state as a conservative foundation to advance liberal values. Yet, the excesses of liberalism began eviscerating the conservative foundation of the West and fuelled its descent into excessive materialism, radical individualism and freedom from religion. The West that Russian conservatives admired throughout the nineteenth century no longer existed, and is thus no longer an attractive role model.

Western conservatism had a strong liberal origin. American conservatism and liberalism had a common purpose during the struggle for independence from the British, in terms of establishing independence based on liberal virtues. This secession from Britain did not entail a cultural revolution; rather, it represented organic change by establishing new political structures consistent with the liberal ideology espoused by Britain. American conservatism maintained a libertarian wing that advocated for radical individualism.

Yet, a split between the conservative impulses to cement the collective and the liberal objectives of elevating the individual above the collective. The United States focused on developing into a distinctive ethno-cultural social group, which was achieved by demanding a White Anglo-Saxon Protestants (WASP) majority as the condition for obtaining statehood in the union (Glazer 1983). Christianity took a central part in the education system as the foundation of shared morality.

Throughout the nineteenth century, the United States remained highly critical of free-trade as a disruption to communities and traditional values. In 1895, Theodore Roosevelt depicted free-trade as a threat to moral cohesion of the state: "Thank God I am not a free-trader. In this country pernicious indulgence in the doctrine of free trade seems inevitably to produce fatty degeneration of the moral fibre" (Eckes 1999: 30). President Eisenhower portrayed the societal disruption of open markets as a necessary evil due to the Cold War, and regretted that free-trade should be tolerated as "all problems of local industry pale into insignificance in relation to the world crisis" (Eckes 1995: 165).

The twentieth century transformed the United States as its liberal creed was heightened in the struggle against fascism and communism, and the century ended in the victory of liberalism as a state ideology. The United States transformed as a state that based in liberal ideals on an ethno-cultural and religious core that had practised the economic nationalism of Alexander Hamilton. As liberalism became a puritan force that transformed its society, even conservatism as an ideology underwent revolutionary change.

The cultural revolution of the 1960s presented conservatives with a challenge. Conservatism can be said to have begun its decline with the cultural revolution of the late 1960s as key pillars of society began to be dismantled, with liberalism challenging the family, religion and the nation. The ability of conservatives to counter-balance these developments collapsed in the 1980s.

The conservative revolution had its origin in the political economy of the 1980s under Reaganism and Thatcherism. The capitalist system from 1945 to the 1980s has been characterised as "embedded liberalism", which is a reference to Polanyi's argument that the market was disembedded from society during the nineteenth century (Ruggie 1982). Embedded liberalism denotes balancing free trade with welfare programmes and other social responsibilities of the state. Under embedded liberalism, the Political Right could defend traditional values and communities, while the political Left could redistribute wealth. In response to the economic stagnation of the 1970s,

Reagan advocated for economic liberalism. Increased market efficiency would thereby cause neglect of social responsibilities in terms of preserving traditional values and communities.

Reagan (1984) recognised the importance of traditional values and Christianity to ensure the United States does not get "mired in the material", which would result in "coarsening of the society" and "a nation gone under". A schism in American conservatism thus emerged as the unfettered market became a leading conservative virtue, although refusing to recognise that it dismantles traditional communities, family values and the collective. The conservative revolution along neoliberal ideology altered the fundamental meaning of conservatism in the United States and the wider West. Economists such as Friedrich von Hayek and Milton Freedman made neoliberal economics the hallmark of American conservatism. A neoliberal consensus subsequently formed as in open markets competitiveness relied on the political Left no longer redistributing wealth from capital to labour, while the political Right could not protect traditional values from market forces. Nations gradually transformed from states with economies to economies with states, where economic determinism reduced every societal question into profit.

The second schism in American conservatism derives from the issue of empire. Classical conservatives sought to prevent that the United States followed the path of Rome as the American Empire erodes the American Republic, as the government grows and relies increasingly on universalism. George Washington cautioned not to "entangle our peace and prosperity in the toils of European ambition, rivalships, interest, humor, or caprice", and Thomas Jefferson advocated for a foreign policy based on "peace, commerce, and honest friendship with all nations, entangling alliances with none". By contrast, neoconservatives believe that sustaining US primacy and reshaping the world in its own image was at the centre of conservatism. Classical conservatives, such as George Kennan, argued the Cold War had perverted the meaning of American conservatism. Kennan had cautioned against the excesses of ideology about the inherent goodness of one's own political system as it can manifest itself in "self-righteousness" and "moral crusades" (Booth and Wheeler 2008: 98). The idea that the United States should impose revolutionary change on the rest of the world through a militaristic and imperial means would not only be destructive for the world, it would also erode the power of the United States. Kennan often quoted John Quincy Adams about the danger of being "in search of monsters to destroy".

For neoconservatives, the preservation of frontiers is expected to keep the state focused and unified towards a shared goal. Attention is diverted away from internal problems during times of expansion. Fredrick Jackson Turner (2008 [1893]) "frontier thesis" argued that the western frontier had mitigated the consequences of individualism and decadence was concealed by the optimism of the great future. Once the United States reached the Pacific Coast, it had to continue establishing new frontiers by venturing into the Pacific. Once a civilisational hegemony is established, the society enters a period of stability and prosperity that fuels ideals of perpetual peace. However, the "golden age" is deceptive as stability and prosperity are largely superficial (Quigley 1961: 159). The meaning, purpose and unity that existed during struggle and expansion ends, and in victory, there is hubris, hedonism, nihilism, materialism and moral corruption (Toynbee 1946; Quigley 1961; Glubb 1976). Much like a star, a civilisation shines the strongest when decay has already begun. Similar to the final years of ancient Rome, the West celebrates frivolity and superficial culture as progress. During the supposed height of the West's civilisational advancements and realisation of its ideals, society succumbs to emotional solitude, social safety nets collapse, the people seek refuge in substance abuse, obesity proliferates and indebtedness cripples communities, while shopping and shallow entertainment distract from growing nihilism (Luttwak 1999: 207–208).

George Kennan believed that the idea of a victory in the Cold War had to be reassessed, as the 1990s demonstrated that the conflict had fundamentally transformed the United States into a sick society. The excesses of liberalism had placed the United States on the path of "unrestrained decadence", which had already manifested itself in a "pathological preoccupation with sex and violence, the weird efforts to claim for homosexuality the status of a proud, noble and promising way of life" (Kennan 2014). The decadence of the United States was comparable to the Soviet Union:

> Americanism, like Bolshevism, is a disease which gains footing only in a weakened body. I have lost my sympathy for the Europeans who protest against the influx of American automobiles and American phonograph records. If the Old World has no longer sufficient vitality, economic and cultural, to oppose these new barbarian invasions, it will have to drown in the flood, as civilizations have drowned before it. (Kennan 2014: 53)

The contemporary cosmopolitan elites in the West display contempt for traditional culture with striking similarity as Peter the Great did for Russian culture. The social fabric of Western societies has undergone profound change over the past decades. Individualism has triumphed over the community, trust has continued declining, Christianity and traditional values have faltered, and families have broken down. Sergei Karaganov, an influential Russian scholar and presidential advisor, argued that the attractiveness of the West had diminished as the West does not have anything more to teach Russia:

> Karaganov opines that Russia and the majority of Europeans want to be part of the Europe of Konrad Adenauer and Charles de Gaulle. As Europe has betrayed its cultural and Christian heritage, Karaganov argues: "For the next decades, Europe will not be a model that is attractive to Russia". (Spiegel 2016)

CONCLUSION

The liberal revolution of the 1990s was immensely destructive to conservative values. However, the subsequent calamity contributed to generate interests in conservative policies as people tend to embrace tradition as a refuge for order during crises.

Russia was in dire need to restore a collective identity, and in its absence, the country almost fragmented into sub-national identities based on different ethnicities and faith. Weakened communities and spiritual emptiness fuelled socio-economic problems such as alcoholism, drug abuse, abortions and broken families. Liberal economics contributed to de-industrialise Russia and create excessive dependence on the West. Russians also must reopen the concept of the nation as Moscow shed its empire and was left with what resembles a nation-state. The centuries-old issue of defining the nation impacts the identity of Russia and its relations with neighbouring states.

Liberalism also proved unable to transform the international system. Rather than becoming an instrument to transcend confrontational power politics, liberalism became an instrument of power politics as altruistic internationalism became subservient to competing national causes. Liberalism translates into sovereign inequality and overlapping authorities that fuel new wars.

A conservative post-mortem of Russian liberalism and the liberal international order suggests that the state and the international system must be organised along distinctive entities pursuing organic growth. While liberalism has largely been discredited by the end of the 1990s, the liberal international order would last until the end of 2010s.

NOTE

1. Recognition of Russian-speakers as citizens of Estonia and Latvia was not a condition for closing the OSCE mission or to obtain EU membership; EU referendums were accepted without the participation of "non-citizens"; and the European Parliament grants Latvia and Estonia voting power for citizens that are not recognised; and the EU has not mitigated the situation by for example recognizing Russian as an official language.

Chapter 8

The Return of Russian Conservatism under Putin

INTRODUCTION

Russian conservatism in the twenty-first century is tasked with overcoming both the communist and liberal revolution of the former century. By the time Putin took the presidency in December 1999, Russia seemed ripe for yet another revolution. Yeltsin's entire liberal platform that had charted Russia's post-Soviet path had failed spectacularly. In terms of domestic issues, the socio-economic collapse had discredited liberal reforms that fuelled chaos rather than restoring order. The liberal revolution of the 1990s had also reaffirmed an old assumption that the alternative to a strong state is anarchy. In terms of foreign policy, the belief that a post-imperial Russia would be embraced by the West had been proved wrong as a new Europe was being created without Russia.

Conservatism became a third way to escape liberalism and without falling back on communism. Yet, Russia is not returning to nineteenth-century conservatism as the past century must be incorporated into the new national consciousness and identity. The twentieth century became a torturous trial for Russia with revolutions, civil war, collectivisation, terror, purges, and Marxist oppression, which was finally relieved by a disasterous liberal revolution. However, conservatives cannot merely eradicate the twentieth century from the national memory and identity as this would represent a revolutionary act by neglecting the principle of organic growth. Contemporary Russian conservatism aims to dig deep roots as the past disruptive century can be digested if it is placed in the historical context of the past millennium. Furthermore, deep roots are required as Russia enters the Fourth Industrial Revolution as the growing ability of digital technologies to manipulate the physical world will transform industry and society.

This chapter will first assess the rediscovery and resurgence of conservatism after the Cold War. The Cold War dualism of liberalism versus socialism has been rejected since they both represent progressive ideologies that neglect that the instinctive is imperishable. The initial pragmatic conservatism then began transitioning towards conservatism as a state ideology. Second, Russia's efforts to deal with its revolutionary past are explored. The Soviet legacy has not been denounced altogether; rather, Moscow has sought to salvage what it can to avoid making conservatism a revolutionary movement. Attempting to turn back the clock is in itself a revolutionary act and an impossibility. Both socialism and liberalism now belong in the national history of Russia, although Russia can avoid being excessively defined by these periods by positioning it within the wider context of Russia's thousand-year-long history. Last, Russian conservatism has been greatly influenced by the mutual othering with the West. A reinvented ideological divide in Europe and the West's encroachment of the Russian World are fuelling resentment towards liberal ideals. It is concluded that modern Russian conservatism has changed greatly from the nineteenth century. Russian conservatism is largely focused on processing a century of revolution and reforming itself due to the loss of empire and the autocracy.

CONSERVATISM AS THE ALTERNATIVE TO THE DUALISM OF THE COLD WAR

Russian politics from the late 1980s and the 1990s were largely polarised between a dichotomy between democrats versus communists and liberals versus patriots (Prozorov 2005: 122). The failure of the liberal revolution then left a political vacuum to be filled by radical alternatives. The Cold War dualism between liberalism and communism immediately made the latter the main alternative. The Communist Party emerged as the largest nation-wide opposition. The great irony was that the revolutionary Communist Party attracted due to a sense of certainty in the familiar and traditional. Communism represented some stability and a proven force to push against the rule of the oligarchs within Russia, and the West's efforts to construct a hegemonic world order by imposing a "new Treaty of Versailles" on Russia to perpetuate its weakness.

Conservatism resurfaced already in the early 1990s to move beyond the ideological dualism that defined the Cold War. Russia's tradition of conservatism was subsequently emerging as a third way, which opposed both the Marxist and liberal revolutionaries. In the 1970s, Solzhenitsyn (1978: 26) had cautioned against the artificial ideological dualism between capitalism and communism as it obscured the importance of preserving the traditional and instinctive:

We have placed too much hope in political and social reforms, only to find that we were being deprived of our most precious possession: our spiritual life. In the East, it is destroyed by the dealings and machinations of the ruling party. In the West, commercial interests tend to suffocate it. This is the real crisis. The split in the world is less terrible than the similarity of the disease plaguing its main sections.

Solzhenitsyn (1978: 26) argued that the Enlightenment of the eighteenth century and Marxism share an affinity for "spiritualized humanism" by advocating "endless materialism" and "freedom from religion". Herein lies a pernicious similarity between the West and East:

At first glance it seems an ugly parallel: common traits in the thinking and way of life of today's West and today's East? But such is the logic of materialistic development. The interrelationship is such, too, that the current of materialism that is most to the left always ends up by being stronger, more attractive, and victorious, because it is more consistent. Humanism without its Christian heritage cannot resist such competition. We watch this process in the past centuries and especially in the past decades, on a world scale as the situation becomes increasingly dramatic. Liberalism was inevitably displaced by radicalism, radicalism had to surrender to socialism, and socialism could never resist Communism.

Solzhenitsyn became a supporter of President Putin as he believed that unlimited rights should not be equated to freedom, rather excessive individualism would unravel the order required for freedom to be sustainable. Unlimited rights were referred to as the liberty of cavemen, and the Orthodox Church was praised for upholding religious and national sensitivities. Solzhenitsyn, therefore, posited it was tantamount that Russia finds its particular path to democracy and does not emulate the West. These views reflect an old debate about the meaning of citizenship in terms of a balance between rights and responsibilities. Excessive rights liberate the individual from its responsibilities towards the community and thus erode the main institutions that can uphold rights and freedoms.

In the aftermath of the Cold War, Huntington (1993: 191) similarly cautioned against what referred to as the Single Alternative Fallacy:

There is the argument that the collapse of Soviet communism means the end of history and the universal victory of liberal democracy throughout the world. This argument suffers from the Single Alternative Fallacy. It is rooted in the Cold War assumption that the only alternative to communism is liberal democracy and that the demise of the first produces the universality of the second.

Conservative forces had a strong role in ending communism as the sole vision and alternative was not merely Western liberalism. For example, the strike by Donbas coal miners against the government in 1989 came from a very conservative region (Crowley 1995). Similarly, the Russian Orthodox Church provided significant backing for Yeltsin as he faced the threat of removal by the Soviet authorities (McDougall 1998). Following the collapse of the Soviet Union, the Orthodox Church became an invaluable source for stabilising a new national identity and restore civil society (Daniel 2006).

EARLY CONSERVATIVE PRAGMATISM

Prominent Russian scholars such as Richard Sakwa (2014: 27) have characterised Putin as a liberal-conservative. The conservatism of Putin has not been constant as he has overseen great changes during more than two decades as the president of Russia. Initially, Putin's conservatism was more liberal before gradually shifting towards the right in response to changes to the domestic and the international system.

As Putin took over the presidency, he made the "Russia at the Turn of the Millennium" speech on 30 December 1999, which seemingly suggested a continuity of the liberalism and universalism that characterised the Yeltsin era:

> Russia is completing the first transitional phase of economic and political reforms. Despite all the difficulties and mistakes, we have now arrived on the main track, on which is the whole of humanity. Only this way, as is clearly evident by international experience, offers a real prospect of dynamic economic growth and improving living standards for the people. There is no alternative. . . . We can hope for the future if we can organically synthesise the universal principles of market economy and democracy with the Russian reality. (Putin 1999)

However, reforms were required to transform Russia into a modern European state. Putin's main reforms to Yeltsin's policies towards the West was to reject the student-teacher format for cooperation that required Russia to make unilateral concessions, which only weakened the state and reduced its ability to obtain a seat at the table in Europe. Case in point, the liberalisation of the energy industry had fuelled the rise of oligarchs that were courted by Western governments. Putin restored the state's control over its strategic industries, mainly energy resources, and endeavoured to negotiate a seat at the table and inclusion in Europe from a position of strength.

Moscow's rejection of the apprentice role to Western civilisation and liberal hegemony triggered a fierce response from the West. Putin was vilified and Russia was Putinised, as all Russian policies were depicted as a character flaw of the president and a rejection of democratic values. However, the conservative input by Putin was even welcomed by parts of Russia's liberal elite. Yegor Gaider, the first prime minister of Russia, argued in 2001 that Putin replacing the revolutionary change of the 1990s with evolutionary change was necessary to bring about much-needed stability (Prozorov 2005).

Yet, Putin continued to articulate the liberal and European ambitions of Russia. Reminiscent of Peter the Great, Putin (2000: 169) argued that Russia was primarily a European state as opposed to Asian: "We are a part of the Western European culture. No matter where our people live, in the Far East or the south, we are Europeans". During the State of the Nation address in 2005, Putin largely defined Russia as a liberal European state:

> Above all else Russia was, is and will, of course, be a major European power.... For three centuries, we – together with the other European nations – passed hand in hand through reforms of Enlightenment, the difficulties of emerging parliamentarism, municipal and judiciary branches, and the establishment of similar legal systems. Step by step, we moved together toward recognizing and extending human rights, toward universal and equal suffrage, toward understanding the need to look after the weak and the impoverished, toward women's emancipation, and other social gains. (Putin 2005)

Yet, Putin sought to decouple liberal ideals from power politics by rejecting the fundamentals of liberal hegemony. Putin repudiated that there was a singly democratic model even within the West. Making a conservative approach to democracy, Putin frequently argued that each country should have the right to experiment with the development of a democratic model that takes into account their unique history and character.

Putin's evolutionary approach to democratisation and modernisation was initially termed *managed democracy*, which was then conceptualised more clearly as *Sovereign Democracy*. Sovereign democracy was a conservative response to the contradictions of liberal hegemony that advocated democracy managed under the supervision of the West. Russia's sovereign democracy was based on the simple recognition that democracy cannot exist without sovereignty. As Charles de Gaulle uttered in a radio broadcast in 1942: "Democracy and national sovereignty are the same thing." Furthermore, democratisation and modernisation should not be conflated with Westernisation. Conservatism instructs Russia to define democracy consistent with its distinctive culture and traditions, rather than allowing for democracy to become an instrument to import Western values and culture.

While Sergei Uvarov had redefined the concept of nationalism for Russia in opposition to the French Revolution, Putin sought to conceptualise democracy against the liberal international order.

Furthermore, Russian conservatism in opposition to Western liberal hegemony leans towards Eurasianism. The conservative Eurasianist, Alexandr Panarin (2002), argues that the military and cultural hegemony of the United States has made the process of globalisation immensely destructive. A conservative alternative requires a balance of power through civilisational pluralism, which incentivises Russia to disassociate itself from the West and form partnerships in the east.

TOWARDS THE ESTABLISHMENT OF A CONSERVATIVE STATE IDEOLOGY

The Russian state is moving towards conservatism as a state ideology. While conservatism was defined by Sergei Uvarov by "Autocracy, Orthodoxy and, Nationality", the new post-monarchy Russian conservatism deals with other challenges that explain the focus on tradition, orthodoxy, family and nationality. A new strand of conservatism was required that maintains the transcendent such as the Orthodox Church, yet is capable of accommodating modern economic realities and technological modernisation. The national idea had to be built on defining Gemeinschaft and encode it as an official state ideology.

Yeltsin argued already in 1998 that the absence of ideology in Russia was problematic as there had been an ideology in each epoch throughout the twentieth century (Slade 2007: 45). Putin's policy manifesto in 1999, "Russia at the Millennium", attempted a centrist position to bridge modernity and universalism with tradition and distinctiveness. The manifesto posited that Russian modernisation would implement universal principles of democracy and market economy on the foundation of Russia's thousand-year-long traditions. Putin is frequently quoted proclaiming that Russia's transition to democracy is a permanent national choice, albeit rejecting any universalist formulas as Russia "will not become a second edition of, say, the US or Britain, where liberal values have deep historic traditions" (Putin 2000: 14).

Exhausted by the ideological turmoil of the past and in dire need of improved living conditions, Russians were averse to ideological ideals in the 1990s (Hanson 2003). The end of communism was liberating to Russia, as the communist ideology had been constraining and often obstructed the ability to advance national interests. Putin (2000) unequivocally denounced the inflexible and constraining dogmas of ideology. Some scholars are thus sceptical about the depth of Russian conservatism, such as Trenin (2007), who argued that Russia is led solely by profit and pragmatism to the extent ideas barely have any significance.

Putin was, indeed, initially averse to official state ideology. At the turn of the century, Russia was in dire need of a pragmatic centrist to bring together a deeply divided nation and a state that no longer fulfilled basic duties. Putin could not afford further political fragmentation by denouncing the communists, nationalists or liberals. As a pragmatist, Putin had initially been adamant to resist committing to an ideology. A possible explanation for his aversion to ideology was the memory of the constraining impact of Marxism that obstructed Moscow from pursuing its national interests. In the 1990s, it had become evident that pursuing national interests to deliver tangible goods to the population and strengthen Russia in the international system was imperative to survive as a state.

Albeit, as Russia stabilised and recovered, Putin recognised the value of ideology. Ideologies are helpful to formulate a common political language, a unifying national idea, and a social contract, and to mobilise the public. The absence of political ideology and reliance on pure pragmatism to advance national interests diminishes soft power (Rutland and Kazantsev 2016: 400). From the early 2000s, Russia began leaning towards a "third way", an older tradition of liberal conservatism (Sakwa 2002: 460). Other forces emerged that pushed Russia in a conservative direction. In 2003, the conservative Motherland Movement, founded by Sergei Glazyev and Dmitri Rogozin, won an unexpected victory in the 2003 elections. The defeat of the liberals marked an important victory for conservatism. Yet, advancing Russia will eventually require establishing a common cause with liberals to prevent the polarisation of Russia.

Putin can be compared to liberal-conservatives such as Boris Chicherin, Semyon Frank and Peter Struve. Chicherin's theory that a strong central government was required to advance gradual liberal reforms and advance the rule of law is especially a trait of Putin. Once becoming president, Putin famously declared that he would establish a "dictatorship of law". This was achieved by centralising power to constrain and defeat the criminal oligarchs and radical opposition that had festered during the chaos of the 1990s (Gill 2006). By 2011, the gravitation towards a conservative political economy became more evident as Putin (2011a) took the central stage in celebrating and quoting Pyotr Stolypin: "Give Russia 20 years of internal and external peace and quiet and it will change beyond recognition". Putin has supported gradual and evolutionary socio-economic reforms and modernisation, and sternly rejected disruptive revolutionary change (Polyakov 2015).

Putin has been directly involved in erecting statues of Russian historical figures in Moscow and across the country. Statues of Vladimir the Great, Ivan the Terrible, Alexander II, Pyotr Stolypin, Alexander III and other Russian leaders tend to spark a national conversation and awareness of Russian history. In 2005, the remains of Ivan Ilyin and the White Army General Anton Denki were returned to Russia and reburied in the famous Donskoy Monastery in Moscow. Putin had arranged and attended the reburial and personally paid for the renovation of Ilyin's tomb. Restoration of statues, churches and advocacy of conservative philosophy indicates that the state strongly believes that Russia needs to know its past to have a future.

From Putin's third term in 2012, his conservative leanings became more profound, and speeches expressed the value of faith and tradition. In a 2013 interview, Putin defined himself as a pragmatic conservative:

> I think it is perfectly possible to say that I am a pragmatist with a conservative bent. . . . Conservatism certainly does not mean stagnation. Conservatism means reliance on traditional values but with a necessary additional element aimed at development. It seems to me that this is an absolutely essential thing. And as a rule the situation in the world, in almost every country, is such that conservatives gather the resources, the funds, and the potential for economic growth. Then the revolutionaries come along and they destroy all this one way or another. (Polyakov 2015: 6)

Putin (2013a) argued that Russian conservatism was not about nostalgia or preventing modernisation, rather "speaking in the words of Nikolai Berdyaev, the point of conservatism is not that it prevents movement forward and upward, but that it prevents movement backward and downward, into chaotic darkness and a return to a primitive state". A conservative political economy also appears to be in the making. Putin (2013a) cautions against unfettered markets and economic determinism as a strain on the collective and sustainable growth:

After all, in the end, economic growth, prosperity and geopolitical influence are all derived from societal conditions. They depend on whether the citizens of a given country consider themselves a nation, to what extent they identify with their own history, values and traditions, and whether they are united by common goals and responsibilities. In this sense, the question of finding and strengthening national identity really is fundamental for Russia.

The caution against returning to a primitive state resembles the warnings of Plato that the excesses of democracy and liberty eventually deconstruct society. Plato argued that liberty has no limits, and will continuously seek to liberate the individual from all external authorities that define the collective. Liberty eventually dismantles societal institutions as "the son is on a level with his father, he having no respect or reverence for either of his parents; and this is his freedom. . . . Citizens chafe impatiently at the least touch of authority" (Plato 2008: 216). Contemporary liberals strive towards equity by elevating the interests of ethnic, religious, gender and sexual minorities, which undermines the central features of the majority that defines the common and unifying history, tradition and faith of the nation. A durable conception of democracy must be conservative that "does now allow the minority to trample down and dishonour everything that is dear to the majority" (Narochnitskaya 2014). Similar sentiments were also expressed by President Putin (2013b), who advocated rolling back the excesses of liberalism:

> Without the values embedded in Christianity and other world religions, without standards of morality that have taken shape over millennia, people will inevitably lose their human dignity. We consider it natural and right to defend these values. One must respect every minority's right to be different, but the rights of the majority must not be put into question.

Putin (2013b) also criticised the cultural and moral relativism advanced by excessive liberalism:

> Today, many nations are revising their moral values and ethical norms, eroding ethnic traditions and differences between peoples and cultures. Society is now required not only to recognise everyone's right to the freedom of consciousness, political views and privacy, but also to accept without question the equality of good and evil, strange as it seems, concepts that are opposite in meaning.

These ideas were formalised into Russia's official document on the *Foundations of the State Cultural Policy* of 2014, which stated that "Russia must be viewed as a unique and original civilization", which requires "the rejection of such principles as multiculturalism and tolerance" for those "imposing alien values on society". In 2014, the Kremlin distributed three conservative books to senior officials: Nikolai Berdyaev's *Philosophy of Inequality*, Ivan Ilyin's *Our Tasks* and Vladimir Solovyov's *The Justification of the Good*.

THE REVOLUTIONARY CENTURY IN THE CONTEXT OF A THOUSAND YEARS OF HISTORY

The turbulent and divisive twentieth century is easier to absorb into the national consciousness and identity if it is placed within the wider unifying narrative of Russia's thousand-year-long history. Contemporary Russian conservatives are faced with the challenge of establishing continuity in its revolutionary and disruptive history, which demands nothing less than constructing a bridge between the ideas and norms of Kievan Rus, the Russian Empire, the

Soviet Union and the Russian Federation. The long historical memory assists in unifying contemporary Russia with the shared consciousness and morality of the transcendental values.

The Kremlin supports the restoration of grand narratives about the history, soul and identity of Russia to use the common past to navigate into the future. Historical continuity is vital that harmonises the past with a forward-looking vision for the future. The pressing need to modernise requires Russia to remake traditions and rural values in the new forms of urban society (Remizov 2010). Yet, without a past, Russia risks being without a future. In the tradition of Catherine the Great to Sergei Uvarov, the education system is central to reforms. The dual role of history is recognised by the education system, which should educate the new generations of the past and also instil patriotism.

Putin (2012) cautioned that Russia had to overcome the narrow historical memory centred on the Soviet and post-Soviet history as "Russia did not begin in 1917 or 1991". Reviving Russia's pre-communist ideas and historical memory is imperative as Russia cannot "resurrect her civic self-consciousness unless it understands that the country's history enjoys one thousand years of historic development" (Putin 2012). The twentieth century had been brutal for Russian organic development due to the collapse of the state in both 1917 and 1991, which caused a loss in the historical continuity and national spirit (Putin 2013b).

The state initiates symbols and traditions to revive the historical memory of Russia. Case in point, the commemoration of the October Revolution was replaced with National Unity Day in 2005, which celebrates the defeat of Polish-Lithuanian occupation forces from Moscow in November 1612 and thus ending the Time of Troubles.

Reviving the historical legacy of Kievan Rus creates ambiguous relations with Belarus and Ukraine. Elevating the significance of Russia as the successor state of Kievan Rus is feared to de-legitimise a separate history and identity of Ukraine and Belarus, and suggests that their natural state is in union with Russia (Wanner 2010). Solzhenitsyn (1998) similarly cautioned against the complexities in the national question: "It is useless to tell Ukrainians that we all descended, by birth and spiritually, from Kiev, and it is just as useless to expect Russians to recognise the fact that people beyond the Dnieper River are different".

The Russian Orthodox Church remains a major unifying conservative institution that has had a central stage throughout Russian history. Conservatism builds legitimacy by linking the past to the future, and the Orthodox Church became an increasingly important institution to restore the necessary continuity in the national identity, and revive spirituality. The Church makes statements that adhere to the idea that Russian civilisation has a special role in the world, the community is recognised as indispensable, and the excesses of liberalism are in no uncertain terms frowned upon.

The Orthodox Church also has a central role in restoring law and order. Conservatism does not aim to restore order by solely banning immoral and destructive behaviour as it represents a form of external compulsion. Rather, conservatism aims to foment the values and morals of people to enable the practice of restraint as an internal compulsion. For example, conservatives are often inclined towards banning abortion, although the reliance on state coercion will only push the practice underground if the law is deemed to be illegitimate. It is therefore imperative to gradually build moral codes that reject killing unborn babies as the ban on abortion would be built on the moral codes of society.

Religious practices and church attendance faltered during the communist era, and the state now zealously supports the revival of the Orthodox Church. Russian society is increasingly filled with Orthodox symbols, traditions and popular rituals such as swimming in icy rivers on the day of Epiphany to mark the baptism of Jesus. While church attendance is still low, Orthodox traditions are gradually seeping into everyday life and culture. Furthermore, the number of parishes in the Russian Orthodox Church increased gradually from 7,000 in 1992 to 38,000 in 2019. In 1931, one of the most iconic and majestic Cathedrals in Russia, the *Cathedral of Christ the Savior*, was destroyed and replaced with a swimming pool on the order of Stalin. By 2000, the Cathedral had been rebuilt.

In the late 1990s, approximately half of adult Russian citizens identified as Orthodox Christians, and since the 2000s, this number has increased to 70–75 per cent (Friedrich-Ebert-Stiftung 2020: 121). For many Russians, affiliation with the Orthodox Church has been an issue of identity rather than spirituality, although spirituality may follow as church attendance has been growing steadily. Young Russians, twenty-five to twenty-nine years old, are more likely to identify as Orthodox Christians and the spiritual interest appears to correlate with the establishment of families.

CONSERVATIVES SALVAGING PARTS OF THE REVOLUTIONARY SOVIET LEGACY

How do conservatives respond to revolutionary periods of their history? Organic change is imperative, and revolution is therefore the antithesis to conservatism. However, eliminating seven decades of communist history from the national memory and consciousness is similarly a revolutionary act. Much like nineteenth-century conservatives such as Grigoryev and Dostoyevsky sought to harmonise pre-Petrine and post-Petrine Russia to form a unifying national narrative, Moscow now has to harmonise pre-Soviet, Soviet and post-Soviet ideas and identities.

Following the collapse of the Soviet Union, some conservative ideas appear to have shaped decisions as Russia abandoned Marxist ideology but preserved some of the symbols for continuity. The national symbols of independent Russia included both Soviet and Imperial Russian components. The Russian Federation introduced the double-headed eagle as its coats of arms that built on the former imperial coats of arms abolished following the Bolshevik Revolution. However, the red star of the communists is still commonly used as a national symbol. Likewise, the melody of the Soviet anthem has been kept, albeit the lyrics were altered.

A key challenge for Russian conservatism is to respond to the decadence under the Soviet Union and the liberal revolution of the 1990s, and assess what could be salvaged (Remizov 2010). Preserving the distinctive traditions of Russia and not succumbing to universalism also required salvaging some of the social policies, ideals and achievements from the Soviet period. Reinventing post-communist society becomes problematic as the period was an extreme aberration in Russian history and there is not much of the experience that could be salvaged.

The Soviet Union industrialised rapidly and achieved technological sovereignty. Russia still benefits from technological sovereignty in areas such as space exploration and its weapon industry. However, technological sovereignty came at a heavy cost due to the economic inefficiency of the Soviet system and the decoupling from Western markets. Furthermore, the victory in the Second World War was an important achievement that continues to shape the national identity, which Russians paid for with an untold human cost.

The conservative inclination towards salvaging something from the Soviet Union has also given impetus to revive Eurasianism. The Soviet Union as radical left-wing Eurasianism has Eurasian features that can be salvaged to support conservative Eurasianism. Russia can also claim ownership of the rise of Eurasia. Karaganov (2020) argues that the Soviet Union was central to decolonisation and it mid-wifed the rise of Asia by depriving the West of the ability to impose its will on the world through military force, which the West had done from the sixteenth century until the 1940s.

Conservatives zealously opposed communism, although it would not be feasible for Moscow to confess, denounce and repent for all the crimes of the Soviet Union to the extent of post-war Germany. Condemning decades of Russian history is destructive, as Russia cannot start writing its own history from a blank piece of paper. Moscow has thus taken a nuanced approach to deal with Soviet crimes as opposed to the West's push for a blanket condemnation of the entire Soviet history. The achievements of the Bolshevik Revolution are upheld, yet the betrayal of the people is condemned.

Subsequently, religious institutions are offered special protection and support due to the suppression by the communist authorities.

Most importantly, Moscow identifies the culprit and victims of the crimes committed. Culprits of the worst crimes are recognised to be Stalin, and the people who suffered most from his reign were the Russian people. During the Cold War, Solzhenitsyn advocated that the term and characterisation of "captive nation" by the United States should also be applied to the Russian nation as it suffered like the nations under communist rule. Moscow's denunciations of Stalin increased from 2007 as Russia strengthened its internal cohesion and the confidence of the Kremin grew. The Russian leadership, including Putin, have on many occasions condemned the crimes of Stalin and constructed a memorial to his victims. In 2009, Putin also denounced the Molotov-Ribbentrop Pact as immoral. The Orthodox Church also became vocal in denouncing Stalin as a "spiritually-deformed monster" (Sherlock 2011: 98).

A nuanced approach was also developed to deal with foreign powers such as Poland. Yeltsin has opened the Soviet archives in 1990 that confirmed Soviet culpability for the killings of Polish officers in the Katyn forest, which Moscow condemned as a horrible Stalinist crime. Putin even stood alongside the Polish Prime Minister, Donald Tusk, in March 2010 in commemoration of the Katyn massacre as an effort to heal the wounds of the past and find some reconciliation.

Managing historical narratives was also imperative in the post-Soviet space as it laid the foundation for the present. Following the collapse of the Soviet Union, Posen (1993: 39) cautioned that against blaming Russia for Stalinist crimes and failed policies in Ukraine:

> If Ukraine begins to blame the famine on Russians, this could be quite dangerous politically. If, instead, the famine continues to be blamed on a Communist Party headed by a renegade Georgian psychopath, then this experience will cause less trouble.

REINVENTING THE IDEOLOGICAL DIVIDE: LIBERALISM VERSUS CONSERVATISM

The liberal inclinations of the West culminated in a lack of empathy for Russia's conservative path and the efforts to salvage parts of the Soviet legacy to be included in the national identity. Russia's reluctance to condemn and repudiate its entire Soviet history is commonly depicted in the West as an effort to whitewash Stalin. In reality, the Russian government is rehabilitating the public image of conservatives, the White Russians and the Tsarist history that had tarnished by the communists.

The West has been re-interpreting history to fit liberal ideology and the power structures it sustains. In the early years of the Cold War, the US government deliberately used the label "totalitarianism" to propagandise the similarities between the Soviet Union and Nazi Germany, and neglect the differences, for the purpose of transferring the hatred of Nazi Germany to Soviet Union (Adler and Paterson 1970). Case in point, the shared Second World War narrative focusing on the collective victory over fascism is rewritten by the EU by reframing it as a conflict between liberalism and totalitarianism. This tactic has again been picked up by both Washington and Brussels. In 2008, Brussel passed a resolution that equated Nazi Germany with the Soviet Union (European Parliament 2008). The EU's decision to attack the key historical event of the Russian collective consciousness was reasoned with support for the liberal order as the historical revisionism would contribute to "rooting democracy more firmly and reinforcing peace and stability in our continent" (European Parliament 2008). In 2019, the EU went even further by passing a resolution that blamed both the Soviet Union and Nazi Germany for the outbreak of the Second World War due to the Molotov-Ribbentrop Pact.

The politicisation of history neglected the West refused to establish an alliance with the Soviet Union against Nazi Germany. Instead, the West appeased Germany in Munich in what Moscow believed was designed to direct German troops towards the Soviet Union, which became a key reason for Moscow to sign its own agreement with Germany. The former UK prime minister Stanley Baldwin is even recorded professing his hope that the Nazis and Soviets would destroy each other (Hitchens 1999: 158). The Molotov-Ribbentrop Pact of 1939 aimed to achieve the same as the Rapallo Treaty of 1922, to prevent Western European maritime power from provoking a clash between two major Eurasian land powers. The efforts to denigrate Russia's dominant role in the defeat of fascism caused a retreat from seeking a middle ground, and the Kremin is instead casting blame on countries such as Poland for emboldening the antisemitism of the Nazis, making its own deal with Hitler and annexing territory from Czechoslovakia after Munich.

Effort in the West to criminalise Soviet history is instrumental to sever the common history between Russia and its neighbours and erect new ideological dividing lines to replace the communist-capitalist divide. President Medvedev argued that Russia had to oppose attempts by the West to rewrite and criminalise Russian and Soviet history, and even constructed a commission to "counter attempts to falsify history to the detriment of Russia" (Russian Federation 2009). Putin (2020) made a conservative argument against the West's re-writing of history: "This is the memory march that symbolizes our gratitude, as well as the living connection and the blood ties between generations". The German foreign minister Haiko Maas (2020) recognised that resentment towards Russia lingered in Central and Eastern

Europe as Soviet liberation was followed by another form of subjugation. However, Mass (2020) nonetheless criticised the anti-Russian historical revisionism of the West:

> The repeated attempts in recent months to rewrite history so disgracefully requires is to speak up loud and clear – something that should not actually be necessary in view of irrefutable historical facts – and to leave no doubt whatsoever that Germany alone unleashed the Second World War.

The West and Russia have gradually "othered" each other in terms of ideology as each side reinvents themselves in opposition to the other. The West reaffirmed its liberal virtues in direct opposition to an anti-liberal strawman identity that was assigned to Russia. For example, in the run-up to the 2014 Sochi Olympics, the West celebrated its tolerance towards homosexuality by chastising Russian "anti-gay laws" and even partially boycotting the event. The ideological othering of Moscow neglected that Russia does not criminalise homosexuality, unlike more than eighty countries in the world that included India and other states that would not be reprimanded similarly. The new ideological divide between the West and Russia is harmful as it pushes each side to an extreme. Liberalism and conservatism are contradictory, yet they balance each other to position the state and society between stasis and transformation.

POST-IMPERIAL CONSERVATISM: DEFENDING "ISLAND RUSSIA"

Conservatism in Russia has historically been challenged by the continuous impulse for expansion. The open Eurasian geography without natural defences has made control over the periphery and gradual expansion a defensive strategy, and the vast expanse made it possible to absorb invading forces and cut off their supply chains. Yet, continuous expansion created even longer and less defendable borders. Russian security considerations altered as its security was increasingly based on hegemony in Eurasia, and thus attracting the unwanted attention of Britain and then the United States. From a conservative perspective, the continued expansion of borders altered the ethno-cultural make-up of Russia and even civic ideals. However, the continuous frontier also instilled a sense of purpose.

The Russian Federation in the twenty-first century no longer has the potential to dominate the Eurasian landmass. The conservatism Russia, while divided by various strands, leans primarily towards cementing the transition from an empire to a civilisation state. Post-imperial Russia had to make its peace with existing borders, while recognising that Russia is not a traditional Westphalian state as ethnic, cultural and historical bonds cross the newly established borders. Influential Russian moderates such as Sergei Karaganov and Andranik Migranyan argued in 1992 in favour of a middle road to avoid instigating tensions. They argued that borders should not be changed based on ethnicity or language, although it was incumbent upon the United States and the West to recognise that Russia has "vitally important interests" in the post-Soviet space (Tolz 1998: 1002).

Russia began inventing a conservative identity for itself from the early 2000s by propagating the ideas of Russian World (Russki Mir) to address the complex history of the region that cannot be delineated with clear-cut national borders. The Kremlin advocated the concept of a Russian World that is tied together by a shared history, culture, orthodox faith and use of the Russian language. The focus on linguistics is not unique to Russia as British conservatives tend to seek unity and common purpose with the English-speaking world (Hannan 2013), while France efforts to maintain its influence in Africa largely centres of promoting the continued use of the French language. The Russian World aimed to strike a balance between the distinctive and the universal. The ideas built on nineteenth- and twentieth-century Russian conservative ideas of Danilevsky, Leontiev, Berdyaev, Ilyin and others.

These ideas have influenced post-imperial Russian policy, which has neither the intention nor the capacity to dominate its external periphery. Even the Central Asian states cautiously diversify their economic connectivity to avoid excessive reliance on Russia. The implication of Russia's smaller power status is a break in its long foreign policy tradition. In the absence of hegemony, power maximisation does not equate to security maximisation. Ensuring stability in Central Asia requires the development of security architecture and a geoeconomic region in cooperation with other large powers.

The civilisational state had strong similarities with the influential *Island Theory* by Vadim Tsymbursky (1993) that emerged in the early 1990s. Tsymbursky's theory called for Russia to establish itself as an island state to overcome the history of security through expansion. The loss of territory created a long belt of weaker states that did not pose a threat and thus recasting Russia as a virtual island – Estonia, Latvia, Lithuania, Belarus, Ukraine and Moldova were positioned along the western border; Georgia Armenia and Azerbaijan along its south-western borders; and Kazakhstan, Uzbekistan, Kyrgyzstan, Tajikistan and Turkmenistan shielding Russia's southern borders.

An immense opportunity arose from yet again being disconnected from Europe and return to its natural condition on the Eurasian steppes. The geographical distance from the West would enable Russia to end its fixation on either emulating the West or building its organic identity in opposition to the West. Furthermore, constructing Russia as a virtual island without any pressing external threats would enable Russia to relax its foreign policy and direct its resources to domestic development (Tsymbursky 1993). The popular vision for a new future reversed the historical impulse of expanding to augment security, as this would merely place Russia closer to Western powers. Tsymbursky (1993) cautioned that if the West would intrude upon the Island Russia by expanding into Ukraine, then Russia should intervene and establish the regions east of the Dnieper River as independent states. A great challenge would then be to not succumb to imperial impulses by absorbing these regions into Russia as it would merely move Russia closer to the West. Instead, Russia should enforce the independence of neighbouring states as a buffer against the West.

Western expansion to the east with the EU and NATO encroached on Island Russia and necessitated a response. Simply cementing Russian control over the periphery is not even a possibility as the shared neighbourhood is divided between either integrating only with the West by decoupling from Russia, or finding a balance between the West and Russia. Moscow demanded a halt to Western expansionism and neutrality is therefore the only policy available. Russia therefore advocates a neutral belt of states that neither side will dominate (Diesen 2020b). The EU-Russia Common Spaces Agreement of 2005 committed both sides to "promote [regional cooperation and integration] in a mutually beneficial manner, through close result-oriented EU-Russia collaboration and dialogue, thereby contributing effectively to creating a greater Europe without dividing lines and based on common values" (Kremlin 2005).

Consistent with the agreement of a belt of neutral states, Moscow announced that the concept of *spheres of influence* was replaced with *spheres of interests*. Spheres of influence denote an exclusive of dominant Russian influence in its neighbouring states. The concept of spheres of interests suggests that recognition by other great powers for Russia's legitimate security interests in its immediate neighbourhood, which must be taken into account when engaging with states along its borders (Trenin 2009). Russia demands that foreign powers recognise the complex human, economic, political, historical and security links between the states in the post-Soviet space. Russia does not demand dominance of exclusive influence, yet the zero-sum initiatives that cement Western spheres of influence are not accepted under the concept of spheres of interests. Foreign Minister Sergei Lavrov (2008a) argued that "we cannot agree when attempts are being made to pass off the historically conditioned mutually privileged relations between the states in the former Soviet expanse as a 'sphere of influence'".

The Ukraine crisis of 2014 was caused by an infringement on Island Russia as the West supported a coup that was linked to severing relations with Russia and pivoting to the West. The zero-sum approach to European integration and support for nationalising the Russian Orthodox Church in

Ukraine are seen as efforts to make Ukraine into an anti-Russian bastion, another Poland.

The Ukraine crisis brought the unresolved and divided elements of the question of Russia. If Russia was a part of Europe, why should it resist Western expansionism to the East? The nationalists and imperialists were divided in terms of Russia's position towards Ukraine. The imperialists believed that bringing Ukraine back into the Russian fold was necessary to restore Russian greatness. By contrast, the nationalists argued in favour of defending and incorporating ethnic Russians that were suppressed by Ukraine. The nationalists only wanted Crimea as the holy land of Russia and an imperative to maintain a formidable maritime corridor in the Black Sea (Lukyanov 2014). The historical accident of losing the peninsula, strong cultural ties, ethnic composition and clear geographical delineation of Crimea ensured that it did not establish a precedent.

Putin leaned towards the nationalists by only laying claim to Crimea, and with the future option of supporting independent regions in eastern Ukraine if the West continues its incursion. Putin (2014a) issued what could be interpreted as a stern warning following the Maidan coup in 2014 and Russia's subsequent reunification with Crimea:

> After the revolution, the Bolsheviks, for a number of reasons, may God judge them, added large sections of the historical South of Russia to the Republic of Ukraine. This was done with no consideration for the ethnic make-up of the population, and today these areas form the southeast of Ukraine.

CONCLUSION

Modern Russian conservatism has to reinvent itself as Russia and its position in the world has undergone a fundamental change over the past century of revolutions. Russia is no longer burdened with empire and conservatives are tasked with transitioning towards a civilisation state. Conservatives therefore lean towards concepts such as the *Russian World* that supports the preservation of existing international borders, yet recognises ethnic, cultural, historic and religious ties. Russia has also shed the autocracy and is experimenting with democratic governance that adapts to its distinctive, geography, history and traditions. Instead of merely preserving its historical memory and religion, Russia must rediscover and revive the pre-Soviet history and the societal role of the Orthodox Church. Furthermore, Soviet history itself must be incorporated into the national narrative. The continuity in Russian conservatism is the mutual othering of the West. Much like in the early nineteenth century, the export of the West's liberal revolutionary movements shapes Russian conservativism as an ideological balance.

Chapter 9

The End of the Occidental Era and the Birth of Greater Eurasia

INTRODUCTION

Russian conservatism is undergoing drastic change as a Eurasian political economy is emerging. Russian conservatism has historically struggled with the inability to balance continuity and change. The subsequent curse has been stagnation until Russia is compelled to periodically catch-up with the West with rapid, disruptive and even revolutionary change. The failure to pursue organic change by balance preservation with modernisation is largely caused by Russia's geography. The geographical manifestation of gemeinschaft and gesellschaft as an Eastern versus Western identity and outlook has been the source an imbalance and fierce pendulum swings throughout Russian history.

The development of Eurasianism has gradually developed economic viability. During the rule of Paul I at the turn of the nineteenth century, a Eurasian strategy emerged to conquer British India by land to circumvent Britain's economic-military supremacy by ruling the seas. In the 1860s and 1870s, Eurasianism was revived in a geoeconomic format. Russia endeavoured to establish direct physical trade links with India and relied on railroads to incrementally cemented its control over Central Asia. The Russian Trans-Caspian railway in the 1880s pushed south towards India in what became known as the Russian-British Great Game. By the 1890s, Russian railroads similarly connected European Russia with the Pacific Coast in what was feared by the British to threaten its global power based on control over the seas.

The Eurasianism of Trubetskoi and Savitsky in the 1920s builds on key ideas from Mackinder's Heartland Theory that viewed geostrategic rivalry primarily as a struggle between maritime powers and land-powers. However, the conflict took on primarily a militarised format during the Cold War. Following the Second World War, the United States replaced Britain's rule of the world's seas and established land-based military forward deployments on the Western (Western Europe), Eastern (Eastern Asia) and Southern (Middle East) inner periphery of the Eurasian continent.

After the Cold War and the failed endeavour to construct Greater Europe with the West, Russia began a pivot to Asia to construct a Greater Eurasia. The Eurasian continent has two geoeconomic centres of power, Europe and East Asia. Russia's Greater Eurasia concept aims to connect Europe and Asia economically into one supercontinent and thus transition away from the dual periphery of these centres of power and towards the centre of a new regional construct.

From a conservative perspective, the political economy of Greater Eurasia enables Russia to overcome its historical obsession with the West and establish an organic Russian path to modernisation. Control over strategic industries, transportation corridors and financial instruments insulates Russia from foreign influence and instead promotes Russian leadership on the global stage. Furthermore, infrastructure projects to connect European Russia with Siberia and Pacific Russia are also imperative to unite the large territory.

This chapter first defines the concept of industrialised conservative political economy. Conservatism has instinctively hostile roots towards liberal economics and industrialisation as it tears away at traditions, family values and gemeinschaft-based communities. Yet, economic stagnation and industrial infancy merely result in excessive dependence on foreign powers to the extent political independence and cultural sovereignty cannot be sustained. The middle-road is economic nationalism that ensures the key economic infrastructure is incorporated into nation-building.

Second, the political economy of conservative Eurasianism builds is defined here has economic nationalism applied to Halford Mackinder's Heartland Theory. The historical struggle between continental powers and maritime powers as outlined by Mackinder is fundamentally shaken by the rise of Asia and "the rest", which subsequently also alters the concept of Eurasianism. Strong incentives are emerging to construct a Eurasian political economy that makes Russia's geography an asset rather than a vulnerability.

Third, the geoeconomics of Greater Eurasia seeks to rewire global value chains and challenge the Western-centric organisation of the international economy. Cooperation between Russia and China is established in all three geoeconomic pillars of powers: strategic industries / technological platforms, transportation corridors and financial instruments.

It is concluded that Russia's geoeconomic strategy for Greater Eurasia can establish an organic path to development that builds a competitive economic model based on Russia's unique traditions and institutions.

THE FAILED POLITICAL ECONOMY
OF GREATER EUROPE

The political economy of Greater Europe was flawed contributing to unfavourable asymmetrical interdependence with the West, and the need to remake Russia as a Western European maritime power.

Yeltsin's rush to the West caused the neglect of relationships in the East as Moscow feared close relations with Central Asia and even China could slow down the pivot to Europe (Tsygankov 2006: 58). Yeltsin's leaning-to-one-side policy had the opposite effect as an asymmetrical interdependent partnership developed due to the excessive economic dependence on the collective West as a more powerful partner (Cheng 2009: 127). Subsequently, the West had strong incentives to exclude Russia from key institutions and instead engage Russia in asymmetrical formats where the West maximises its collective bargaining power against Russia that stands alone. The West was "Russia's only choice – even if tactical – thus provided the West with a strategic opportunity. It created the preconditions for the progressive geopolitical expansion of the Western community deeper and deeper into Eurasia" (Brzezinski 2009: 102). Russia's significance in the world was subsequently expected to wither away as it became a geostrategic "black hole" at the periphery of both Europe and Asia (Brzezinski 1997: 87).

Yeltsin eventually recognised the need to diversify Russia's partnerships to reduce dependence on an expansionist West. In the 1980s, Moscow had feared long-term threats emerging from the south and east rather than the West, although NATO expansion "pushes Russia towards China instead of drawing Russia towards Europe and America" (Waltz 2000: 30). Yeltsin replaced the liberal prime minister Andrei Kozyrev with the conservative Eurasianist Yevgeny Primakov, who advocated defending Russia's distinctiveness by looking to the east. Yeltsin also appeared to drift towards a new civilizational strategy after recognising that his neo-Petrine policies had failed. Yeltsin proclaimed Russia had to take a step away from the West: "After all, we are a Eurasian state" (Tsygankov 2006: 66). Russia's National Security Concept of 1997 identified Russia as an "influential European and Asian power". However, Primakov's Eurasianism was ahead of its time as it did not have the political economy behind it. Primakov advocated for a Moscow-Beijing-New Delhi alliance, although its partners neither had the capacity nor intention to challenge the Western-centric global economy. Primakov's Eurasianism was also feared to instigate conflict with a powerful and unified West.

Russia's aspirations to merely be a "normal European power" was reversed as NATO expansion fuelled a new consensus in Moscow that Russia was destined to remain a great power (Pouliot 2010: 179). Left outside Europe, it was recognised that Russia would need great power capabilities to ensure it could uphold an independent foreign policy and resist the intrusive influence by the West. Kozyrev similarly argued already in March 1994 that Russia was "doomed to be a great power" as "some people in the West have succumbed to the fantasy that a partnership can be built with Russia on the principle of 'if the Russians are good guys now, they should follow us in every way'" (Pouliot 2010: 178).

Primakov later argued that Russia's great power status was a historical mission that Russia yet again had the responsibility to take upon itself, not as an empire but as "the holder of international equilibrium of power" (Tsygankov 2006: 71). While Russia was too large to be included in a wider West, it would succumb on the outside if it remained too weak. Putin summarised his thoughts on the topic by arguing: "Either Russia will be great or it will not be at all" (Shevtsova 2003: 175). Putin sought to integrate with Europe from a position of strength to ensure equality. As late as January 2014, a month before the coup in Ukraine, Moscow was advocating a Greater Europe consisting of a free-trade zone from Lisbon to Vladivostok (Putin 2014b).

After the Western-backed coup in Ukraine in 2014, Moscow largely reached a consensus that the gradual integration into the West had been a dangerous illusion and the Greater Europe initiative had to be declared dead. Even the former Russian foreign minister Igor Ivanov who had been an ardent supporter of Greater Europe, announced it had been a failure. Ivanov (2015) instead threw his support for Greater Eurasia as Moscow set its eyes on the East: "Russia is no longer the eastern flank of the failed Greater Europe and is becoming the western flank of the emerging Greater Eurasia".

It was widely expected in the West that the post–Cold War generation of young Russians would view the West more favourably. However, the young Russians growing up under liberal internationalism and NATO expansionism have adopted a very sceptical view of the West. Polling data from 2020 by the Levada Center and the Fredrich Ebert Foundation reveal that only 35 per cent of young Russians consider Russia to be a European country. And 58 per cent either disagreed or strongly disagreed with the statement that Russia is a European country. Despite not having grown up during the Cold War, the young Russians are more sceptical of the United States and distrust NATO more than any other international organisation. The expectation of continued division and bellicosity is evident as 42 per cent believe that relations with the West "will always be marked by mistrust" (Friedrich-Ebert-Stiftung 2020).

THE POLITICAL ECONOMY OF EURASIANISM

Does Eurasia represent an economically backward initiative or a geoeconomic project to revolutionise global power? Russia was for centuries cut off from the main maritime corridors and became economically backward as a land-based power. Obtaining access to the Volga, the Baltic Sea and the Black Sea required conflict. However, as its territory expanded, it began reaching the periphery of Eurasia and connect it with infrastructure, Russia could reorganise global power politics. By the mid-seventeenth century, Russia was approaching Chinese borders, and in 1689 Russia had reached the Bering Strait. In 1689, Russia and China signed the Treaty of Nerchinsk, which established their first common border.

The Eurasianism of Trubetskoi and Savitsky appears to be strongly influenced by the ideas of Halford Mackinder concept of the Eurasian Heartland. The curse of Russian history was diagnosed as attempting to modernise along the line of Western European maritime powers, which made the Eurasian geography of Russia a weakness. The Eurasian political economy aimed to embrace Russia's Eurasian distinctiveness and develop a political economy accordingly. Savitsky argued that maritime powers had a proclivity towards imperialism. A self-sufficient Eurasian continental market was the solution to imperialism and slavery.

Savitsky explained the First World War and largely predicted the Second World War in 1919 as he argued the maritime containment of land-powers would push Germany to expand eastwards. Savitsky believed, in the Mackinder tradition, that alignment with Germany was the best option for Russia as continental powers must align their interests to balance oceanic powers.

Mackinder, representing the interests of the main oceanic power of his time, advocated that Britain should construct a European security structure that facilitates zero-sum interests between Germany and Russia to prevent cooperation. Yet, Germany and Soviet Russia reached an agreement with the Treaty of Rapallo already in 1922 that denounced all territorial and financial claims. In his paper, "Geographical and Geopolitical Foundations of Eurasianism", Savitsky (1997) argued that Russia was the true "Middle Kingdom" that could bring together Eurasia to oppose oceanic imperialism.

The three great Eurasian powers, the Scythians, Huns and Mongols, had all destabilised and fragmented as they had not reached and controlled the maritime borders of Eurasia. The fourth great Eurasian power, the Russian Empire and the Soviet successor, drew strength from the same Eurasian systemic incentives or geostrategic "rhythms". Yet, the Soviet Union was also destined to also stagnate, fragment and collapse unless it could reach the Eurasian maritime borders.

Russia's long history of moving towards European maritime corridors as the arteries of international commerce and military strength. However, as its control over the Eurasian landmass increased, Russia began reaching the maritime periphery of the Eurasian supercontinent. George Kennan (1951: 5) repeated Mackinder's warnings about Russian land power over Eurasia: "No single Continental land power should come to dominate the entire Eurasian land mass" as it would lead "on an overseas expansion hostile to ourselves and supported by the immense resources of the interior of Europe and Asia".

In *Exodus to the East*, Savitsky (1996) argued that maritime transportation made geography a central component for economic advancements. Since Peter the Great, the British had pushed back against Russia's efforts to establish itself as an Oceanic economy. Savitsky believed that Russia should recognise its continental geography and adapt to it by constructing a self-sufficient continental economy. Attempting to compete for maritime corridors placed Russia at a disadvantage against the Europeans. By contrast, the political economy of Eurasia strives towards using the Eurasian geography as a competitive advantage and not a handicap (Savitsky 1921).

THE COLD WAR GEOPOLITICS OF
THE EURASIAN HEARTLAND

Mackinder's view of competition over Eurasia had been preoccupied with both economic connectivity and military power. The rule of maritime powers, either British or American, depends on preventing one Eurasian land power from establishing hegemony or an alliance of Eurasian land-powers from establishing collective rule over Eurasia.

The analytical framework addressed the British-Russian rivalry that had continued throughout the nineteenth century and into the twentieth century. Mackinder's Heartland Theory had a geoeconomic vector as railways were feared to negate the significance of maritime power in international commerce. During the Cold War, the Heartland Theory remained influential, although the United States had displaced Britain, and it took on a more militaristic approach as the Soviet Union relied less on economic statecraft.

Spykman (1942) developed the "Rimland Theory" as an extension of Mackinder's Heartland Theory. His ideas became very influential to the point that the US strategy was referred to as the Spykman-Kennan thesis of containment (Parker 1985). The dominance of maritime powers would be preserved with "forward deployments" in the coastal periphery of Eurasia – Western Europe, East Asia and the Middle East. Spykman (1942: 182) posited that it was the historical responsibility of the United States to encircle and contain Russia:

> For two hundred years, since the time of Peter the Great, Russia has attempted to break through the encircling ring of border states and the reach the ocean. Geography and sea power have persistently thwarted her.

The ideas of Mackinder and Spykman were preceded by the influential work of Alfred Thayer Mahan in the 1890s, an influential US Navy Admiral. In *The Influence of Sea Power upon History*, Mahan's (2013) advocated for the United States to establish itself as a sea power like the British Empire to dominate international commerce. Mahan depicted the United States as a continent-sized island relying on sea power to maintain a balance of power in Europe and Asia to prevent any one state or group of states from challenging the United States. A powerful US navy, in partnership with the UK, was deemed to be imperative to contain the Western maritime edges of the Eurasian continent (Mahan 2013). Spykman (2008: 470) advocated that the United States "will have to adopt a similar protective policy toward Japan" to preserve a balance of power in the Far East to preclude the rise of China.

The US offshore strategy as a maritime power had the key objective of ensuring that a hegemon did not emerge in Eurasia, which is ensured by instigating division and a natural balance of power (Van Evera 2006: 88; Posen 2014). The offshore balancer can stay outside major wars for most of their duration to save treasury and blood, and then enter the war towards the end to ensure the outcome is a politically divided continent with a natural balance of power (Mearsheimer and Walt 2016: 78). The offshore balancer must remove its physical presence once a post-war settlement had been made. If not, the presence will exhaust the wealth of the offshore balancer and incentivise cooperation among Eurasian land-powers to balance its intrusive presence.

Friedman (2014) argues that preventing one power or coalition of powers from dominating Europe or Eurasia was the primary motivation for the United States to enter both the First and Second World War. During the Second World War, the offshore balancer strategy was fittingly expressed by Truman in 1941: "If we see that Germany is winning the war we ought to help Russia, and if Russia is winning, we ought to help Germany and in that way let them kill as many as possible" (Gaddis 2005: 4).

The analytical framework of the Heartland Theory was further invigorated in the United States with the ascendance of the Soviet Union after the Second World War (Blouet 2005: 6). The severely skewed balance of power in Europe, due to the victory of the Soviet Union, had made the prospect of Soviet dominance in Eurasia a possibility. Thus, temporary US forward deployments on the Eurasian continent was deemed necessary, which broke with the traditional policies of an offshore balancer. Before becoming president, Dwight Eisenhower cautioned in 1951: "If in ten years, all American troops stationed in Europe for national defence purposes have not been returned to the United States, then this whole project will have failed" (Carpenter 1992: 12).

The containment strategy against the Soviet Union has subsequently even been referred to as the "Spykman-Kennan thesis of containment"

(Parker 1985). George Kennan, the "architect of containment", argued primarily for economic containment by denying the Soviet Union more than one centre of industrial and economic potential to establish a "Eurasian balance of power" (Gaddis 1982: 38). The ideas behind the Heartland Theory emerged in US National Security Council reports from 1948 and onwards as a central theoretical component to containing the Soviet Union (Gaddis 1982: 57–58). President Reagan confirmed the relevance of the Heartland Theory in the US National Security Strategy:

> The United States' most basic national security interests would be endangered if a hostile state or group of states were to dominate the Eurasian landmass – that area of the globe often referred to as the world's heartland. We fought two world wars to prevent this from occurring. And, since 1945, we have sought to prevent the Soviet Union from capitalizing on its geostrategic advantage to dominate its neighbors in Western Europe, Asia, and the Middle East, and thereby fundamentally alter the global balance of power to our disadvantage. (White House 1988: 1)

HEGEMONY AFTER THE COLD WAR

After the Cold War, the United States did not retreat to its offshore balancing strategy. The prospect of security through global hegemony convinced Washington that the expenditures and alienation of Eurasian land-powers were worth the risk. A draft of the US Defense Planning Guidance, leaked in 1992, stipulated: "It is improbable that a global conventional challenge to the US and Western security will re-emerge from the Eurasian heartland for many years to come". The main objective of US post–Cold Strategy to prevent a Eurasian challenger was outlined:

> This is a dominant consideration underlying the new regional defense strategy and requires that we endeavor to prevent any hostile power from dominating a region whose resources would, under consolidated control, be sufficient to generate global power. These regions include Western Europe, East Asia, the territory of the former Soviet Union, and Southwest Asia. (*New York Times* 1992)

The hegemonic strategy of the United States after the Cold War was defined by Brzezinski (1997: 40): as "to prevent collusion and maintain security dependence among the vassals, to keep tributaries pliant and protected, and keep the barbarians from coming together" (Brzezinski 1997b: 40). Rather than transcending the power politics of the past, the American unipolar moment was largely reliant on maintaining divisions between Eurasian powers by organising the continent based on conflicting interests (Friedman 2014). Brzezinski advised that ideally the disintegration of the Soviet Union would be followed by the disintegration of Russia into a "loosely confederated Russia – composed of a European Russia, a Siberian Republic, and a Far Eastern Republic". The ideas of Brzezinski represents a continuation of Mackinder's (1919: 205–215) advocacy of breaking up Germany and Russia into states associated in a loose federation to prevent the emergence of future Eurasian rivals to dominance by the maritime powers.

Washington organised its dominance over Eurasia through "system-dominance", which denotes the offer of patronage to regional powers that commit to the US-centric international system (Schweller 1999: 41; Katzenstein 2005: 57; Buzan 2005). Germany and Japan are the principal nodes on the western and eastern edge of Eurasia (Bretherton and Vogler 1999: 66–67). The partnerships entailed some trade-offs, as the United States supported the development of the EU to contain Russian influence, while the collective bargaining power of the EU also scaled back US influence (Katzenstein 2005: 50). The struggle to establish a viable node at the southern edge, in the Middle East, has been a costly endeavour.

The only two independent poles of power in the post–Cold War era were Russia and China, which had to be contained (Katzenstein 2005: 5; Buzan 2005). Asymmetrical interdependence was established with both Russia and China through an international division of labour that ensured the United States and the West remained at the higher echelons of global values chains.

By the late 1980s, the West established a modern core-periphery structure of the global economy akin to the British repeal of the Corn Laws in 1843. Unlike the nineteenth century, the modern economy is not simply divided by the export of manufactured goods versus natural resources. Rather, the digitalisation of the economy resulted in a move towards a post-industrial society where knowledge economies occupied the high-value component of global values chains (Bell 1976). The US government provided strong economic support for its tech companies through direct and indirect subsidies through new patents law with universities and the commercial application of military funding (Benner 2002: 70; Perelman 2003). The subsidy of the tech sector deviated significantly from the liberal economics the United States propagated (Block 2008).

Once superiority was established in digital technologies, the United States began pushing a new format for free trade. Technological corporations in the United States, Western Europe and Japan began to merge and restructure their supply chains and business operations in the 1980s. With the support of governments, the West and Japan were consolidating control over research, development, marketing and intellectual property rights, and began shedding the low-profit sectors of the economy that could easily be diversified

(Prechel 2000). The United States opened its low-skilled manufacturing and assembly for competition, and in return sought to prevent other states from catching up by demanding that patent laws were extended and enforced more vigorously (Sell 2003; Shadlen 2005). The trade-related intellectual property rights thus became the foundation for the repeal of the Corn Laws 2.0.

Russia fell into the "liberal division of labour trap" that does not use state-intervention to develop a comparative advantage higher in global value chains. Subsequently, Russia became an exporter of natural resources and began to rapidly de-industrialise throughout the 1990s and losing the techno-logical sovereignty it had built up during the Soviet era. The West still sought to reduce reliance on Russia's main strategic industry, energy, as it created European dependence on Russia. In the new international division of labour, China became the factory for Western technologies with China. Put simply, the United States would innovate new technologies such as the iPhone, and the Chinese could produce and assemble in return for opening their markets to the United States.

PUSHING RUSSIA TOWARDS CHINA

The post–Cold War strategy of preserving a division between Germany and Russia as land-powers neglected that the international distribution of power was rapidly changing. In the past, pushing Russia into Asia would relegate Russia to economic obscurity and eliminate its status as a European power. With geoeconomic power shifting rapidly to the East, the rules of the game have changed. The West is pushing Russia closer towards China at the worst possible time in history, as the West's 500-year-long dominance is coming to an end.

China has been amassing geoeconomic power and preparing to challenge the geoeconomic leadership of the United States by restructuring the global economy. Looking east, Russia no longer sees solitude and isolation on disconnected steppes of Eurasia. Instead, Russia looks towards China and other giants in the east that seek to integrate the Eurasian continent with new industries, transportation corridors and financial instruments. Rather than dis-appearing into Asia, Russia is finding a Eurasian path to modernisation and diversification away from excessive economic reliance on the West. Rather than leaving Europe, Russia will have greater bargaining power and skew the balance of dependence on the old continent.

The ability to disrupt economic connectivity between Russia and China is more difficult than between Russia and Germany where buffer states have been created. Russia and China share a long border and the partnership is therefore less vulnerable to competition in transit states. Central Asia is the most likely venue for rivalry, although there are great incentives for harmonising the competing formats for Eurasian integration. While the West has the explicit objective of decoupling or "liberating" the shared neighbourhood from Russian influence, China benefits from Russian connectivity in the region and therefore seeks to avoid antagonising Moscow. Among the Chinese population, there is also a very favourable view of Russia and admiration for the decisive leadership against the Western expansionism (Lukin 2020).

China's dissatisfaction with the US-led international economic order differs from that of Russia. China initially adapted to the international division of labour set under US hegemony until it had grown powerful and then transitioned to a Listian development strategy. In the 1970s, China opened its markets to the world and espoused the idea of pursuing a "peaceful rise". The neo-mercantilist policies of wage suppression and currency devaluation enabled China to maximise exports and minimise imports. The reduced standard of living was an investment in the future as China accrued productive capacity and large amounts of foreign reserves. China climbed global value chains as the profits from the trade gap were invested in the form of subsidies for its industries and acquisitions of strategic industries abroad. Furthermore, China could take advantage of its huge market size by demanding the transfer of knowledge and know-how from foreign companies as a condition for access to the large Chinese market. Beijing also engaged in theft of intellectual property rights and reverse engineered foreign technologies to escape core-periphery relations.

As China climbed up global value chains and amassed great wealth, the US-led international economic system did not reform to reflect the new international distribution of power. The Chinese concept of a peaceful rise is a dual process as the United States would have to be willing to accommodate China by sharing power in a multipolar system (Buzan 2010: 5). Instead, the United States began to reassert its control over the geoeconomic levers of power following the global financial crisis of 2008–2009. The United States began negotiating the Trans-Pacific Partnership (TPP) agreement, which had the purpose of marginalising China's economic power in the region. As Obama (2016) wrote in an op-ed: "the world has changed. The rules are changing with it. The United States, not countries like China, should write them". American cyber-espionage intensified; Washington became more ambiguous about its commitment to the One-China policy and the status of Taiwan; Obama announced the military pivot to Asia; reforms to the International Monetary Fund (IMF) continued to be delayed; and the United States encouraged ASEAN to develop into an anti-Chinese bloc. Under Trump, these initiatives only intensified as the United States began repatriating global supply chains and pushing allies to suspend reliance on Chinese technologies.

CHINA AND RUSSIA DEVELOP A
EURASIAN "AMERICAN SYSTEM"

Both Russia and China are pursuing a Listian development model akin to Hamilton's three-pillared American System. With striking similarities to the American and German policies of the nineteenth century, Russia and China are developing strategic industries / high-tech products, transportation corridors and financial instruments. The combined effort by the two Eurasian giants to construct the geoeconomic pillars for a Greater Eurasia to displace the Bretton Woods system has been termed "Kissinger's worst nightmare" (Burrows and Manning 2015: 3).

The Russian concept of a Eurasianist political economy largely conforms with the Chinese Shanghai Spirit that propagates positive-sum solutions in Eurasia. The Shanghai Spirit is commonly dismissed in the West as propaganda, yet it conforms with the ideas of the Savitsky that suggests maritime powers are inclined towards imperialism. Savitsky (1921) argued that maritime power relied on creating divisions in Eurasia to rule from the maritime edges of the supercontinent, which was juxtaposed with Eurasianist landpowers who are dependent on seeking cooperation and harmonising interests to administer the continent.

STRATEGIC INDUSTRIES

Both China and Russia aim to leap forward as the world enters a new industrial revolution defined by digital technologies manipulating the physical world. Falling behind on the industrial revolution devastated both Russia and China. Russia's humiliating defeat to the British in the Crimean War (1853–1856) diminished its position in Europe. Likewise, China's defeat to Britain in the Opium Wars (1839–1842; 1856–1860) transformed China from one of the largest to one of the weakest economies in the world. The ensuing *Century of Humiliation* then lasted until the Communist Revolution.

From the 2000s, China gradually caught up with the West and established technological sovereignty as its key strategic industries are all domestic. Beijing's aspiration to surpass US technological leadership was evident in 2015 with *The Made in China 2025 Initiative*, an ambitious and well-funded industrial policy which aims to establish technological leadership in 5G technology, automation, robotics, artificial intelligence and other innovative technologies. The EU's Chamber of Commerce in China reprimanded China for the robust industrial policy as it rendered European companies unable to compete (European Union 2017). A completely autonomous digital ecosystem has been developed where the leading digital platforms are Chinese. The term "splinternet", denotes the Balkanisation of the internet as China and Russia nationalists the digital space by decoupling from the US-led internet.

The modern conservatism of Russia aims to incorporate traditions and expertise of the past, while concurrently adapting to a rapidly changing world. The new conservatism recognises that stability ultimately depends on Russia also ensuring socio-economic and political stability by strengthening its geoeconomic position in the international system (Chebankova 2016). Russia has a much weaker position than China, although it is moving towards "technological preparedness", which enables Russia to implement technological innovations abroad into its domestic ecosystem to advance technological sovereignty. The major digital platforms are domestic, and Russia has sought partnership with China in areas such as e-commerce and operating systems where its capabilities have been lacking.

Moscow recognises that the world is entering another industrial revolution and funds are subsequently directed to develop "technological sovereignty" to prevent excessive dependence on foreign powers. Putin cautioned against extreme core-periphery relations emerging from excessive reliance on foreign technologies in the new industrial revolution: "If someone can provide a monopoly in the field of artificial intelligence, then the consequences are clear to all of us: he will rule the world" (Bendett 2019). Russia is advancing a largely successful import substitution programme in strategic industries such as agriculture and high-tech industries, which received greater focus following the West's anti-Russian sanctions since 2014. While Western powers initially deluded themselves with the idea that the Russian-Chinese partnership was merely a "marriage of convenience", they soon took notice that it has evolved into a strategic high-tech partnership and area establishing a space for technological sovereignty within artificial intelligence, digital platforms, e-commerce, telecommunications, biotechnology and other key areas (Bendett and Kania 2019).

TRANSPORTATION CORRIDORS

Russia's is developing physical connectivity across Eurasia with transportation corridors and energy pipelines. An east-west corridor is established to improve connectivity between Europe with East Asia, and a north-south corridor is developed for more competitive routes between India, Iran and Russia. The diversification of economic connectivity and energy supplies away from Europe also enables Russia to establish sovereign control over its economic activities and reduce foreign influence. These initiatives aim to benefit and be harmonised with China's trillion-dollar Belt and Road Initiative (BRI) that connects Eurasia by both land and sea. Furthermore, with approximately $200 billion invested in digital infrastructure in the Digital Silk Road, China is connecting the world with undersea cables and broadband.

Russian-Chinese cooperation for Eurasian formats in Central Asia is vital for both east-west and the north-south economic connectivity in Eurasia. Western maritime powers have since the 1990s sought to control the energy resources in Central Asia. The West aimed to marginalise both Russia and Iran by establishing an energy corridor through Georgia and Azerbaijan to access Central Asia. This corridor followed the path as the Batumi-Baku rail corridor that Mackinder recommended that Britain take control over during the Russian Revolution to scale back the Soviet presence in the Caspian region. A second energy corridor has been planned since the 1990s from Turkmenistan through Afghanistan, Pakistan and India (TAPI pipeline). The EU's INOGATE initiative explicitly aims to marginalise Russian participation in regional energy infrastructure and is complemented with the EU's Transport Corridor Europe-Caucasus-Asia (TRACECA) to develop transportation corridors that circumvent Russia. The trend towards marginalising Russia has since been reversed as Russia and China establishes collective leadership in the region.

The east-west corridor is developed by improving the Trans-Siberian railway and the Baikal-Amur railway. Additional routes also pass from China through Central Asia before cutting into European Russia and Europe, with Kazakhstan being a central node in the Eurasian transportation infrastructure. The use of routes from Pacific Russia is promoted by building and modernising ports along the Russian Pacific Coast in Nakhodka, Vostochny, Vanino and Zarubino.

The east-west corridor also has a maritime component with Russian "Northern Sea Route" through the Arctic. Mackinder (1919: 198) described the absence of maritime corridors in the Eurasian heartland as key in the containment of European land-powers:

> There flow across that plain some great navigable rivers; certain of them go north to the Arctic Sea and are inaccessible from the ocean because it is cumbered with ice, while others flow into inland waters, such as the Caspian, which have no exit to the ocean.

With the Arctic becoming more accessible due to the retreating ice, the Russian Arctic has the potential to become a major transportation corridor due to faster and cheaper transit. Furthermore, it would be the only strategic maritime transportation corridor outside of US control. Russia and China are also cooperating in the Arctic to develop the infrastructure required for transportation and energy extraction in the high north. China even incorporated the Arctic into its Silk Road concept when its first White Paper on the Arctic was released in January 2018, which conceptualised a "Polar Silk Road" in partnership with Russia (PRC 2018).

The North-South Transportation Corridor (NSTC) was initially signed by Russia, Iran and India, although it took on more members and began gathering a momentum a decade later. NSTC is a multi-modal network consisting of seaports, rail and road to bypass the Suez Canal to save time and money with more competitive physical connectivity. The 7,200 km long corridor between St. Petersburg and Mumbai enables Russia to construct a more multipolar Eurasia to ensure power does not concentrate excessively in either the United States or China. Yet, the project does not undermine China as the intersection between the East-West corridor and the North-South can be mutually complementary and creates more economic dynamism to the region. Russia devoted much more focus and funds to the NSTC after the West's anti-Russian sanctions that commenced in 2014. The efficiency and competitiveness of the NSTC is undermined by the West's sanctions against Iran and the tensions between Ukraine and Russia following the coup in 2014.

FINANCIAL INSTRUMENTS

Domestic and regional financial instruments are imperative for Russia to ensure greater ownership over its own modernisation process, a condition for a conservative political economy. Excessive financial dependency on foreign powers was a key weakness during modernisation in the late nineteenth century under the conservative development policies of Sergei Witte. Unlike the American national bank and the French Crédit Mobilier, Russia was not successful in mobilising the funds of its middle class to reduce reliance on foreign finance.

The lesson appears to have been learned by Russia in the twenty-first century. A conservative fiscal policy resulted in Russia paying down its foreign debts. After five years of anti-Russian sanctions that were aimed to crush the Russian economy, Forbes reported in 2019 that Russia had become "bullet-proof" for investors (Rapoza 2019). By late 2019, the Russian GDP at purchasing power parity (PPP) was the sixth largest in the world and almost surpassing Germany.

Russia has engaged in a forceful de-dollarisation campaign by reducing its dollars in reserves and trade. Gold has been important to diversify away from the US dollar and to enhance the stability of its own currency. Russia's gold reserve in January 2008 was 457 tonnes, and in 2020, it surpassed 2,300 tonnes. Russia is therefore on the path of becoming the third-largest holder of gold as both Italy and France have just in excess of 2,400 tonnes each. The ability to reduce trade in dollars has been augmented by the strategic partnership with China, which is actively seeking to internationalise the yuan and decouple from the dollar. The petro-dollar is thus challenged as the world's largest energy exporter and importer are working towards settling their energy trade in domestic currencies. Both Russia and China are seeking to decouple from the use of dollars in trade with third countries as the new practices are implemented.

New investment banks are established or in the process of being established through the Eurasian Economic Union, the Shanghai Cooperation Organisation, BRICS and other arrangements that seek to emulate the success of the Chinese-led Asia Infrastructure Investment Bank (AIIB) launched in 2015. A synergy effect is pushed as the major modernisation initiatives and infrastructure projects are aimed to be financed by Russian or Eurasian banks. For example, the Russia-China Investment Fund (RCIF) the China-Eurasian Economic Cooperation Fund (CEF) share investment projects to harmonise Russia's Eurasian Economic Union with China's BRI. Both Russia and China have developed alternatives to the SWIFT international transaction system, new rating agencies and smaller cooperative initiatives such as UnionPay-MIR debit card to end the use of American cards. Furthermore, cooperation in digital economic platforms is enabling Russia to transition away from former banking technologies were it was lagging. Platforms such as WeChat or Sesame, which are being emulated by Russian counterparts, are redefining financial services and will likely outperform traditional banks (Lipton et al. 2016: 17).

THE GEOECONOMIC BALANCE OF DEPENDENCE IN EURASIA

In the early 1990s, Eurasian ideas were already re-emerging in Russia. For example, Vladimirtsov's *The Life of Genghis Khan* from 1922 was reprinted, which argued that Genghis Khan had a strong and positive influence on the political culture of Russia. Yet, the world and Russia had changed drastically, and the questioned to be asked was – what does a conservative political economy look like?

With the rise of Asia, Eurasianism became an ideology of multipolarity. The balance of dependence logic works in Russia's advantage as a Eurasian balancer. Even in relations with China, the presence of other major powers supports the harmonisation of interests. For example, Russia and China have great incentives to harmonise competing interests in Central Asia as without rivalry "Moscow and Beijing would have Central Asia as well as Mongolia to themselves, effectively shutting out all external powers from the heart of Eurasia" (Lukin 2015: 201).

For post-Soviet Russia, the balance of power logic for Eurasian Russia is fundamentally different than for European Russia. With China being the dominant power in Asia, other states in the region have strong systemic incentives to accommodate Russia and augment economic connectivity to ensure that Russia does not become excessively reliant on a more powerful China.

Case in point, Japan is under great pressure to improve relations and develop economic cooperation with Russia to ensure that Russia's pivot to Asia does not merely become a pivot to China. If Russia becomes economically too dependent on China, Moscow would be less able to remain neutral in the conflicts between China and Japan (Diesen 2018). Similarly, India has strong incentives to support Russia's development of the Northern Sea Route through the Arctic to ensure it does not become solely a Russian-Chinese project.

Relations between Russia and the West will also ultimately change with the rise of Eurasia. The West's hostile strategy to Russia is conditioned on the idea that Russia has nowhere else to go, and must accept whatever the West offers in terms of "partnership". The rise of the East fundamentally alters Moscow's relationship with the West by enabling Russia to diversify its partnerships. Panarin argues that a Eurasian Russia will present Germany with an ultimatum: "whether to build the heartland *together with* Russia, or Russia will build it with China in an *alternative* form".

This resembles an ultimatum that former US national security advisor Zbigniew Brzezinski argued that the United States was faced with due to the rise of China. The United States could either accept and facilitate the emergence of a multipolar world and use its leverage to shape new infrastructure that maintains US leadership as the first among equals, or the United States could attempt to prolong unipolarity but then rival powers would construct a multipolar world without Washington's input and possibly in opposition to the United States (Brzezinski 2009). To prevent an alliance against the United States, it was imperative that Washington "fashion a policy in which at least one of the two potentially threatening states [China and Russia] becomes a partner in the quest for regional and then wider global stability", which subsequently marks the end of US global domination (Brzezinski 2016).

The neo-Eurasianists tend to be dismissive of unified Slavdom. Panarin is sceptical about the future of Slavic states in Eastern Europe as their destiny will continue to be defined by the historical competition between Germany and Russia, which suggests they will not find unity and thus remain less relevant. The main relevance and value of the Slavic states derive from the Western efforts to make the Slavic states a frontline against Russia. Resolving the tensions among the Slavs would therefore have to be facilitated through Greater Eurasia as it is aimed to cancel the unipolar project and mitigate tensions with Germany.

A COMMON EURASIAN HOME

Eurasianism entails reorganising relations with Europe in a wider format as opposed to decoupling from Europe. Gorbachev's concept of a Common European Home was a format for accommodating both capitalism and socialism in Europe to end the militarised bloc politics. Peaceful coexistence was based on the analogy of a common house with separate rooms for the competing ideologies. Gorbachev's Common European Home was ultimately defeated by the US concept of Europe Whole and Free that aimed to integrate the continent within one "room" with liberalism written on the door. The concept of a European Whole and Free implied unipolarity as the United States was the ideological champion of liberalism, and it manifested itself through NATO expansionism.

Russia's Greater Eurasia Initiative can be conceptualised as a Greater Eurasian Home. Instead of accommodating capitalism and socialism, the Common Eurasian Home is a conservative construct that houses civilizational diversity. Eurasian history and spirit are believed to have equipped Russia with the ability to work with other civilisations without denigrating their distinctiveness. Putin has at various times spoken at the Organisation of the Islamic Conference (OIC) about Russia's history as a bridge between the Christian World and the Islamic World, and harmonious relations between the Russian Orthodox Church and Islam (Tsygankov 2006).

Eurasianism offers a conservative approach to cooperation and globalisation that seeks to conserve civilisational distinctiveness in a multipolar format. According to Panarin, Moscow must "propose to the peoples of Eurasia a new, powerful, superenergetic synthesis" based on "people's conservatism" and "civilizational diversity" (Hahn 2018: 17). In the tradition of Mackinder, Panarin suggests that the failure to reach a post–Cold War settlement with the West should lend support to cultivate China as "a partner in the heartland" to form a Sino-Russian Union (Hahn 2018: 10).

Europe is conceptualised as the western peninsula of Greater Eurasian or the Common Eurasian Home, which suggests that conservatives and Westernisers can find common ground. Russia's Eurasian identity encompasses the Rus from the north, Byzantium from the south, the nomadic Golden Horde and Tatars from the east, and Europe in the West. The political economy of Greater Eurasia is being structured as a more feasible format for integration with Europe by developing more favourable symmetry. Even the Eurasian Economic Union as a central component of Greater Eurasia is envisioned by Putin (2011b) as an instrument for integrating with Europe as equals:

> In our view, the solution could be the elaboration of common approaches "at the grassroots level", as the saying goes. At first, within the existing regional

structures – the EU, NAFTA, APEC, ASEAN, and others – and then, by means of dialog between them. It is precisely from such integrative "bricks" that a world economy of a more stable character could be formed. For example, the two biggest associations on our continent – the European Union and the Eurasia n Union now being formed – basing their collaboration on the rules of free trade and the compatibility of systems of regulation, are objectively capable, including through relations with third countries and regional structures, of extending these principles to the entire area – from the Atlantic to the Pacific. To an area that will be harmonious in its economic nature, but polycentric from the point of view of specific mechanisms and executive decisions. It will then be logical to begin a constructive dialog on the principles of collaboration with the states of the Asia-Pacific Region, North America, and other regions.

Eurasianism can harmonise conservative interests with Russian westernisers as integration with the West is premised on the preservation of Russia's civilisational distinctiveness. The use of collective bargaining power even ensures a more feasible format for cooperation by ensuring more symmetrical interdependence. Putin (2011b) argued the EAEU is an instrument for integration with Europe:

> The Customs Union, and later, the Eurasian Union, will now become a participant in the dialog with the EU. In this way, membership of the Eurasian Union, apart from the direct economic benefits, will allow each of its members to integrate more quickly, and from stronger positions, into Europe.

The Eurasian land-powers will eventually incorporate Europe and other states on the inner periphery of Eurasia. Political loyalties will incrementally shift as economic interests turn to the east, and Europe is gradually becoming the western peninsula of Greater Eurasia.

First, the strategic industries of Europe are becoming increasingly dependent on the east. Germany, France, Britain and other major states are cooperating with China's Huawei to install 5G technology. Similarly, Turkey and Serbia purchased the S-400 missile defence system. Second, transportation corridors are required as European connectivity diversifies with rival land- and maritime transportation corridors. The Port of Piraeus has become China's main maritime bridgehead into Europe, which is connected with Central Europe and comes full circle by connecting with Eurasian land-corridors. Italy, Greece, Poland, Austria, Luxemburg and Switzerland have joined the Chinese BRI. Third, new financial instruments are restructuring international finance. In 2015, all major European powers joined the Chinese-led AIIB. All of the aforementioned developments took place despite US objections and threats of sanctions.

The rise of the east creates systemic incentives for the fragmentation of the Western-centric geoeconomic infrastructure. The United States is devoting its focus primarily towards East Asia and to loose interests in Europe. With the relative power of the United States in decline, Europe is also under growing pressure to halt its expansion and find a settlement with Russia. At the Munich Security Conference in February 2020, the French president argued that Europe cannot continue to depend on US protection, and he recognised the need to include Russia in the European security architecture to reduce the zero-sum structures. This is reminiscent of Merkel's argument in 2017 that "Europeans must take our destiny into our own hands" and Germany's traditional caution that a Europe without Russia risks becoming a Europe against Russia.

CONCLUSION

Von Clausewitz, a Prussian general and military theorist, famously wrote: "To achieve victory we must mass our forces at the hub of all power and movement, the enemy's centre of gravity". The centre of gravity concept is a reference to the source of strength. The main adversaries of Russia draw their strength from the three-pillared geoeconomic instruments to administer Eurasia from the maritime periphery, which is also why they become the principal adversaries. Constructing a Eurasian continental political economy based on its own strategic industries, physical connectivity and financial mechanisms is a necessity to successfully manage change and organic growth. Russia ending its more than three-centuries long Occidental Era may paradoxically improve relations with the West by improving the symmetry in relations.

Chapter 10

Russia as an International Conservative Power

INTRODUCTION

Russian conservatism has historically been confronted with a dilemma of taking on a domestic or universal cause. The domestic path suggested that Russia should insulate itself from the turbulence from abroad, while the universal mission sought to save Europe from itself. Russia developed an international conservative position throughout history by assuming the role of "Third Rome" after the fall of Constantinople; by opposing the French Revolution in a coalition with European monarchies; by conquering Paris after Napoleon had been pushed out from Russian territory; and by providing military support against the European revolutions in 1848. The contemporary crisis in Western liberalism is yet again presenting Russia with the dilemma between either shielding itself from the disruptions and chaos abroad or positioning itself as an international conservative power tasked with also restoring the international order.

Russian international conservatism is currently finding supporters and opposition in both the East and the West. In the East, there is an appetite for establishing a less Western-centric approach to international cooperation that dismisses sovereign inequality and accommodates civilizational diversity. The soft power of Russian conservatism in the West is paradoxical as it entails culturally detaching Russia from the West. Russian liberalism does not produce much soft power as Russia would merely play second fiddle to the West by emulating the universal values championed by the West. By contrast, Russian conservatism addresses weaknesses of excessive liberalism that emerges in the West. Russia establishes a common cause with Western conservatives by embracing its own distinctive culture and pursuing an organic path towards change and modernity.

This chapter first explores Russia's pre-communist role as an international conservative power. Russia's appeal to conservatives around the world derives from both the support for cultural similarities and the rejection of universalism. Second, populists are emerging across the world who redefine the main division in the world away from liberalism versus authoritarianism to national-patriotism versus cosmopolitan-globalism. Last, Russian soft power emerges from its international conservative position. It is concluded that Russian international conservatism is attracting allies across the world, although it also makes Russia a more obvious target as the Western political establishments seek to defend liberal hegemony.

CONSERVATIVES OF THE WORLD UNITE!

The West has for centuries mirrored itself in pre-communist Russia. For Western liberals seeing the world through the lens of the Enlightenment, Russia was commonly dismissed as economically backward, barbaric and underdeveloped. For Western conservatives that feared the social costs caused by the extremes of the Enlightenment, the decadence of excessive individualism of materialism was often contrasted with the collectivism and spirituality that defined Russia.

Historically, pre-communist Russia was commonly the go-to-country for Western conservatives. The appeal can be explained as Russia was late to industrialise; the complex history that made it less able to assimilate into Europe; the geographic vastness preserved gemeinschaft and agrarian society; or the prolonged use of communes conserved spirituality. Whatever the source of Russian conservatism, Western conservatives have historically looked towards Russia to rediscover something they lost along the way of industrialisation and rapid modernisation. Russia's role in Europe has traditionally been depicted as a gemeinschaft power to balance the excesses of gesellschaft in Western Europe. Khomyakov opined that Russia had to preserve its spirituality and community that would also enable it to save the West from its own decadence.

The French philosopher and diplomat Joseph De Maistre blamed the excessive rationalism and decline of Christianity for the destruction of revolutionary France. Much like other Western conservatives, De Maistre sought to look towards Russia to recapture the untarnished culture and re-energise France. His great disappointment was thus the Russians were rapidly seeking to emulate the decadent path of France. Many conservatives in nineteenth-century Britain were similarly fascinated with and admired Russia for preserving tradition and spiritual communities. By the late nineteenth century, the churches of England and Russia created closer ties based on a shared Christian faith to mitigate the tensions from the Great Game (Hughes 2004).

Haxthausen (1856) similarly wrote extensively on the societal value of Russia's rural communities as a source of unity and purpose, which he attempted to introduce into European social thought. As a German Catholic, Haxthausen found a solid common conservative ground with Russian Slavophiles. The complex political and economic structures in Germany were believed to fuel nihilism and cultural decay. Haxthausen believed that Russia's struggle was to find its path to modernisation built heavily on its native institutions, and above all unity thorough the Orthodox Church. Haxthausen (1856: 353) was thus deeply sceptical of the Europeanisation of Russia as it corrupted its spirit and aptitude for organic growth.

> The Old Believers are in general much more simple, moral, sober and reliable than the other Russian peasants; indeed, one may say that the closer the Russian approaches the Old Believers in manners, dress and habits the better he becomes. On the other hand, when the Russian peasant becomes Europeanised, cuts off his beard, puts aside his native dress and builds a modern house he is no longer to be trusted. He has, as a rule, become a rogue.

When civilisations crumble, people have historically looked towards an external power to infuse the civilisation with new energy. When decadent civilisation decline, they usually look towards a civilisation at the periphery for cultural renewal (Toynbee 1946: 30; Quigley 1961: 148). Spengler (1922) believed that the West was degenerating and looked towards Russia as a source of spiritual revival. Like Slavophobic German nationalist, Spengler deemed Russia to be an Asianised civilisation that at the forefront of a revolt against the white European world. Yet, Spengler's depiction of Russia as a primitive civilisation was not intended as derision. Instead, Russia was portrayed by Spengler as a youthful civilisation, which he contrasted with the ageing and decadence of the West. Unlike the German nationalists who believed that Slavs could not manage their own state, Spengler revered the Russian soul and cultural vigour that made it the prime successor of the decadent West.

The great irony of George Kennan as the author of the Long Telegram and intellectual architect of the containment policy was his immense attraction towards Russia. Kennan (1972: 116) expressed admiration for pre-communist Russia: "There was some mysterious affinity which I could not explain even to myself." Kennan largely despised the Marxists for destroying one of the most important the spiritual centres and captivating cultures of the world.

The current revival of affinity towards Russian conservatism in the West can appear to be a contradiction as it historically entails becoming "less European" by taking on a more Eurasian identity. However, by recognising the distinctiveness of Russia and rejecting universalism, Moscow establishes common cause with classical conservatives around the world. Russian conservatives have similarly looked towards and admired Western conservatives as intellectual brethren. The richness of European culture was deeply appreciated, although considering it was in a state of decay. Conservatives such as Konstantin Leontyev expressed great admiration for European civilisation, yet believed it had exhausted its energy and was reaching towards the end of its life. The commonality of the French language in Russia made intellectuals more exposed to ideas of French conservatives in the early nineteenth century, which paradoxically inspired Russians to assert their cultural autonomy and pushing back on the intrusiveness of French culture on Russian society (Freeden 1996: 133–134).

Russia also advances its conservative ideals in foreign affairs. Case in point, Russia promoted a declaration in the Organization for Security and Cooperation in Europe (OSCE) and the UN against "the problem of Christianophobia". Moscow argued that the persecution of Christians in the Middle East and North Africa has not received the same focus and protection as other religious groups (Lavrov 2014). Moscow's conservative philosophy is also directed towards the failings of liberalism in the West and the wider world. Putin responded to the crisis in Western liberalism and the liberal international order ahead of the G20 meeting in June 2019 by declaring:

> The liberal idea has become obsolete. It has come into conflict with the interests of the overwhelming majority of the population. . . . Deep inside, there must be some fundamental human rules and moral values. In this sense, traditional values are more stable and more important for millions of people than this liberal idea, which, in my opinion, is really ceasing to exist.

RISE OF THE POPULISTS

The resurgence of Russian conservatism is occurring at a time when Western liberalism is descending into crisis and populism is filling a political vacuum. The West prospered by accommodating a balance between conservatism and liberalism. The nation-state represents a conservative construct that harnesses the instinctive tribalism in human nature by defining the collective by the shared ethno-cultural core and civic ideals. The nation-state became a robust vessel to advance individual rights and freedoms, which restrained the authority of institutions representing the collective. The liberal-conservative balance prevented the conservatism from descending into stagnation, xenophobia and authoritarianism, while it ensured liberalism from not deconstructing the key institutions that represent the collective. Over the past decades, liberalism began decoupling from the nation-state as the individual was to be liberated from the arbitrary authority of Christianity, ethnicity, culture, history, gender and other institutional scaffolding of society. The decoupling of liberalism and conservatism eliminated the sense of common cause and each side increasingly perceive the "other" as delegitimate by attacking what is revered.

Much focus has been devoted to the affinity of Western right-wing populists towards Russia. Yet, the common depiction of a xenophobic and Islamophobic alliance of convenience between the West's Political Right and Russia is deeply flawed. Russia's Eurasianist Conservatism recognise its Muslim Tatar population to be native to the land, and Moscow is reaching favourably out to the Islamic world to engage other Eurasian civilisations in a multipolar format. Furthermore, Russia finds support from both the Political Right and the political Left across the West. As the crisis of neoliberalism collapses the political centre across the West, the anti-Russian platform is undermined. Liberalism has become the principal foundation for Western unity and the ideological platform for maintaining a divided Europe.

The populist rejection of the neoliberal idea is fragmenting the foundation of Western unity and fuelling support for Russia. The rise of populism is therefore commonly depicted and delegitimised as a grand Russian conspiracy, as Russia is blamed for the upset in almost every election and referendum in the West. However, contemporary populism, much like populism in the late nineteenth century, functions as a corrective mechanism to the excesses of liberalism. As neoliberalism is increasingly rejected in domestic policies, it is also rejected as the ideology justifying the redevising of Europe.

Populism is a contested concept, but it is usually defined as nativist, authoritarian, and anti-establishment (Pauwels 2011; Mudde 2016: 4). The terms populism is therefore mostly used derogatory intention due to the negative connotations. However, the nativist and authoritarian inclinations of populists is a corrective mechanism to the erosion of in-group loyalty and authority as central pillars of conservative morality that focuses on the preservation of the social group. Similarly, the anti-establishment sentiment is a response to the polarisation of society between the cosmopolitan liberal elite and the "people" left behind from the forces of globalisation and thus seeking refuge in traditional institutions and values.

Populists are voted into power due to some powerful undercurrents in human nature that are neglected. The Enlightenment and the industrial revolution tasked the state with managing change as rational industrial society began deviating from instincts in human nature. The transition from autonomous agricultural work in traditional communities to complex industrial societies placed responsibility upon states to ensure the new builds on the experiences of the past. The liberal format for globalisation inevitably undermines conservatism as it homogenises the world and advances radical individualism. The West is gradually less defined by civilisational ideas with roots to the past, as progressive ideologies of liberalism and socialism undermine the concept of legitimacy being based on traditions and a shared past.

Managing change entails positioning society between continuity and change by balancing the tradition with the modern. When liberalism decouples from conservatism and the nation-state, society inevitably polarises. Democracy itself depends on conservative principles that uphold the nation-states as the collective. National unity is a required foundation for democracy as political pluralism must rest within "accepted boundaries" defined by commonality and consensus (Diamond 1990: 49). Polarisation eventually tears away at democracy as common interests, political principles and accountability are replaced with loyalty to party membership.

The kinship that previously defined the nation-state as a community degrades into a physical space inhabited by random people with little in common, which thus creates fragmentation. Liberalism challenges the legitimacy of the nation-state as an infringement upon liberalism by perpetuating tribalism, while conservatism recognises that tribalism is a human instinct that is managed within the nation-state. Globalism is based on the erroneous assumption that the erosion of the nation-state will result in the transition to a "global village", which neglects that social groups are defined by distinctiveness and in-group loyalty. Instead, the nation-state fragments into smaller tribes. Hobsbawm (2007: 93) observed that "the process that turned peasants into Frenchmen and immigrants into American citizens is reversing, and it crumbles larger nation-state identities into self-regarding group identities".

The populists may not have all the answers and can be very misguided. An unsavoury strand of populism often emerges when liberalism and conservatism polarise, as the divisive environment motivates some conservatives to repudiate liberal principles and thus neglect the need to temper the excesses of conservatism. For example, most conservatives do not reject the liberal arguments of feminism as an expression of equal worth, opportunity and fairness, or the liberal argument for respecting minority cultures. However, conservatives walk a fine line by restricting the excesses, which are defined by destructive impact on the in-group loyalty and authority of collective institutions. The excesses of feminism can undermine the family as an indispensable institution in society, while excessive protection of minority cultures can undermine assimilation as the foundation of social capital (Haidt 2012: 309). This nuance can erode when liberalism undermines the key institutions valued by conservatives, which then creates an equally radical counter-position on the Political Right. A conservative backlash is emerging as evident by countries all over the world enacting laws to protect their flags and anthems.

Mudde (2016: 30) argues, "The populist surge is an illiberal democratic response to decades of undemocratic liberal policies", which consisted of a

neoliberal consensus among the elites on issues such as immigration, economics and integration. When those who did not benefit from globalisation
began to question increasingly uneven economic distribution, the replacement of national culture with multiculturalism, and mass immigration, they
were confronted with a liberal ideological mantra that denounced opposition
and complaints as backwardness caused by dangerous tribalism. The intellectual source of liberal intolerance is outlined in Marcuse's (1969) concept of
Repressive Tolerance, which stipulates that "the objective of tolerance would
call for intolerance" towards the Political Right and the conservative majority
that sustains oppression.

The polarisation of Western society bears resemblance to Russia's past. In
the early eighteenth century, Peter the Great launched a Cultural Revolution
that neglected conservative principles by decoupling Russia from its past,
which increasingly polarised the cosmopolitan Europeanised elites from
the people. The cosmopolitan and globalist elites in Western states are now
similarly breaking with their own population by the effort of creating a new
future untainted by the past.

Panarin (2001) predicted a new divide in the world between "economic
man" of excessive liberalism and "social man" that upholds the social responsibilities of conservatism. "Economic man" is represented by globalist elites
advancing a post-modernist view of the world, in which Darwinist natural
selection elevates the hedonistic and vain who are committed to materialism
and radical individualism. By contrast, "social man" aims to restore harmony
and stability in the society by reviving the role of tradition, religion and
morality to survive modernity.

An increasingly contemptuous relationship emerges between the cosmopolitan elites, which prospered from globalisation, and the working-class
that has been disadvantaged by liberal globalism and thus seek refuge in
traditional values. Instead of recognising the economic hardship and loss
of national culture, the "petulant, self-righteous, intolerant" liberal elites
expressed contempt for the traditional: "'Middle America' – a term that has
both geographic and social implications – has come to symbolise everything
that stands in the way of progress: 'family values', mindless patriotism, religious fundamentalism, racism, homophobia, retrograde views of women"
(Lasch 1996: 28–29).

The cosmopolitan elites display a common misconception that there is
a linear advancement of liberty as individualism eschews the authority of
the collective. However, coexistence is imperative as the collective sets the
foundation for individualism to exist. An instinct deeply embedded in human
nature is activated when the collective order that defines "us" is threatened.
Suddenly, demands are triggered for rejecting tolerance for what deviates
from the collective and instead embrace authoritarianism (Stenner 2005).

As Plato cautioned, democracy is followed by tyranny as the people look towards a strongman to restore order. Almost two decades before the election of Donald Trump, Rorty (1998) observed that the neoliberal consensus was creating a political vacuum left that would likely be filled by a strongman:

> Members of labor unions, and unorganized and unskilled workers, will sooner or later realize that their government is not even trying to prevent wages from sinking or to prevent jobs from being exported. Around the same time, they will realize that suburban white-collar workers – themselves desperately afraid of being downsized – are not going to let themselves be taxed to provide social benefits for anyone else. At that point, something will crack. The nonsuburban electorate will decide that the system has failed and start looking around for a strongman to vote for – someone willing to assure them that, once he is elected, the smug bureaucrats, tricky lawyers, overpaid bond salesmen, and postmodernist professors will no longer be calling the shots. . . . Once the strongman takes office, no one can predict what will happen.

In 1989, Fukuyama announced the ideological victory of liberalism as the "end of history". Almost three decades later, Fukuyama (2018) recognised that liberalism fails to address central questions about human nature, such as what creates a sense of purpose and community. A post-mortem of the neoliberal system is needed in the West to assess the consequences of shedding conservative principles that have traditionally coexisted with liberalism in the West. Neoliberalism endowed the West with a pedagogic mission and restructured the relationship with Russia and the wider world in a teacher-student format. Infatuated with the mission of remaking the world in the West's image, the West itself began to crumble. The failure to explore and address the internal contradictions of the neoliberal system was largely due to the need to propagate it. As Oscar Wilde famously wrote, "The nuisance of the intellectual sphere is the man who is so occupied in trying to educate others, that he has never had any time to educate himself".

NATIONAL-PATRIOTISM VERSUS COSMOPOLITAN-GLOBALISM

The capitalism-communist divide of the Cold War was soon thereafter recast as a liberal-authoritarian divide as an ideological scaffolding to maintain Western unity and continue the division of Europe. With the decline of classical conservatism, a political vacuum is filled by right-wing populists who seek to revive classical conservatism. The populists are rejecting the division of the world between liberalism and authoritarianism, and are instead viewing the main dividing lines as national-patriotism versus cosmopolitan-globalism. Through this prism, Russia transitions from being the main adversary to become an indispensable ally.

The dividing lines of conservative ethos versus progressive ideologies were already re-established among Russian scholars in the 1970s. Veche, a conservative journal that emerged in the early 1970s, attempted to reintroduce Russians to Slavophile ideas. Veche denounced cosmopolitanism for its spiritual emptiness and called on the reintroduction of orthodox values into society. According to the American conservative Patrick Buchanan (2013), Putin is following this tradition. Buchanan (2013) applauds Putin for rejecting the radical secularism of the West:

> He is seeking to redefine the "Us vs. Them" world conflict of the future as one in which conservatives, traditionalists, and nationalists of all continents and countries stand up against the cultural and ideological imperialism of what he sees as a decadent west.

Buchanan, an anti-communist during the Cold War who advised Richard Nixon, Gerald Ford and Ronald Reagan, now envisions the new struggle of the world through a different prism. Buchanan (2014) argued that Putin is

> tapping into the worldwide revulsion of and resistance to the sewage of a hedonistic secular and social revolution coming out of the West. In the culture war for the future of mankind, Putin is planting Russia's flag firmly on the side of traditional Christianity.

Samuel Huntington (2004) recognised that the rise of a neoliberal elite was polarising society and creating new dividing lines. Ordinary people rely on the preservation of national identity, culture, traditional values, and manufacturing jobs. By contrast,

> for many elites, these concerns are secondary to participating in the global economy, supporting international trade and migration, strengthening international institutions, promoting American values abroad, and encouraging minority identities and cultures at home. The central distinction between the public and elites is not isolationism versus internationalism, but nationalism versus cosmopolitanism. (Huntington 2004: 5)

The criticisms of the EU by Russian and European conservatives are gradually converging. Initially, both Russia and the European conservatives lambasted efforts by Brussels to monopolise on the contested concept of "Europe" to establish narrow narratives on issues such as European integration (Diez

1999; Malcolm 1995). From London, the criticism against Brussels focused on equating European integration with the transfer of sovereign powers from democratic nation-states to an EU bureaucracy. In Moscow, the criticism was directed towards the exclusion of Russia, which resulted in European integration becoming a zero-sum process akin to Cold War bloc politics.

The rise of populists has added a shared critique – the homogenising process of EU members that diminish the cultural diversity within the bloc. The elites in Brussels became a representation of the detached cosmopolitan elites that despised the nation and traditional culture, which is commonly compared to the politburo in Russia's past. Anti-establishment parties across Europe often contrast the conservative ethos of Russia with the EU as a community of bankers rather than people, and denounce "Merkel's Europe of the banks" (Braghiroli and Makarychev 2016: 219). Italia Liberia submitted a constitutional bill to the Supreme Court on 27 May 2020 that called for a referendum on the withdrawal of Italy from the EU. Gian Luca Toppi, a lawyer that contributed to the bill, argued from a conservative perspective that there are "harmful effects of participating in a Union without a soul and based only on finance".

Western conservatives commonly make comparisons between the EU and the Soviet Union as both deconstructs the national distinctiveness to develop a larger construct based on universalism. On the Russian side, Narochnitskaya (2014) similarly argued:

> Europe is ruled by a post-modernist, almost Trotskyist, left-libertarian elite. During Soviet times, the Central Committee Propaganda Department advocated the Marxist-Leninist utopia, which called for everybody to be granted an equal share of bread and expected all nations to merge and fuse on this basis. The Brussels propaganda department proposes something similar: it aspires to give everyone similar democracy and human rights and hopes that everybody will think the same about the meaning of life. Both universalist projects completely ignore fundamental differences in religious and philosophical worldviews of peoples and nations.

The advances of reason and individualism at the peril of the instinctive and communitarian fuel nihilism across the world. Al Gore (2013: 367), the former US presidential candidate, argued that identity crises are emerging across the planet in which "we begin to value powerful images instead of tested truths" to rediscover "who we are":

> The resurgence of fundamentalism in every world religion, from Islam to Judaism to Hinduism to Christianity; the proliferation of new spiritual movements, ideologies, and cults of all shapes and descriptions; the popularity of New Age Doctrines and the current fascination with explanatory myths and

stories from cultures the world over – all serve as evidence for the conclusion that there is indeed a spiritual crisis in modern civilisation that seems to be based on an emptiness at its center and the absence of a larger spiritual purpose.

While Russian soft power attracts some segments of Western conservatives, it also makes Russia a prime target to retain the liberal international order. The inability to identify the flaws of excessive liberalism results in Western political elites continuing to treat the growing crisis as an abnormality and look for simplistic answers to overcome populism. In the United States, the Trump phenomenon was attempted to be explained as a Russian conspiracy in the RussiaGate proceedings that only further reduced public trust in the political-media establishment (Cohen 2018). In Europe, the faltering of the political centre is also treated as a grand Russian conspiracy to "weaken the West from within". After decades of interfering in the domestic affairs of other states under the banner of liberalism, the political-media establishment in the West has rediscovered the principle of sovereignty and seeks to defend itself from external influence.

RUSSIAN CONSERVATISM AS SOFT POWER

There has been a liberal democratic bias in the concept of soft power, which has neglected the growing attraction and soft power of Russian conservatism (Keating and Kaczmarska 2019). Liberal democratic ideals were deemed to be the main, if not only, source of soft power due to its universalism. Albeit, Russian conservatism as soft power has gradually been formalised into policies that recognise international competition will be fought with ideas.

In the early 2000s, Russia began to actively employ conservative principles to wield soft power to push back against Western expansionism. Putin (2012b) defined soft power as "the promotion of one's own interests and approaches through persuasion and attraction of empathy towards one's own country, based on its achievements not only in the material sphere but also in the spheres of intellect and culture". Instead of measuring civilisation by their ability to emulate universal Western liberalism, Russia's Foreign Minister Sergei Lavrov (2008b) opined:

> As regards the content of the new stage in humankind's development, there are two basic approaches to it among countries. The first one holds that the world must gradually become a Greater West through the adoption of Western values. It is a kind of "the end of history." The other approach – advocated by Russia – holds that competition is becoming truly global and acquiring a civilizational dimension; that is, the subject of competition now includes values and development models.

The Russian Foreign Policy Concept of 2013 similarly recognised in the tradition of Huntington that competition would begin to orient around civilisational ideas:

> For the first time in modern history, global competition takes place on a civilizational level, whereby various values and models of development based on the universal principles of democracy and market economy start to clash and compete against each other. Cultural and civilizational diversity of the world becomes more and more manifest. (RF 2013)

The conservatism of the Kremlin identifies a liberal threat from following the liberal path of the West. However, by cautioning against the excesses of liberalism in the West, Putin is implicitly also appealing to the West and the rest of the world. Putin (2013b) opined:

> We see that many Euro-Atlantic states have taken the way where they deny or reject their own roots, including their Christian roots which form the basis of Western civilization. In these countries, the moral basis and any traditional identity are being denied – national, religious, cultural, and even gender identities are being denied or relativised. There, politics treats a family with many children as juridically equal to a homosexual partnership; faith in God is equal to faith in Satan. The excesses and exaggerations of political correctness in these countries indeed leads to serious consideration for the legitimization of parties that promote the propaganda of paedophilia. The people in many European states are actually ashamed of their religious affiliations and are indeed frightened to speak about them. Christian holidays and celebrations are abolished or "neutrally" renamed, as if one were ashamed of those Christian holidays. With this method one hides away the deeper moral value of those celebrations. And these countries try to force this model onto other nations, globally. I am deeply convinced that this is a direct way to the degradation and primitivization of culture. This leads to deeper demographic and moral crisis in the West. What can be better evidence for the moral crisis of human society in the West than the loss of its reproductive function? And today nearly all "developed" Western countries cannot survive reproductively, not even with the help of migrants.

Putin (2013a) announced that Russian conservatism enjoyed great support in the world, irrespective of opposition by Western liberal elites.

> We know that there are more and more people in the world who support our position on defending traditional values that have made up the spiritual and moral foundation of civilisation in every nation for thousands of years: the values of

traditional families, real human life, including religious life, not just material existence but also spirituality, the values of humanism and global diversity.

POST-SOVIET CONSERVATISM

A key civilisational theme evolved that referred to the Russian World (Russki Mir), which differs from Western civilisation. The Russian World encompasses the linguistic and cultural space of Russia and the millions of ethnic Russian compatriots abroad. In the annual Federal Assembly Speech of 2007, Putin (2007) argued the Russian language is a central component for the shared cultural space of the Russian World: "The Russian language not only preserves an entire layer of truly global achievements but is also the living space for the many millions of people in the Russian-speaking world, a community that goes far beyond Russia itself."

The cultural links take on various formats. The core of the Russian World was Belarus and Ukraine as the fellow successor states of Kievan Rus. The post-Soviet space is defined by shared history, culture, traditions and language. The orthodox faith is the source of a religious and cultural with the space in Greece and Cyprus, while Serbia is also tied to Russia by pan-Slavic sentiments and historical ties. However, Russia also seeks common ground and cooperation based on Christianity with the West, and based on conservative values and civilisational distinctiveness with the entire world.

EUROPEAN CONSERVATISM

The neoliberal consensus has opened a political vacuum that is currently being filled by the populists on both the Political Right and the political Left. These new political groups also tend to be very critical of the neoliberal architecture of Europe, as a Europe without Russia inevitably becomes a Europe against Russia.

Case in point, in Germany both Die Linke on the Political Left and AfD on the Political Right share favourable views of Russia. The German populists deem Russia to be "an attractive partner with similar cultural traits as Europe," and there is a strong appeal due to the populist ideal of "sovereign nation states furthering their interests without reference to universal values or prior institutional commitments" (Chryssogelos 2010: 273). In Austria, the Freedom Party's ascendance to power elevated similar Russia-friendly political figures.

Political forces in France are also pushing against the neoliberal consensus and thus finding a common cause with Russia. Marine Le Pen, the former presidential candidate and leader of National Front, argued that "the divide is no longer between the right and the left, but between the patriots and the globalists. . . . It's a choice of civilisation. I will be the president of those French who want to continue living in France as the French do" (Noack and Birnbaum 2017). Le Pen lambasted the EU and NATO for undermining traditional culture and family values, which she contrast with Moscow's political platform and Putin as the defender of "the Christian heritage of European civilization" (Polyakova 2014). Le Pen argued that France had to recognise the fundamental changes in the world: "A new world has emerged in these past years. . . . It's the world of Vladimir Putin, it's the world of Donald Trump in the US. I share with these great nations a vision of cooperation, not of submission" (Henley 2017). Le Pen eventually lost to Emmanuel Macron in the 2017 presidential election. Albeit, the Gaulinist spirit of France is even returning to the establishment political class. Macron (2020) argued that the liberal format for globalisation appeared to have exhausted itself:

> There were real successes. It got rid of totalitarians, there was the fall of the Berlin Wall 30 years ago and with ups and downs it brought hundreds of millions of people out of poverty. But particularly in recent years it increased inequalities in developed countries. And it was clear that this kind of globalisation was reaching the end of its cycle, it was undermining democracy.

In Italy, Russia-friendly political groups came to power in early 2018 with the coalition of Lega and the Five Star Movement. Matteo Salvini, the deputy prime minister of Italy, proclaimed that "Russia represents the future" and even wore a t-shirt with the picture of President Putin in the European Parliament. Salvini also expressed his cultural affinity towards Russia by arguing "I feel at home in Russia in a way that I don't in other European countries" (Squires 2018). The Italian right-wing party Fronte Nazionale applauded Russia's "courageous position against the powerful gay lobby" (Shekhovtsov 2014). Roberto Fiore, the leader of the Italian right-wing party Forza Nuova, argued that "Moscow is the Third Rome, and the role of Russia in history is to revive Christianity" (Anzar 2015).

An important exception is Poland, where conservatives and nationalists are a deep mistrust towards Russia. Polish conservatives therefore commonly criticise other European conservatives for their Russophone sentiments. Yet, there are nonetheless some cracks emerging in the anti-Russian consensus. Lech Walesa, the leader of the Solidarity movement and the first democratically elected President of Poland, argued that the animosity and divisions between Russia and Poland should be resolved. Walesa also blamed the United States and Europe for their efforts to keep the historical wounds open:

Every time we ran into a disagreement between us, there were always some third parties profiting from it. They took advantage of our differences and disagreements. The time has come for us to put an end to this and build good relations. . . . If we could come to an agreement with Russia, it would shock all of Europe and the US. They use the discord between us to their advantage. (RT 2020)

HUNGARIAN CONSERVATIVES

While Russia traces its Eurasian origin to the Mongols in the thirteenth century, Hungarian Turanism builds on the national idea of its people being descendants of the Huns. The Huns emerged from the Eurasian steppes in the fifth century and brought havoc to the Roman Empire. Hungarian Turanism had its heyday in the second half of the nineteenth century and first half of the twentieth century. Turanism initially had its appeal as an eastern idea in opposition to a threat from the Slavs, and also incorporated Finns and Estonians as Ural-Altaic peoples united by language. In the more modern application, Turanism is used in opposition to Western dominance and can be linked to Russia. Previously, German and French scholars seeking to exclude Russia from Europe used the term "Turanism" to refer to an Asiatic Russia.

These ideas are seeing a revival in Hungary. Prime Minister Viktor Orban argued: "Hungarians see themselves as the late descendants of Attila the Hun" and Hungarians should therefore take pride to be the most western Eastern people. Turanism is a conservative stance in opposition to the liberal excesses of the West, and aligns Hungary closer to Russia and Turkey as Eurasian powers. Hungary even attained an observer status in the assembly of "Turkic speaking countries" consisting of Turkey, Azerbaijan, Kazakhstan, Kyrgyzstan and Uzbekistan.

As a crisis of liberalism ravages, a Europe detached from its past and in disarray, the effort in Hungary to become "more European" appears to be reversing. Orban accused the liberal EU elites of having betrayed the cultural and religious traditions of the continent. Orban (2014) advocated illiberal democracy consistent with conservative principles, and cautioned that liberal democracies "will not be able to sustain their world-competitiveness in the following years" and "today, the stars of international analyses are Singapore, China, India, Turkey, Russia". Furthermore, Orban had expressed his admiration and support for Moscow's concept of sovereign democracy. The political economy of Hungary is also changing with its "Eastern Opening" (Keleti Nyitás) initiative that aims to reduce its excessive economic dependence on the West by establishing closer economic connectivity with the east.

EURASIAN CONSERVATISM

Russian conservatism has much in common with its Asian counterparts, where modernisation was also conflated with westernisation. Asia also struggled to develop an organic path to modernity as the national culture was uprooted to accommodate foreign culture. The conservative challenge in the East was therefore to oppose two extreme groups: the revolutionaries seeking to uproot the national culture to modernise, and those who rejected modernity altogether.

In the 1980s, a new cultural conservatism began to emerge in China at the time when classical conservatism began to be discarded in the West (Cha 2003: 482). Confucianism represents conservative ideas advocating that social integration, stability and harmonious relationships require respect for tradition and social hierarchy. While Confucian values are strong in China, they are also found in other East Asian states such as Japan and Korea (Zhang et al. 2005).

China has to some extent become a very conservative country. The rapid and disruptive developments in China over the past decades created incentives to revive Confucianism to ensure that the objectives of morality and harmony are not lost on the path to modernity (Bell 2010). Rather than transcending the concept of the nation, the Chinese state has embarked on traditional nation-building by homogenising China into a more cohesive tribe based on a shared ethno-cultural core. The Chinese government advocates assimilation of both Tibet and Xinjiang by advocating Han Chinese to relocate to the region and scaling back on the region distinctiveness. The main objective of the Chinese Communist Party is not to promote communism abroad, but to revive Chinese civilisation and restore its status from before the Opium Wars. Eurasianism also has a strong appeal as it is feared that the United States will launch a modern Opium War to weaken China and usher in another Century of Humiliation.

Indian conservatism is currently expressed through Hindu nationalism and traditionalism to homogenise the population. This strand of conservatism represents a common contradiction found in the conservatism of multi-ethnic and multi-religious states. Hindu nationalism aptly defines the social group and links it to religion as the transcendent source of tradition and spirituality. However, defining India solely by Hinduism becomes a revolutionary movement as it breaks with the past. India's conservative challenges should not be simplified, yet it resembles the historical difficulties of Russian conservatives to identify the nation and collective to be preserved. Despite its difficulties and internal contradictions, the rise of Hindu nationalism is a conservative reaction to social and cultural change in India and the liberal international order. India also has systemic incentives to embrace a Eurasian political economy. India promotes formats for economic connectivity in Eurasia to skew the balance of dependence and prevent the Eurasian continent from becoming too reliant on China. For example, India engages in the North-South Transportation Corridor with Iran and Russia, various connectivity initiatives with Central Asia, the Go East policy to connect with South-East Asia, and seemingly in defiance of geography even seeks a role in the Russian Northern Sea Route through the Arctic.

CONCLUSION

History is repeating itself as Russian conservatism is yet again transitioning towards an international mission. Speeches by the political leadership and strategic documents of the Russian Federation affirm that cooperation and competition in the world will focus increasingly on civilisational ideas. Russia is positioning itself as a champion of conservatism that repudiates the notion that unfettered liberalism can deliver purpose for the individual and stability for the international system. Russian is returning to its pre-communist role as an international conservative power that continues the historical task of saving Europe from itself. However, Russia's post-Soviet conservatism positions Russia as both the "real Europe" and a Eurasian power.

Conservatives around the world find unity in the rejection of universalism and support for cultural distinctiveness and civilisational pluralism. Europe has prospered under a liberal-conservative balance that positioned society between change and continuity, where Russia historically has been a conservative anchor that resisted the excesses of liberal revolutionary developments. Conservatives in the East see Russia taking a leading role in the rejection of liberal hegemony. Classical conservatives and populists in the West tend to view the world as a national-patriotism versus cosmopolitan-globalism divide, which implies that Russia transitions from being an adversary to becoming an ally.

Russia's international conservatism presents several challenges and risks. Instability and chaos are likely awaiting as neoliberalism is faltering, and Russia should be cautious about standing too close during the transition to an unknown future. The association with populists and politically immature forces abroad could implicate Russia in conflicts it should insulate itself from. Populists in both the West and the East should not be trusted as history provides many examples about the dangers of attempting to preserve and revive what has already been lost. Furthermore, the elites of the neoliberal order that seek to revive the liberal-authoritarian divide will continue to use Russia as an external threat to establish domestic solidarity. Several Western states are already showing indications of being *irrational*, which is defined by realists as having rivalry in domestic politics influencing or dictating foreign policy.

Conclusion

Taming Russia's Revolutionary Impulses

The evolution of Russian conservatism demonstrates that the principles of conservatism have remained constant, yet the policies have changed to adapt to the developments and challenges of Russia. Conservatism is theorised here as a paradox since it is based on a universal feature entrenched in human nature, which is the instinctive need to organise in distinctive social groups that pursue organic change. Russian conservatism can therefore be compared with conservatism in other countries as they are based on the same principles, which is to reject universalism to uphold civilisational distinctiveness.

Two major challenges for Russian conservatism has been discussed in this book. First, Russia's historical vulnerability to revolutionary change has always complicated organic change. Following each disruptive period, conservatives must incorporate the revolutionary changes and identity into its national narrative and identity. Second, a Russian path to organic change has lacked a viable political economy, and Russia has instead attempted to modernise by emulating the West, irrespective of the different geography and history.

From its conception, Russia had a complex origin due to the strong influences of Slavdom, the Nordic Rus and the Byzantine Empire. The fragmentation of Kievan Rus and subsequent Mongol occupation diminished the Europeanness of Russia and its economic prowess by being cut off from major maritime corridors as the arteries of international trade. The Mongol Yoke and the conquest of Tatar kingdoms in the mid-sixteenth century resulted in ambiguity about the nation due to the multi-ethnic character of Russia and its belonging to Europe. The Orthodox Church and autocracy, which were strengthened after the Mongol Yoke and defensive expansionism subsequently became the domineering conservative policies as the representative of the collective. The Orthodox Church also is especially vital as the source of morality and legal foundations, as well as defining the commonality and difference between Russia and Europe.

The reason of the Enlightenment and spirituality of the counter-Enlightenment movement manifested itself as a western versus eastern identity, which caused more disruption and societal divisions than in its European counterparts. Modernisation was thus conflated with the Europeanisation of Russia. Peter the Great undertook a great leap towards modernity and detached Russia from organic growth. Russia established itself as a European maritime power and modernised its industries. Yet, the Cultural Revolution aimed to make Russia more European created a deep division and antagonism between the cosmopolitan and Europeanised elites, and the peasantry that identified by the land and traditional values. The neglect of organic change created a vacuum filled by conservative Slavophiles who sought to represent the peasantry and Russia's cultural and political distinctiveness.

Likewise, the French Revolution could not be implemented in Russia due to ambiguity about the nation. The official conservatism was developed by Sergei Uvarov, who countered the French Revolutionary slogan "liberty, egalitarianism, and fraternity", with the Russian conservative alternative: "orthodoxy, autocracy and nationality". Russian history had been and continued to be defined by a clear pattern – internal division created chaos domestically and emboldened expansionism by neighbouring states.

Over the next decades, conservatism branched in different directions due to the complex historical roots of Russia and ambiguity of the nation. Some conservatives romanticised pre-Petrine reforms, although nostalgia corrupts as setting the clock back is a revolutionary act. Other conservatives sought to bridge the divide with the Europeanised elites by recognising that Russia had both a pre-Petrine and post-Petrine past. Some conservatives envisioned drastic changes that were aligned with geostrategic objectives – such as the Pan-Slavs advocacy for resolving the nationality question by unifying the Slavs, or the conservative argument for retaking Constantinople.

The Eurasianists emerged as a new conservative strand following the Bolshevik Revolution. Eurasianism was able to address the revolutionary changes throughout Russian history by defining the nation as of Slavic origin that merged with Turkic, Ugro-Finnic and other ethnic components on the Eurasian steppes that transformed Russia. Eurasianism also responded to the revolutionary changes of the Soviet Union and positioning itself as a conservative exit strategy once the Marxist experiment would eventually fail due to its internal contradictions.

Furthermore, the Eurasianists political economy began to take shape with the industrialisation in the second half of the nineteenth century. Rather than organising its economy according to the model of Western maritime powers, the Eurasianists built on Russia's distinctiveness by seeking advantage as a land power as an organic path to modernity. Russia has been denied direct access transportation corridors by Western maritime powers since the Treaty of Stolbovo in 1617, which only intensified after Peter the Great established a presence on the Baltic Sea. The Eurasianist leaned towards establishing a continental economy to negate the rule of maritime powers.

The Soviet Union was replaced by a liberal revolution at both the domestic and international level, which also neglected key conservative principles. However, Russia has drifted back to its conservative Eurasianist inclinations. Post-Soviet Russia has a more homogenous ethno-cultural core, yet it continues to define itself as a multi-ethnic state and the collective is defined within the narrative of a civilisation state. Parts of the Soviet legacy and the liberal revolution have been salvaged to the extent it conforms with conservative principles. Yet, the past revolutionary century will not define Russia, as Moscow's conservative government under Putin are striving towards putting the past century in the context of Russia's thousand-year-long history. The only constant has been the Orthodox Church, which is reintroduced into Russian culture and all aspects of life.

Furthermore, the Eurasianist political economy has winds in its sails as the 500-year history of dominance by Western maritime powers has come to an end. The rise of the East, especially China, is unravelling the Western-led political economy. Unlike the maritime powers that ruled from the Eurasian periphery by dividing Eurasian powers, the Eurasian strategy is believed to rely on cooperation and harmonisation of interests.

The historical challenge for Russian conservatives, to establish an organic path to modernity, appears to be within reach. Eurasian partnerships are established to develop technological sovereignty, transportation corridors and financial instruments outside the control of the West. The dichotomy between western reason and modernity versus eastern spirituality had come to an end, and the conservatives can manage change in terms of balancing reason and instinct, the modern and traditional, the individual and collective.

Analysing the evolution of Russian conservatism is necessary to understand Russia, although it also generates many questions: Is it possible to establish international unity based on the rejection of universalism? Should international cooperation be premised on the preservation of civilisational pluralism? If so, can Western conservatives find a common cause with Russian conservatism in the format of a Common Eurasian Home?

Bibliography

Adams, B., 1897. *The Law of Civilisation and Decay*. London: The Macmillian Company.

Adler, L. K. and Paterson, T. G., 1970. Red fascism: The merger of Nazi Germany and Soviet Russia in the American image of totalitarianism, 1930's–1950's. *The American Historical Review*, vol. 75, no. 4, pp. 1046–1064.

Albright, M., 1998. Interview on NBC-TV "The Today Show" with Matt Lauer, *US Department of State Archive*, 19 February 1998.

Andrew, J., 1982. *Russian Writers and Society in the Second Half of the Nineteenth Century*. New York: Springer.Aron, R., 2017. *Peace and War: A Theory of International Relations*. London: Routledge.

Ascher, A., 2002. *PA Stolypin: The Search for Stability in Late Imperial Russia*. Stanford, CA: Stanford University Press.

Ashworth, W. J., 2017. *The Industrial Revolution: The State, Knowledge and Global Trade*. London: Bloomsbury Publishing.

Azar, I., 2015. Europe's far right flocks to Russia International conservative forum held in St. Petersburg, *Meduza*, 24 March 2015.

Badmaev, V., 2015. Eurasianism as a 'philosophy of nation', in Dutkiewicz, P. and Sakwa, R. (eds.), *Eurasian Integration: The View From Within*. London: Routledge, pp. 31–45.

Baker, J., 2002. Russia in NATO? *The Washington Quarterly*, vol. 25, no. 1, pp. 95–103.

Bartlett, R., 1990. *Land Commune and Peasant Community in Russia: Communal Forms in Imperial and Early Soviet Society*. New York: Palgrave Macmillan.

Bell, D., 1976. The coming of the post-industrial society. *The Educational Forum*, vol. 40, no. 4, pp. 574–579.

Bell, D., 2010. *Confucian Political Ethics*. Princeton, NJ: Princeton University Press.

Bendett, S., 2019. Putin drops hints about upcoming national AI strategy, *Defense One*, 30 May 2019.

Bendett, S. and Kania, E. B., 2019. A new Sino-Russian high-tech partnership: Authoritarian innovation in an era of great-power rivalry, *Australian Strategic Policy Institute*, October 2019.

Benner, C., 2002. *Work in the New Economy: Flexible Labor Markets in Silicon Valley*. Malden, MA: Blackwell Publishing.

Berdyaev, N., 1923. *Filosofiya neravenstva: Pisma k nedrugam po sotsialnoi filosofii* [Philosophy of Inequality: Letters to the Enemies of Social Philosophy]. Obelisk, Berlin.

Berdyaev, N., 1947. *The Russian Idea*. London: Geoffrey Bles Ltd.

Berryman, J., 2002. British imperial defence strategy and Russia: The role of the royal navy in the far east (1878–1898). *International Journal of Naval History*, vol. 1, no. 1, pp. 44–62.

Blackwell, W. L., 2015. *Beginnings of Russian Industrialization, 1800–1860*. Princeton, NJ: Princeton University Press.

Blair, T., 1999. The Blair doctrine, *Public Broadcasting Service*, 22 April 1999. Block, F., 2008. Swimming against the current: The rise of a hidden developmental state in the United States. *Politics & Society*, vol. 36, no. 2, pp. 169–206.

Bloom, A., 2008. *The Closing of the American Mind*. New York: Simon & Schuster.

Booth, K. and Wheeler, N. J., 2008. *The Security Dilemma: Fear, Cooperation and Trust in World Politics*. Basingstoke: Palgrave Macmillan.

Boterbloem, K., 2018. *A History of Russia and Its Empire: From Mikhail Romanov to Vladimir Putin*. New York: Rowman & Littlefield Publishers.

Bova, R., 2015. *Russia and Western Civilization: Cutural and Historical Encounters: Cutural and Historical Encounters*. London: Routledge.

Braghiroli, S. and Makarychev, A., 2016. Russia and its supporters in Europe: Trans-ideology a la carte. *Southeast European and Black Sea Studies*, vol. 16, no. 2, pp. 213–233.

Brandenberger, D. L. and Dubrovsky, A. M., 1998. 'The people need a tsar': The emergence of national Bolshevism as Stalinist ideology, 1931–1941. *Europe-Asia Studies*, vol. 50, no. 5, pp. 873–892.

Bretherton, C. and Vogler, J., 1999. *The European Union as a Global Actor*. London: Routledge.

Brezhnev, L. I., 1980. *Socialism, Democracy and Human Rights*. Oxford: Pergamon Press.

Broers, M., Hicks, P. and Guimera, A., 2012. *The Napoleonic Empire and the New European Political Culture*. London: Palgrave Macmillan.

Brzezinski, Z., 1997. *The Grand Chessboard: American Primacy and its Geopolitical Imperatives*. New York: Basic Books.

Brzezinski, Z., 2009. *The Choice: Global Domination or Global Leadership*. New York: Basic Books.

Brzezinski, Z., 2016. Towards a global realignment, *The American Interest*, 17 April 2016.

Brzezinski, Z., 2017. How to address strategic insecurity in a turbulent age, *The Huffington Post*, 3 January 2017.

Buchanan, P., 2013. Is Putin one of us? *Official Website of Patrick J. Buchanan*, 17 December 2013.

Buchanan, P., 2014. Whose side is god on now, *Official Website of Patrick J. Buchanan*, 4 April 2014.

Burbank, J., 1986. *Intelligentsia and Revolution*. New York: Oxford University Press.

Burckhardt, J., 2010. *The Civilisation of the Renaissance in Italy*. New York: Dover Publications.

Burke, E., 1790. *Reflections on the French Revolution*. London: Seeley, Jackson, and Halliday.

Burke, E., 1792. *The Works of Edmund Burke*. London: J. Dodsley, Pall Mall.

Burke, E., 1796. *Letters on Regicide Peace*. Indianapolis: Liberty Fund.

Burrows, M. and Manning, R. A., 2015. Kissinger's nightmare: How an inverted US-China-Russia may be a game-changer, *Valdai Paper*, no. 33, 9 November 2015.

Bush, G., 1992. Address before a Joint Session of the Congress on the State of the Union, *The American Presidency Project*, 28 January 1992.

Buzan, B., 2005. The security dynamics of a 1+4 world, in Aydinli, E. and Rosenau, J. N. (eds.), *Globalization, Security, and the Nation State: Paradigms in Transition*. Albany: State University of New York Press, pp. 177–198.

Buzan, B., 2010. China in international society: Is "peaceful rise" possible? *The Chinese Journal of International Politics*, vol. 3, no. 1, pp. 5–36.

Byrnes, R. F., 1968. *Pobedonostsev: His Life and Thought*. Bloomington: Indiana University Press.

Carpenter, T. G., 1992. *A Search for Enemies: America's Alliances After the Cold War*. Washington, DC: Cato Institute.

Carson, D. A., 2012. *The Intolerance of Tolerance*. Cambridge: Wm. B. Eerdmans Publishing.

Cha, S. H., 2003. Modern Chinese confuscianism: The contemporary neo-confusian movement and its cultural significance. *Social Compass*, vol. 50, no. 4, pp. 481–491.

Chaadaev, P., 1965. Philosophical letters, in Edie, J. M., Scanlan, J. P., Zeldin, M. B. and Kline, G. L. (eds.), *Russian Philosophy*. New York: Quadrangle.

Chamberlain, L., 2020. *Ministry of Darkness: How Sergei Uvarov Created Conservative Modern Russia*. London: Bloomsbury Publishing.

Chang, H. J., 2002. *Kicking Away the Ladder: Development Strategy in Historical Perspective*. New York: Anthem Press.

Chebankova, E., 2016. Contemporary Russian conservatism. *Post-Soviet Affairs*, vol. 32, no. 1, pp. 28–54.

Cheng, J. Y. S., 2009. Chinese perceptions of Russian foreign policy during the Putin administration: U.S.-Russia relations and "strategic triangle" considerations. *Journal of Current Chinese Affairs*, vol. 8, no. 2, pp. 145–168.

Cherniavsky, M., 1968. Ivan the terrible as renaissance prince. *Slavic Review*, vol. 27, no. 2, pp. 195–211.

Cheshire, H. T., 1934. The expansion of imperial Russia to the Indian border. *The Slavonic and East European Review*, vol. 13, no. 37, pp. 85–97.

Chesterton, G. K., 2002. *Chesterton Day by Day: The Wit and Wisdom of GK Chesterton*. New York: Inkling Books.

Christoff, P. K., 2019. *An Introduction to Nineteenth-Century Russian Slavophilism: Iu. F. Samarin*. London: Routledge.

Chryssogelos, A. S., 2010. Undermining the west from within: European populists, the US and Russia. *European View*, vol. 9, no. 2, pp. 267–277.

Churchill, W. S., 2013. *The World Crisis: The Aftermath* (vol. 4). New York: Rosetta Books.

Cohen, S. F., 1980. *Bukharin and the Bolshevik Revolution: A Political Biography, 1888–1938*. Oxford: Oxford University Press.

Cohen, S. F., 1984. The friends and foes of change: Reformism and conservatism in the Soviet Union, in Hoffmann, E. P. and Laird, R. F. (eds.), *The Soviet Polity in the Modern Era*. New York: Aldine de Gruyter, pp. 85–104.

Cohen, S. F., 2018. *War With Russia?: From Putin & Ukraine to Trump & Russiagate*. New York: Simon & Schuster.

Conrad, J., 1996. *Heart of Darkness*. London: Palgrave Macmillan.

Cooley, A. and Nexon, D., 2020. *Exit from Hegemony: The Unraveling of the American Global Order*. Oxford: Oxford University Press.

Coser, L. A., 1951. Some aspects of Soviet family policy. *American Journal of Sociology*, vol. 56, no. 5, pp. 424–437.

Crowley, S., 1995. Between class and nation: Worker politics in the New Ukraine. *Communist and Post-Communist Studies*, vol. 28, no. 1, pp. 43–69.

Daniel, W. L., 2006. *The Orthodox Church and Civil Society in Russia*. College Station: Texas A&M University Press.

Danilevsky, N., 2013. *Russia and Europe: The Slavic World's Political and Cultural Relations with the Germanic-Roman West*. Bloomington, IN: Slavica Publishers.

Deneen, P. J., 2018. *Why Liberalism Failed*. New Haven, CT: Yale University Press.

Diamond, L. J., 1990. Three paradoxes of democracy. *Journal of Democracy*, vol. 1, no. 3, pp. 48–60.

Dickinson, A., 2000. Quantifying religious oppression: Russian orthodox church closures and repression of priests 1917–41. *Religion, State & Society*, vol. 18, no. 4, pp. 327–335.

Diesen, G., 2016. *EU and NATO Relations with Russia: After the Collapse of the Soviet Union*. London: Routledge.

Diesen, G., 2017. *Russia's Geoeconomic Strategy for a Greater Eurasia*. London: Routledge.

Diesen, G., 2018. The geoeconomics of the Russian–Japanese territorial dispute. *Asian Survey*, vol. 58, no. 3, pp. 582–605.

Diesen, G., 2019. Russia as an international conservative power: The rise of the right-wing populists and their affinity towards Russia. *Journal of Contemporary European Studies*, vol. 28, no. 2, pp. 1–15.

Diesen, G., 2020a. Narrowing the deepening division between the West and Russia, in Grigoryev, L. and Pabst, A. (eds.), *Global Governance in Transformation: Challenges for International Cooperation*. London: Springer, pp. 59–72.

Diesen, G., 2020b. Neutral power Russia? in Reginbogin, H. and Lottaz, P. (eds.), *Permanent Neutrality*. Lanham, MD: Lexington Books.

Diesen, G. and Keane, C., 2017. The two-tiered division of Ukraine: Historical narratives in nation-building and region-building. *Journal of Balkan and Near Eastern Studies*, vol. 19, no. 3, pp. 313–329.

Diesen, G. and Keane, C., 2018. The offensive posture of NATO's missile defence system. *Communist and Post-Communist Studies*, vol. 51, no. 2, pp. 91–100.

Diez, T., 1999. Speaking 'Europe': The politics of integration discourse. *Journal of European Public Policy*, vol. 6, no. 4, pp. 598–613.

Dixon, S., 2015. *Catherine the Great*. London: Routledge.

Dostoyevsky, A., 2001. *Fyodor Dostoyevsky: A Study*. Honolulu: University Press of the Pacific.

Dostoyevsky, F., 1986. *Complete Collected Works in 30 Volumes* [Polnoe Sobranie Sochinenii v Tridtsari Tomah. Leningrad: Nauka.

Dostoevsky, F., 1997. *A Writer's Diary – Volume 2: 1877–1881*. Evanston, IL: Northwestern University Press.

Dostoyevsky, F., 2009a. *Notes From Underground*. Translated by Constance Garnett, Cambridge: Hackett Publishing Company.

Dostoyevsky, F., 2009b. *A Writers Diary Volume – Volume 1*. Evanston, IL: Northwestern University Press.

Dostoyevsky, F., 2016. *The Brothers Karamazov*. Moscow: Aegitas.

Dostoyevsky, F., 2017. *The Possessed*. New York: Simon & Schuster.

Dowler, W., 1982. *Dostoevsky, Grigor'ev, and Native Soil Conservatism*. Toronto: University of Toronto Press.

Durkheim, E., 2005. *Suicide: A Study in Sociology*. London: Routledge.

Earle, E. M., 1943. Friedrich list, forerunner of Pan-Germanism. *The American Scholar*, vol. 12, no. 4, pp. 430–443.

Eckes, A. E., 1999. *Opening America's Market: US Foreign Trade Policy Since 1776*. Chapel Hill: University of North Carolina Press.

Eklof, B., Bushnell, J. and Zakharova, L. G., 1994. *Russia's Great Reforms, 1855–1881*. Bloomington: Indiana University Press.

Engerman, D. C., 2009. *Modernization From the Other Shore: American Intellectuals and the Romance of Russian Development*. Cambridge, MA: Harvard University Press.

Etkind, A., 2011. *Internal Colonization: Russia's Imperial Experience*. Cambridge: Polity Press.

European Parliament, 2008. Written declaration on the proclamation of 23 August as European Day of Remembrance for Victims of Stalinism and Nazism, PE406.730v01-00, 7 May 2008.

European Union, 2017. China manufacturing 2025: Putting industrial policy ahead of market forces, *European Chamber of Commerce*, 7 March 2017.

Evdokimov, P., 2011. *Orthodoxy: The Cosmos Transfigured*. New York: New City Press.

Fagan, P., 1995. The real root causes of violent crime: The breakdown of marriage, family, and community, *The Heritage Foundation*, 17 March 1995.

Ferguson, A., 1767. *An Essay on the History of Civil Society*. Piscataway, NJ: Transaction Publishers.

Finkel, S., 2010. Nikolai Berdiaev and the philosophical tasks of the emigration, in Hamburg, G. M. and Poole, R. A. (eds.), *A History of Russian Philosophy 1830–1939: Faith, Reason, and the Defense of Human Dignity*. Cambridge: Cambridge University Press, pp. 346–362.

Frankl, V. E., 1985. *Man's Search for Meaning*. New York: Simon & Schuster.

Freeden, M., 1996. *Ideologies and Political Theory: A Conceptual Approach*. Oxford: Clarendon Press.

Freud, S., 1963. Reflections upon war and death, in *Character and Culture*. New York: Collier Books.

Friedman, G., 2014. The geopolitics of the United States, part 1: The inevitable empire, *Stratfor*, 4 July 2014.

Friedman, T. L., 1998. Foreign affairs; now a word from X, *The New York Times*, 2 May 1998.Friedrich-Ebert-Stiftung, 2020. Russia's 'generation Z': Attitudes and values 2019/2020, *Friedrich-Ebert-Stiftung*, 2020.

Fukuyama, F., 1989. The end of history? *The National Interest*, vol. 16, pp. 3–18.

Fukuyama, F., 2018. *Identity: The Demand for Dignity and the Politics of Resentment*. New York: Farrar, Straus and Giroux.

Gaddis, J. L., 2005. *Strategies of Containment: A Critical Appraisal of American National Security Policy During the Cold War*. Oxford: Oxford University Press.

Gallagher, J. and Robinson, R., 1953. The imperialism of free trade. *The Economic History Review*, vol. 6, no. 1, pp. 1–15.

Gerschenkron, A., 1962. *Economic Backwardness in Historical Perspective*. Cambridge, MA: Harvard University Press.

Gill, G., 2006. A new turn to authoritarian rule in Russia? *Democratization*, vol. 13, no. 1, pp. 58–77.

Gillespie, D. C., 1989. History, politics, and the Russian peasant: Boris Mozhaev and the collectivization of agriculture. *The Slavonic and East European Review*, vol. 67, no. 2, pp. 183–210.

Glazer, N., 1983. *Ethnic Dilemmas: 1964–82*. Cambridge, MA: Harvard University Press.

Glazyev, S. Y., 1998. *Genocide*. Moscow: Terra Publishing.

Glebov, S., 2017. *From Empire to Eurasia: Politics, Scholarship, and Ideology in Russian Eurasianism, 1920s–1930s*. Ithaca, NY: Cornell University Press.

Glubb, J., 1976. *The Fate of Empires and Search for Survival*. Edinburgh: William Blackwood & Sons Ltd.

Gogol, N. V., 2009. *Selected Passages from Correspondence with Friends*. Nashville: Vanderbilt University Press.

Goldman, W. Z., 1993. *Women, the State and Revolution: Soviet Family Policy and Social Life, 1917–1936*. Oxford: Cambridge University Press.

Gore, A., 2013. *Earth in the Balance: Forging a New Common Purpose*. New York: Routledge.

Grisbrooke, W. J., 1967. *Spiritual Counsels of Father John of Kronstadt*. London: James Clarke.

Gumilev, L., 1989. *Drevniaia Rus' i Velikaia Step*. Moscow: Ast.

Gusev, V., 2001. *Russian Conservatism: Main Directions and Stages of Development* [Russkii Konservatizm: Osnovnye Napravleniya i Etapy Razvitiya]. Tver: Tverskoi Gosudarstvennii Universitet.

Hahn, G. M., 2018. *Ukraine Over the Edge: Russia, the West and the "New Cold War"*. Jefferson, NC: McFarland.

Haidt, J., 2012. *The Righteous Mind: Why Good People Are Divided by Politics and Religion*. London: Penguin Books.

Halperin, C. J., 1987. *Russia and the Golden Horde: The Mongol Impact on Medieval Russian History*. Bloomington: Indiana University Press.

Hamburg, G. M., 1992. *Boris Chicherin & Early Russian Liberalism: 1828–1866*. Palo Alto, CA: Stanford University Press.

Hamburg, G. M., 1998. *Liberty, Equality, and the Market: Essays by BN Chicherin*. New Haven, CT: Yale University Press.

Hamburg, G. M., 2015. Language and conservative politics in Alexandrine Russia, in Offord, D. (ed.), *French and Russian in Imperial Russia: Language Attitudes and Identity*. Edinburgh: Edinburgh University Press, pp. 118–138.

Hamburg, G. M., 2016. *Russia's Path Toward Enlightenment: Faith, Politics, and Reason, 1500–1801*. New Haven, CT: Yale University Press.

Hamilton, A., 1791. Report of manufacturers, communication to the house of representatives, *Washington*, 5 December 1791.

Hannan, D., 2013. *Inventing Freedom: How the English-Speaking Peoples Made the Modern World*. New York: HarperCollins.

Hanson, S., 2003. Instrumental democracy: The end of ideology and the decline of Russian political parties, in Hesli, V. L. and Reissinger, W. M. (eds.), *The 1999–2000 Elections in Russia: Their Impact and Legacy*. Cambridge: Cambridge University Press, pp. 163–185.

Harman, O., 2010. *The Price of Altruism: George Price and the Search for the Origins of Kindness*. New York: W. W. Norton.

Haukkala, H., 2005. The relevance of norms and values in the EU's Russia policy. *Finnish Institute of International Affairs*, UPI Working Paper no. 52, pp. 1–22.

Haxthausen, A., 1856. *The Russian Empire: Its People, Institutions and Resources*. Oxon: Frank Cass and Company Limited.

Heckscher, E., 1955. *Mercantilism*. London: George Allen and Unwin.

Heidegger, M., 1953. *Introduction to Metaphysics*. New Haven, CT: Yale University Press.

Heller, M., 2015. *Histoire de la Russie et de son empire*. Paris: Tempus.

Henderson, W. O., 1975. *The Rise of German Industrial Power, 1834–1914*. Berkeley: University of California Press.

Henley, J., 2017. Le Pen, Putin, Trump: A disturbing axis, or just a mutual admiration society? *The Guardian*, 29 April 2017.

Herder, J. G., 1772. Treatise on the origin of language, in *Philosophical Writings*. Cambridge: Cambridge University Press, pp. 65–164.

Herder, J. G., 1966. *Ideas Upon Philosophy and the History of Mankind*. New York: Bergman Publishers.

Herz, J. H., 1950. Idealist internationalism and the security dilemma. *World Politics*, vol. 2, no. 2, pp. 157–180.

Hill, C., 1972. *The World Turned Upside Down: Radical Ideas During the Puritan Revolution*. Harmondsworth: Penguin.

Hilton, B., 1977. *Corn, Cash, Commerce: The Economic Policies of the Tory Governments, 1815–1830*. New York: Oxford University Press.

Hirschman, A., 1945. *National Power and the Structure of Foreign Trade*. Berkeley: University of California Press.

Hitchens, P., 1999. *The Abolition of Britain: The British Cultural Revolution from Lady Chatterley to Tony Blair*. London: Quartet Books.

Hitchens, P., 2014. Further thoughts on Russia, *Mail on Sunday*, 3 March 2014.

Hobsbawm, E., 2007. *Globalisation, Democracy and Terrorism*. London: Little, Brown.

Hosking, G. A., 2001. *Russia and the Russians: A History*. Cambridge, MA: Harvard University Press.

Hudson, M., 2010. *America's Protectionist Takeoff, 1815–1914: The Neglected American School of Political Economy*. Islet.

Hughes, M., 2000. State and society in the political thought of the Moscow Slavophiles. *Studies in East European Thought*, vol. 52, no. 3, pp. 159–183.

Hughes, M., 2004. The English Slavophile: W. J. Birkbeck and Russia. *The Slavonic and East European Review*, vol. 82, no. 3, pp. 680–706.

Huntington, S. P., 1957. Conservatism as an ideology. *American Political Science Review*, vol. 51, no. 2, pp. 454–473.

Huntington, S. P., 1993. If not civilizations, what? Paradigms of the post-cold war world. *Foreign Affairs*, vol. 72, no. 5, pp. 186–194.

Huntington, S. P., 1996. *The Clash of Civilizations and the Remaking of World Order*. New York: Simon & Schuster.

Huntington, S. P., 2004. Dead souls: The denationalization of the American Elite, *The National Interest*, 1 March 2004.

Ilyin, I., 1956. *Our Tasks: Articles 1948–1954* [Nashi Zadachi: Statii 1948–1954], vol. 1. Paris: Izdatelstvo Obshche-Voennogo Soyuza.

Imbrogno, S., 1986. Family policy in the Soviet Union. *International Journal of Sociology of the Family*, vol. 16, no. 2, pp. 165–180.

Ivanov, I., 2015. The sunset of Greater Europe, Speech at the 20th Annual International Conference of the Baltic Forum "The US, the EU and Russia – The New Reality", 12 September. Riga.

Jung, C. G., 1973. *Letters 1: 1906–1950*. Princeton, NJ: Princeton University Press.

Jung, C. G., 2014. *The Spiritual Problem of Modern Man: Modern Man in Search of a Soul*. London: Routledge.

Karaganov, S., 2006. Dangerous relapses, *Russia in Global Affairs*, 8 May 2006.

Karaganov, S., 2020. The military underpinning of the geopolitical revolution, in Diesen, G. and Lukin, A. (eds.), *Russia in a Changing World*. London: Palgrave Macmillan, pp. 1–22.

Karamzin, N. M., 2005. *Karamzin's Memoir on Ancient and Modern Russia: A Translation and Analysis*. Ann Arbor: University of Michigan Press.

Kassow, S. D., 1994. The university statute of 1863, in Eklof, B., Bushnell, J. and Zakharova, L. G. (eds.), *Russia's Great Reforms, 1855–1881*. Bloomington: Indiana University Press, pp. 247–263.

Katz, M., 2017. *Mikhail N. Katkov: A Political Biography, 1818–1887*. Berlin: Walter de Gruyter GmbH & Co. KG.

Katzenstein, P. J., 2005. *A World of Regions: Asia and Europe in the American Imperium*. London: Cornell University Press.

Keating, V. C. and Kaczmarska, K., 2019. Conservative soft power: Liberal soft power bias and the 'hidden' attraction of Russia. *Journal of International Relations and Development*, vol. 22, no. 1, pp. 1–27.

Kendall, T. D. and Tamura, R., 2010. Unmarried fertility, crime, and social stigma. *The Journal of Law and Economics*, vol. 53, no. 1, pp. 185–221.

Kennan, G. F., 1947. Sources of soviet conduct, *Foreign Affairs*, July 1947.

Kennan, G. F., 1951. *American Diplomacy 1900–1950*. Chicago: University of Chicago Press.

Kennan, G. F., 1972. *Memoirs: 1925–1950*. Boston: Little, Brown.

Kennan, G. F., 1993. *Around the Cragged Hill: A Personal and Political Philosophy*. New York: Norton.

Kennan, G. G., 2014. *The Kennan Diaries*. New York: W. W. Norton & Company, Inc.

Khodarkovsky, M., 1997. Ignoble savages and unfaithful subjects: Constructing non-Christian identities in early modern Russia, in Brower, D. R., Lazzerini, E. J. and Lazzerini, E. (eds.), *Russia's Orient: Imperial Borderlands and Peoples, 1700–1917*. Bloomington: Indiana University Press.

Khomyakov, A., 1895. *Russia and the English Church During the Last Fifty Years*. London: Rivington.

Khristoforov, I., 2002. *Aristocratic Opposition to the Great Reforms: End of 1850– Middle of 1870s* [Aristokraticheskaya Oppozitsiya Velikim Reformam: Konets 1850–Seredina 1870-kh Godov]. Moscow: Institute of Russian History of RAN.

Kipp, J. W. and Lincoln, W. B., 1979. Autocracy and reform bureaucratic absolutism and political modernization in nineteenth-century Russia. *Russian History*, vol. 6, no. 1, pp. 1–21.

Kireevsky, I., 1911. *Polnoe Sobranie Sochinenii*. Moscow: Kaluga.

Kirk, R., 1953. *The Conservative Mind: From Burke to Eliot*. Washington, DC: Regnery Publishing.

Kissinger, H., 1999. Interview with the *Daily Telegraph*, 28 June 1999.

Kissinger, H. A., 1968. The white revolutionary: Reflections on Bismarck. *Daedalus*, vol. 77, no. 3, pp. 888–924.

Kohn, H., 1953. *Pan-Slavism: Its History and Ideology*. Notre Dame, IN: University of Notre Dame Press.

Kortunov, A., 2017. False conflict: Universalism and identity. *Valdai Discussion Club*, 11 October 2017.

Kotkin, S., 2016. Russia's perpetual geopolitics: Putin returns to the historical pattern, *Foreign Affairs*, May/June 2016.

Kremlin, 2005. Road map on the common space of external security, *Presidential Executive Office*, Moscow, 10 May 2005.

Landau, J. M., 1995. *Pan-Turkism: From Irredentism to Cooperation*. Bloomington: Indiana University Press.

Lasch, C., 1996. *The Revolt of the Elites and the Betrayal of Democracy*, New York: W. W. Norton & Company.

Lavrov, S., 2008a. Russian foreign policy and a new quality of the geopolitical situation for diplomatic yearbook 2008, *The Ministry of Foreign Affairs of the Russian Federation*, 15 December 2008.

Lavrov, S., 2008b. Russia and the world in the 21st century, *Russia in Global Affairs*, July/September 2008.

Lavrov, S., 2012. Russia in the 21st-century world of power, *Russia in Global Affairs*, 27 December 2012.

Lavrov, S., 2014. Remarks and responses to reporters' questions by Foreign Minister Sergey Lavrov during a news conference following the OSCE Ministerial Council meeting, Basel, 5 December 2014.

Leontyev, K., 1885. *East, Russia and the Slavs* [Vostok, Rossiya i slavyanstvo]. T.1, Moscow.

Lieven, D., 1998. Russian, imperial and Soviet identities. *Transactions of the Royal Historical Society*, vol. 8, pp. 253–269.

Lieven, D., 2009. *Russia Against Napoleon: The Battle for Europe, 1807 to 1814*. London: Allen Lane.

Lijphart, A., 1969. Consociational democracy. *World Politics*, vol. 21, no. 2, pp. 207–225.

Likhachev, D. S., 1963. Further remarks on the problem of old Russian culture. *Slavic Review*, vol. 22, no. 1, pp. 115–120.

Lippman, W., 2008. *The Stakes of Diplomacy*. New Brunswick, NJ: Transaction.

Lipton, A., Shrier, D. and Pentland, A., 2016. Digital banking manifesto: The end of banks? *Massachusetts Institute of Technology*, pp. 1–20.

List, F., 1885. *The National System of Political Economy*. London: Longmans, Green & Company.

List, F., 2016. *The Natural System of Political Economy*. London: Routledge.

Lossky, N., 1952. *History of Russian Philosophy*. London: George Allen and Unwin.

Lukashevich, S., 1965. *Ivan Aksakov, 1823–1886: A Study in Russian Thought and Politics*. Cambridge, MA: Harvard University Press.

Lukin, A., 2000. *Political Culture of the Russian "Democrats"*. Oxford: Oxford University Press.

Lukin, A., 2015. Eurasian great power triangle, in Klieman, A. (ed.), *Great Powers and Geopolitics: International Affairs in a Rebalancing World*. Ramat-Aviv: Springer, pp. 183–206.

Lukin, A., 2020. *Pivot to Asia: Russia's Foreign Policy Enters the 21st Century*. New Delhi: Vij Books India.

Luttwak, E., 1993. Why fascism is the wave of the future. *London Review of Books*, vol. 16, no. 7, pp. 3–6.

Luttwak, E., 1995. The national prospect, *Commentary Magazine*, 1 November 1995.

Luttwak, E., 1999. *Turbo Capitalism*. New York: HarperCollins Publishers.

Maas, H., 2020. There can be no politics without history, *German Federal Foreign Office*, 7 May 2020.

Mackinder, H. J., 1904. The geographical pivot of history. *The Geographical Journal*, vol. 170, no. 4, pp. 421–444.

Mackinder, H. J., 1919. *Democratic Ideals and Reality*. New York: Henry Holt & Company.

Macron, E., 2020. FT interview: Emmanuel Macron says it is time to think the unthinkable, *Financial Times*, 16 April 2020.

Makarenko, A., 1967. *The Collective Family: A Handbook for Russian Parents*. New York: Doubleday & Co.

Malcolm, N., 1995. The case against 'Europe'. *Foreign Affairs*, vol. 74, no. 2, pp. 52–68.

Mankoff, J., 2009. *Russian Foreign Policy: The Return of Great Power Politics*. New York: Rowman & Littlefield Publishers.

Mann, M., 2005. *The Dark Side of Democracy: Explaining Ethnic Cleansing*. Cambridge: Cambridge University Press.

Mannheim, K., 1936. *An Introduction to the Sociology of Knowledge*. London: Routledge.

Marcuse, H., 1969. Repressive tolerance, in Wolff, R. P., Moore, B. and Marcuse, H. (eds.), *Critique of Pure Tolerance*. Boston: Beacon Press, pp. 95–137.

Martin, A. M., 1998. The family model of society and Russian national identity in Sergei N. Glinka's Russian Messenger (1808–1812). *Slavic Review*, vol. 57, no. 1, pp. 28–49.

Marx, K., 1977. *Critique of Hegel's Philosophy of Right*. Cambridge: Cambridge University Press.

Marx, K., 2008. *The 18th Brumaire of Louis Bonaparte*. Rockville, MD: Wildside Press LLC.

Matlock, J. F., 2010. *Superpower Illusions: How Myths and False Ideologies Led America Astray—And How to Return to Reality*. New Haven, CT: Yale University Press.

Mau, V. and Starodubrovskaya, I., 2001. *The Challenge of Revolution: Contemporary Russia in Historical Perspective: Contemporary Russia in Historical Perspective*. Oxford: Oxford University Press.

McDougall, W. A., 1998. Religion in diplomatic history, *Foreign Policy Research Institute*, 2 March.

McKeown, T. J., 1989. The politics of corn law repeal and theories of commercial policy. *British Journal of Political Science*, vol. 19, no. 3, pp. 353–380.

Mearsheimer, J. J., 2018. *Great Delusion: Liberal Dreams and International Realities*. New Haven, CT: Yale University Press.

Mearsheimer, J. J. and Walt, S. M., 2016. The case for offshore balancing. *Foreign Affairs*, vol. 95, no. 4, pp. 70–83.

Meissner, B., 1977. The Soviet concept of nation and the right of national self-determination. *International Journal*, vol. 32, no. 1, pp. 56–81.

Mezhuyev, B., 2017. 'Island Russia' and Russia's identity politics, *Russia in Global Affairs*, 6 June 2017.

Mill, J. S., 2001. *On Liberty*. Ontario: Batoche Books.

Miller, A., 2008. *Romanov Empire and Nationalism: Essays in the Methodology of Historical Research*. Budapest: Central European University Press.

Mirsky, D. S., 1927. The Eurasian movement. *The Slavonic Review*, vol. 6, no. 17, pp. 311–320.

Mitrokhin, N., 2003. *Russkaya Partiya: Dvizhenie Russkikh Natsionalistov v SSSR 1953–1985*. Moscow: Novoe Literaturnoe Obozrenie.

Mott, W. H., 1997. *The Economic Basis of Peace: Linkages Between Economic Growth and International Conflict*. Westport, CT: Greenwood Publishing Group.

Mudde, C., 2016. Europe's populist surge: A long time in the making. *Foreign affairs*, vol. 95, no. 6, pp. 25–30.

Narochnitskaya, N., 2003. *Rossiya i Russkie v Mirovoi Istorii*. Moscow: Mezhdunar Otnosheniya.

Narochnitskaya, N., 2014. You can not explain the blind that it's dark, *Voyennoye Obozreniye*, 17 January 2014.

Neumann, I. B., 1999. *Uses of the Other: The 'East' in European Identity Formation*. Manchester: Manchester University Press.

Neumann, I. B., 2016. *Russia and the Idea of Europe: A Study in Identity and International Relations*. London: Routledge.

Neumann, I. B. and Pouliot, V., 2011. Untimely Russia: Hysteresis in Russian-Western relations over the past millennium. *Security Studies*, vol. 20, no. 1, pp. 105–137.

New York Times, 1992. Excerpts from Pentagon's plan: "Prevent the re-emergence of a new rival", *The New York Times*, 8 March 1992.

Nietzsche, F., 1967. *The Will to Power*. New York: Random House.

Nietzsche, F., 1968. *Thus Spoke Zarathustra*. London: Penguin Books.

Nikitenko, A., 1975. *The Diary of a Russian Censor*. The University of Massachusetts Press, Amherst.

Nikonov, V., 2017. *Oktyabr' 1917: Kto byl nichem, tot stanet vsem* [October 1917: Who Was Nothing, Will Become Everything]. Moscow: Eksmo.

Noack, R. and Birnbaum, M., 2017. The leading French Presidential Candidates Emmanuel Macron and Marine Le Pen, in their own words, *The Washington Post*, 23 April 2017.

Norman, J., 2018. *Adam Smith: What He Thought, and Why It Matters*. London: Penguin.

Norris, J., 2005. *Collision Course: NATO, Russia, and Kosovo* (Foreword by Strobe Talbott). Westport, CT: Praeger.

Obama, B., 2016. President Obama: "The TPP would let America, not China, lead the way on global trade", *The Washington Post*, 2 May 2016.

Offord, D., 2006. *Journeys to a Graveyard: Perceptions of Europe in Classical Russian Travel Writing*. London: Springer Science & Business Media.

O'Meara, P., 2019. *The Russian Nobility in the Age of Alexander I*. London: Bloomsbury Publishing.

Orban, V., 2014. Full text of Viktor Orbán's speech at Băile Tuşnad (Tusnádfürdő) of 26 July 2014, *The Budapest Beacon*, 26 July 2014.

Panarin, A., 2001. Narod bez elity: Mezhdu otchayaniyem i nadezhdoy [A nation without an Elite: Between Despair and Hope]. *Nash Sovremennik*, no. 11.

Panarin, A., 2002. *Iskusheniye Globalizmom*. Moskva: Eksmo-Press.

Parker, G., 1985. *Western Geopolitical Thought in the Twentieth Century*. New York: Routledge.

Pauwels, T., 2011. Measuring populism: A quantitative text analysis of party literature in Belgium. *Journal of Elections, Public Opinion and Parties*, vol. 21, no. 1, pp. 97–119.

Pearson, T. S., 2004. *Russian Officialdom in Crisis: Autocracy and Local Self-Government, 1861–1900*. Cambridge: Cambridge University Press.

Perelman, M., 2003. *Steal This Idea: Intellectual Property and the Corporate Confiscation of Creativity*. New York: Palgrave Macmillan.

Perelman, M., 2012. The power of economics versus the economics of power. *Challenge*, vol. 55, no. 6, pp. 53–66.

Pipes, R., 1959. *Karamzin's Memoir on Ancient and Modern Russia*. Cambridge, MA: Harvard University Press.

Pipes, R., 1964. Narodnichestvo: A semantic inquiry. *Slavic Review*, vol. 23, no. 3, pp. 441–458.

Pipes, R., 1971. Russian conservatism in the second half of the nineteenth century. *Slavic Review*, vol. 30, no. 1, pp. 121–128.

Pipes, R., 2005. *Russian Conservatism and Its Critics: A Study in Political Culture*. New Haven, CT: Yale University Press.

Pipes, R., 2010. *Property and Freedom*. London: Random House.

Plato, 2008. *The Republic*. Sacramento: Creative Media Partners.

Podberezkin, A. and Pedberezkina, O., 2015. Eurasianism as an idea, civilizational concept and integration challenge, in Dutkiewicz, P. and Sakwa, R. (eds.), *Eurasian Integration: The View From Within*. London: Routledge, pp. 46–60.

Polanyi, K., 1944. *The Great Transformation*. Boston: Beacon Press.

Polyakov, L., 2015. "Conservatism" in Russia: Political tool or historical choice? *Russie. Nei. Vision*, no. 90, pp. 1–20.

Popescu, N. and Wilson, A., 2009. *The Limits of Enlargement-Lite: European and Russian Power in the Troubled Neighbourhood*. London: European Council of Foreign Relations.

Posen, B., 1993. The security dilemma and ethnic conflict. *Survival*, vol. 35, no. 1, pp. 27–47.

Posen, B., 2014. *Restraint: A New Foundation for US Grand Strategy*. London: Cornell University Press.

Posen, B., 2018. The rise of illiberal Hegemony: Trump's surprising grand strategy, *Foreign Affairs*, March/April 2018.

Pososhkov, I., 1987. *The Book of Poverty and Wealth*. Stanford, CA: Stanford University Press.

Pouliot, V., 2007. Pacification without collective identification: Russia and the trans-atlantic security community in the post-cold war era. *Journal of Peace Research*, vol. 44, no. 5, pp. 605–622.

PRC, 2018. China's arctic policy, *The State Council Information Office of the People's Republic of China*, 26 January 2018.

Prechel, H., 2000. *Big Business and the State: Historical Transformation and Corporate Transformation, 1880s–1990s*. Albany: State University of New York Press.

Prozorov, S., 2005. Russian conservatism in the Putin presidency: The dispersion of a hegemonic discourse. *Journal of Political Ideologies*, vol. 10, no. 2, pp. 121–143.

Putin, V., 1999. Russia at the turn of the millennium, 31 December 1999.

Putin, V., 2000. *First Person: An Astonishingly Frank Self-Portrait by Russia's President*. New York: Public Affairs.

Putin, V., 2005. State of the nation address, *Government of the Russian Federation*, 25 April 2005.

Putin, V., 2007. Address to the Federal Assembly, 26 April 2007.

Putin, V., 2011a. Prime Minister Vladimir Putin chairs a meeting of the organising committee for the celebration of Pyotr Stolypin's 150th birthday anniversary, *Government of the Russian Federation*, 13 July 2011.

Putin, V., 2011b. New integration project for Eurasia – A future that is being born today, *Izvestiya*, 4 October 2011.

Putin, V., 2012. Russia and the changing world, *RT*, 27 February 2012.

Putin, V., 2013a. Presidential address to the Federal Assembly, *President of Russia*, 12 December.

Putin, V., 2013b. Meeting of the Valdai International Discussion Club, *Government of the Russian Federation*, 19 September.

Putin, V., 2014a. Address by President of the Russian Federation, Moscow, 18 March 2014.

Putin, V., 2014b. Russia-EU Summit, 28 January 2014.

Putin, V., 2020. Vladimir Putin: The real lessons of the 75th anniversary of world war II, *The National Interest*, 18 June 2020.

Putnam, R. D. and Campbell, D. E., 2010. *American Grace: How Religion Divides and Unites Us*. New York: Simon & Schuster.

Quigley, C., 1961. *The Evolution of Civilisations: A Historical Analysis*. Indianapolis, IN: Liberty Press.

Rabow-Edling, S., 2012. *Slavophile Thought and the Politics of Cultural Nationalism*. New York: State University of New York Press.

Raeff, M., 2012. *Michael Speransky Statesman of Imperial Russia 1772–1839*. London: Springer.

Rancour-Laferriere, D., 1995. *The Slave Soul of Russia: Moral Masochism and the Cult of Suffering*. New York: New York University Press.

Rangsimaporn, P., 2009. *Russia as an Aspiring Great Power in East Asia: Perceptions and Policies from Yeltsin to Putin*. London: Springer.

Rapoza, K., 2019. For Wall Street, Russia has become 'Bulletproof', *Forbes*, 18 November 2019.

Reagan, R., 1984. Remarks at an ecumenical prayer breakfast in Dallas, Texas, *Reagan Library*, 23 August 1984.

Reinert, E., 2005. German economics and development economics, in Reinert, E. and Komo, J. S. (eds.), *The Origins of Development Economics*. London: Zed Books, pp. 48–68.

Remizov, M., 2010. Conservatism and modernity [Koservatizm i sovremennost], in Neklessa, A. (ed.), *Konservatism/Traditsionalizm: Teoriya, Formy Realizatsii, Perspektiva. Materialy Postoyanno Deystvuyushego Nauchnogo Seminara.* Moscow: Nauchny Ekspert.

RF, 2013. Concept of the foreign policy of the Russian Federation, *The Ministry of Foreign Affairs of the Russian Federation*, 18 February 2013.

Riasanovsky, N. V., 1947. The Norman theory of the origin of the Russian state. *Russian Review*, vol. 7, no. 1, pp. 96–110.

Riasanovsky, N. V., 1956. *Russia and the West in the Teachings of the Slavophiles: A Study of Romantic Ideology.* Cambridge, MA: Harvard University Press.

Riasanovsky, N. V., 1959. *Nicholas I and Official Nationality in Russia 1825–1855.* Berkeley: University of California Press.

Riasanovsky, N. V., 1992. *The Image of Peter the Great in Russian History and Thought.* Oxford: Oxford University Press.

Riasanovsky, N. V., 1993. *A History of Russia.* Oxford: Oxford University Press.

Riasanovsky, N. V., 1995. *The Emergence of Romanticism.* Oxford: Oxford University Press.

Ricardo, D., 1821. *On the Principles of Political Economy and Taxation.* London: John Murray.

Richard, C. J., 2012. *When the United States Invaded Russia: Woodrow Wilson's Siberian Disaster.* New York: Rowman & Littlefield Publishers.

Robinson, G. T., 1967. *Rural Russia Under the Old Régime: A History of the Landlord-Peasant World and a Prologue to the Peasant Revolution of 1917.* Berkeley: University of California Press.

Robinson, P., 2019. *Russian Conservatism.* Dekalb: Northern Illinois University Press.

Rogger, H., 1966. Reflections on Russian conservatism: 1861–1905. *Jahrbücher für Geschichte Osteuropas*, pp. 195–212.

Rorty, R., 1998. *Achieving Our Country: Leftist Thought in Twentieth-Century America.* Cambridge, MA: Harvard University Press.

RT, 2020. Europe & US use Russia-Poland discord to their advantage, first post-cold war Polish leader Walesa tells RT, *RT*, 29 February 2020.

Ruggie, J. G., 1982. International regimes, transactions, and change: Embedded liberalism in the postwar economic order. *International Organization*, vol. 36, no. 2, pp. 379–415.

Russian Federation, 2009. Decree of the Russian President: About the Commission under the President of the Russian Federation to counter attempts to falsify history to the detriment of Russia, Moscow, 15 May 2009.

Rutland, P. and Kazantsev, A., 2016. The limits of Russia's 'soft power'. *Journal of Political Power*, vol. 9, no. 3, pp. 395–413.

Sakwa, R., 2008a. Putin's leadership: Character and consequences. *Europe-Asia Studies*, vol. 60, no. 6, pp. 879–897.

Sakwa, R., 2008b. *Russian Politics and Society*. London: Routledge.

Sakwa, R., 2014. *Putin Redux: Power and Contradiction in Contemporary Russia*. London: Routledge.

Sakwa, R., 2017. *Russia Against the Rest: The Post-Cold War Crisis of World Order*. Cambridge: Cambridge University Press.

Saunders, D., 2014. *Russia in the Age of Reaction and Reform 1801–1881*. London: Routledge.

Savitsky, P., 1996. *Exodus to the East*. Bakersfield: Charles Schlacks, Jr. Publisher.

Savitsky, P., 1921. *Kontinent-Okean: Rossiia i Mirovoi Rynok*. Sofia: Iskhod k Vostoku.

Savitsky, P., 1997. *Geographical and Geopolitical Foundations of Eurasianism*. Agraf: Continent EM.

Schimmelpennick van der Oye, D., 2015. Russia, Napoleon and the threat to British India, in Hartley, J. M., Keenan, P. and Lieven, D. (eds.), *Russia and the Napoleonic Wars*. London: Palgrave Macmillan.

Schmidt, R. J., 1956. Cultural nationalism in Herder. *Journal of the History of Ideas*, pp. 407–417.

Schmitt, C., 1986. *Political Romanticism*. Cambridge, MA: MIT Press.

Schweller, R. L., 1999. Realism and the present great power system: Growth and positional conflict over scarce resources, in Kapstein, E. B. and Mastanduno, M. (eds.), *Unipolar Politics: Realism and State Strategies After the Cold War*. New York: Columbia University Press, pp. 28–68.

Scruton, R., 2015. The future of European civilization: Lessons for America, *The Heritage Foundation*, 8 December 2015.

Sell, S. K., 2003. *Private Power, Public Law: The Globalization of Intellectual Property Rights*. Cambridge: Cambridge University Press.

Semmel, B., 1970. *The Rise of Free Trade Imperialism*. Cambridge: Cambridge University Press.

Shadlen, K., 2005. Policy space for development in the WTO and beyond: The case of intellectual property rights, *Global Development and Environment Institute*, Working Paper No. 05–06, Tufts University.

Shekhovtsov, A., 2014. The Kremlin's marriage of convenience with the European far right, *Open Democracy*, 28 April 2014.

Sherlock, T., 2011. Confronting the stalinist past: The politics of memory in Russia. *The Washington Quarterly*, vol. 34, no. 2, pp. 93–109.

Shevtsova, L., 2003. *Putin's Russia*. Washington, DC: The Carnegie Endowment for International Peace.

Shishkov, A. S., 1803. *Rassuzhdenie o Starom i Novom Sloge Rossiskogo Jazika* [Discourse in Old and New Style of the Russian Language]. St. Petersburg: Imperatorskaya Tipographia.

Shulman, S., 2004. The contours of civic and ethnic national identification in Ukraine. *Europe-Asia Studies*, vol. 56, no. 1, pp. 35–56.

Singleton, A. C., 1997. *No Place Like Home: The Literary Artist and Russia's Search for Cultural Identity*. New York: State University of New York Press.

Slade, G., 2007. The Russian idea and the discourse of Vladimir Putin. *Central European University Political Science Journal*, vol. 1, pp. 44–57.

SMH, 1999. No turning back now for alliance, *Sydney Morning Herald*, 31 May 1999.

Smith, A., 2006. *The Theory of Moral Sentiments*. New York: Dover Publications.

Solzhenitsyn, A., 1978. The exhausted west, *Harvard Magazine*, July–August 1978.

Solzhenitsyn, A., 1986. *Warning to the West*. London: Macmillan.

Solzhenitsyn, A., 1998. Ugodilo Zernishko, Promezh Dvuh Zhernovov [The grain fallen between two millstones], *Noviy Mir*, p. 11.

Solzhenitsyn, A. and Tretyakov, A., 2006. Sberezhenie naroda—vysshaya izo vsekh nashikh gosudarstvennykh zadach, *Moskovskie novosti*, 28 April 2006.

Sorokin, P. A., 1941. *The Crisis of Our Age*. New York: E. P. Dutton.

Sowell, T., 2002. *A Conflict of Visions: Ideological Origins of Political Struggles*. New York: Basic Books.

Spengler, O., 1922. The two faces of Russia and Germany's eastern problems, *Politische Schriften*, Munich, 14 February 1922.

Spengler, O., 1991. *The Decline of the West*. Oxford: Oxford Paperbacks.

Spiegel, 2016. We are smarter, stronger and more determined, *Spiegel*, 13 July 2016.

Squires, N., 2018. Italy risks clash with Britain and EU as it threatens to veto renewal of Russia sanctions, *The Telegraph*, 17 October 2018.

Stalin, J., 1981. *The National Question and Leninism: Reply to Comrades Meshkov, Kovalchuk, and Others*. Moscow: Foreign Languages Publishing House.

Starr, S. F., 1972. *Decentralization and Self-Government in Russia, 1830–1870*. Princeton, NJ: Princeton University Press.

Steiner, L., 2011. *For Humanity's Sake: The Bildungsroman in Russian Culture*. Toronto: University of Toronto Press.

Stenner, K., 2005. *The Authoritarian Dynamic*. Cambridge: Cambridge University Press.

Strauss, L., 1953. *Natural Right and History*. Chicago: University of Chicago Press.

Streeck, W. and Yamamura, K., 2005. *The Origins of Nonliberal Capitalism: Germany and Japan in Comparison*. Ithaca, NY: Cornell University Press.

Sullivan, A., 2007. *The Conservative Soul: Fundamentalism, Freedom, and the Future of the Right*. New York: Harper Perennial.

Szlajfer, A., 2012. *Economic Nationalism and Globalization: Lessons from Latin America and Central Europe*. Leiden: Brill.

Szvák, G., 2011. The golden age of Russian historical writing: The nineteenth century, in Macintyre, S., Maiguashca, J. and Pok, A. (eds.), *The Oxford History of Historical Writing – Volume 4: 1800–1945*. Oxford: Oxford University Press, pp. 303–325.

Talbott, S., 2002. *The Russia Hand*. New York: Random House.

Tolz, V., 1998. Forging the nation: National identity and nation building in post-communist Russia. *Europe-Asia Studies*, vol. 50, no. 6, pp. 993–1022.

Tönnies, F., 1957. *Community and Society*. New York: Dover Publications.

Toynbee, J. A., 1946. *Study of History*. Oxford: Oxford University Press.

Trenin, D., 2007. *Getting Russia Right*. Washington, DC: Carnegie Endowment.

Trenin, D., 2009. Russia's spheres of interest, not influence. *The Washington Quarterly*, vol. 32, no. 4, pp. 3–22.

Trenin, D. V., 2011. *Post-Imperium: A Eurasian Story*. Washington, DC: Brookings Institution Press.

Trigos, L., 2009. *The Decembrist Myth in Russian Culture*. London: Palgrave Macmillan.

Trubetskoi, N., 1920. *Evropa i chelovechestvo* [Europe and Mankind]. Sofia.

Tsygankov, A., 2006. *Russia's Foreign Policy: Change and Continuity in National Identity*. New York: Rowman & Littlefield Publishers.

Tsygankov, A., 2009. *Russophobia*. New York: Palgrave Macmillan.

Tsymbursky, V., 1993. Ostrov Rossiya: Perspektivy rossiyskoy geopolitiki (Island Russia: Perspectives on Russian geopolitics). *Polis*, no. 5, pp. 11–17.

US Senate, 1983. Broken families: Hearings before the subcommittee on family and human services, *United States Senate*, 4 October 1983.

Uvarov, S., 1818. Rech prezidenta Imperatorskoy akademii nauk, popechitelia Peterburgskogo uchebnogo okruga v torzhestvennom sobranii Glavnogo pedagogicheskogo instituta [Speech of the president of Imperors Academy of Science, guardian of Petersburg educational district in ceremonial convention of Main Pedagogy Institute], 22 March 1818.

Van Evera, S., 2006. American foreign policy for the new era, in Van Evera, S. (ed.), *How to Make America Safe: New Policies for National Security*. Cambridge: The Tobin Project.

Van Tyne, C. H., 1927. *England and America*. Cambridge: Cambridge University Press.

Verkhovsky, A. and Pain, E., 2010. Civilization nationalism: The Russian version of the «special way», in *Forum noveishei vostochnoevropeyskoy istorii i kultury* [Forum of the Newest East Europe History and Culture], pp. 69–99.

Vernadsky, G., 1947. Reforms under Czar Alexander I: French and American influences. *The Review of Politics*, vol. 9, no. 1, pp. 47–64.

Vico, G., 2002. *Scienza Nuova, The First New Science*. Cambridge: Cambridge University Press.

Voegelin, E., 1974. Reason: The classic experience. *The Southern Review*, vol. 10, no. 2, pp. 237–264.

Volfson, S., 1929. *Sotsiologiia Braka i Semi*. Minsk.Von Laue, T. H., 1954. A secret memorandum of Sergei Witte on the industrialization of imperial Russia. *The Journal of Modern History*, vol. 26, no. 1, pp. 60–74.

Von Mohrenschildt, D. S., 1981. *Toward a United States of Russia: Plans and Projects of Federal Reconstruction of Russia in the Nineteenth Century*. London: Fairleigh Dickinson University Press.

Wade, R. H., 2003. What strategies are viable for developing countries today? The World Trade Organization and the shrinking of 'development space'. *Review of International Political Economy*, vol. 10, no. 4, pp. 621–644.

Walt, S. M., 2018. *The Hell of Good Intentions: America's Foreign Policy Elite and the Decline of US Primacy*. New York: Straus and Giroux, Farrar.

Waltz, K. N., 2000. NATO expansion: A realist's view. *Contemporary Security Policy*, vol. 21, no. 2, pp. 23–38.

Wanner, C., 2010. *Burden of Dreams: History and Identity in Post-Soviet Ukraine*. University Park, PA: Penn State University Press.

Ware, K., 2011. Sobornost and eucharistic ecclesiology: Aleksei Khomiakov and his successors. *International Journal for the Study of the Christian Church*, vol. 11, no. 2–3, pp. 216–235.

Weber, M., 1924. *Gesammelte Auf sditze zur Soziologie und Sozialpolitik*. Tübingen: Mohr.

Weber, M., 1958. *The Protestant Ethic and the Spirit of Capitalism*. New York: Scribner.

White House, 1988. National security strategy of the United States, *White House*, April 1988.

Whitman, A., 1969. Lindbergh traveling widely as conservationist, *The New York Times*, 23 June 1969.

Whittaker, C. H., 1978. The ideology of Sergei Uvarov: An interpretive essay. *The Russian Review*, vol. 37, no. 2, pp. 158–176.

Whittaker, C. H., 1984. *The Origins of Modern Russian Education: An Intellectual Biography of Count Sergei Uvarov; 1786–1855*. Dekalb: Northern Illinois University Press.

Whittaker, C. H., 1992. The reforming Tsar: The redefinition of autocratic duty in eighteenth-century Russia. *Slavic Review*, vol. 51, no. 1, pp. 77–98.

Wiederkehr, S., 2007. Eurasianism as a reaction to Pan-Turkism, in Shlapentokh, D. (ed.), *Russia Between East and West: Scholarly Debates on Eurasianism*. Leiden: Brill, pp. 39–60.

Williams, M. C. and Neumann, I. B., 2000. From alliance to security community: NATO, Russia, and the power of identity. *Millennium-Journal of International Studies*, vol. 29, no. 2, pp. 357–387.

Williams, W. A., 2011. *The Contours of American History*. New York: Verso Books.

Witte, S., 1954. 'Report of the Minister of Finance to his Majesty on the necessity of formulating and thereafter steadfastly adhering to a definite program of a commercial and industrial policy of the Empire. Extremely secret.', in Von Laue, T. H., A Secret Memorandum of Sergei Witte on the Industrialization of Imperial Russia. *The Journal of Modern History*, vol. 26, no. 1, pp. 60–74.

Wortman, R., 1994. *Scenarios of Power: Myths and Ritual in the Russian Monarchy*. Princeton, NJ: Princeton University Press.

Wynot, J. J., 2004. *Keeping the Faith: Russian Orthodox Monasticism in the Soviet Union, 1917–1939*. College Station: Texas A&M University Press.

Wæver, O., 2000. The EU as a security actor: Reflections from a pessimistic constructivist on post-sovereign security orders, in Kelstrup, M. and Williams, M. C. (eds.), *International Relations Theory and the Politics of European Integration. Power, Security and Community*. London: Routledge, pp. 250–294.

Zakharova, L. and Owen, T. C. (eds.), 2005. *Russia in the Nineteenth Century: Autocracy, Reform, and Social Change, 1814–1914*. New York: M. E. Sharpe.

Zevelev, I., 2009. Russia's future: Nation or civilization? *Russia in Global Affairs*, vol. 7, no. 4, pp. 73–87.

Zhang, Y. B., Lin, M. C., Nonaka, A. and Beom, K., 2005. Harmony, hierarchy and conservatism: A cross-cultural comparison of confucian values in China, Korea, Japan, and Taiwan. *Communication Research Reports*, vol. 22, no. 2, pp. 107–115.

Zhivov, V., 2009. *Language and Culture in Eighteenth Century Russia*. Boston: Academic Studies Press.

Zyrianov, P., 1997. The development of the Russian state system in the nineteenth and early twentieth centuries, in Hara, T. and Matsuzato, K. (eds.), *Empire and Society: New Approaches to Russian History*, pp. 107–132. Slavic Research Center, Hokkaido University, Sapporo.

Index

Note: Page numbers followed by "n" denote endnotes.

231